MW01491825

The Murders of Annie Hearn

The Murders of Annie Hearn

The Poisonings that Inspired Agatha Christie

Jonathan Oates

PEN & SWORD TRUE CRIME

An imprint of
Pen & Sword Books Ltd
Yorkshire - Philadelphia

First published in Great Britain in 2024 by
Pen & Sword Military
An imprint of
Pen & Sword Books Ltd
Yorkshire - Philadelphia

ISBN 978 1 39905 656 4

A CIP catalogue record for this book is available from the British Library.

Typeset in INDIA by IMPEC eSolutions
Printed and bound in England by CPI Group (UK) Ltd, Croydon, CRO 4YY

Pen & Sword Books Ltd. incorporates the Imprints of Pen & Sword Archaeology,
Atlas, Aviation, Battleground, Discovery, Family History, History, Maritime,
Military, Naval, Politics, Railways, Select, Transport, True Crime, Fiction,
Frontline Books, Leo Cooper, Praetorian Press, Seaforth Publishing,
Wharncliffe, White Owl and After the Battle.

For a complete list of Pen & Sword titles please contact

PEN & SWORD BOOKS LIMITED
47 Church Street, Barnsley, South Yorkshire, S70 2AS, England
E-mail: enquiries@pen-and-sword.co.uk
Website: www.pen-and-sword.co.uk

or

PEN AND SWORD BOOKS
1950 Lawrence Rd, Havertown, PA 19083, USA
E-mail: uspen-and-sword@casematepublishers.com
Website: www.penandswordbooks.com

This book is dedicated to Mark John Maguire

Contents

Acknowledgements

Many people have helped in the production of this book in numerous ways. Mark John Maguire, whose great YouTube channel, 'They got away with murder', introduced me to the facts of the case, has read the text and provided encouragement. Fellow crime author Dr Anna-Lena Berg has read it (twice) and gave useful and inspirational advice, especially on the medical aspects and on other matters. Another great help was Lindsay Siviter, who, as always, lent relevant material. John Gauss read the text to correct any mistakes in English and grammar as well as providing genealogical advice. Paul Lang provided a copy of the postcard from Bude from his extensive postcard collection. The East Cornwall History Society assisted with two of the pictures. Lucy Bernacki provided additional encouragement and advice.

Introduction

In 1930 and 1931 Britain was gripped by a real-life murder mystery that had all the ingredients of a popular detective novel by an author such as Agatha Christie. There was murder by poison; possibly two or three murders by poison. The chief suspect disappeared before the inquest and it was initially unclear whether she was dead or alive. Then she was found and was arrested. She was charged with two murders and after several appearances at the magistrates' court, was put on trial for her life. The result was both surprising and disappointing.

Yet there has been no film or TV drama about this sensational and ultimately unresolved case. It was covered in an issue of a magazine series about unsolved mysteries published in 1984, and it has appeared in anthologies of Cornish murders and mysteries. There is a lengthy YouTube video which outlines the story and posits a solution. However, it is necessarily abbreviated, providing the narrative and explaining the author's considered theory in about an hour. The first book entirely devoted to the case was published in 2022. There has also been a recent novelisation, *Arsenic and Mercy Quint*.

This book is informed by the copious reporting in both national and local newspapers, chiefly *The Western Morning News*, a Cornish daily, the press in the 1930s being so much more detailed than its successors of today. The text also relies on the Home Office and Assize papers from The National Archives, autobiographical writings by the chief suspect and the memoirs of some of the senior legal and medical figures involved in the case. Sources well known to the genealogist, such as wills, census returns, directories and so on, are also used.

The book begins as the case first became known to the public and describes the death of the victim in 1930. It then works backward to explore the principal characters and their relationships with one another. We then return to 1930 and the inquest of the victim. It will also consider the deaths of others, including family members who may have been the murderer's first victims. By this time, however, the main suspect had disappeared. She did not escape her pursuers, as she was identified by her new employer, arrested and charged with murder. The cut and thrust between the lawyers and the witnesses takes up much of the later chapters.

The final chapter discusses what happened to the main characters in later life. Just as importantly it discusses the mystery that remained after the trial's end. Namely, who really killed Mrs Thomas in 1930, and why? Previous commentators have come to varied conclusions. The book investigates whether there was a hitherto unknown serial killer at work at a time when such people were little known in Britain.

I was drawn to this case by rereading the Agatha Christie novel *Sad Cypress*, published in 1940, which draws on this true tale as part of the fictional story. In part two of the book there is a conversation between Dr Peter Lord and Hercule Poirot. In the kitchen at Hunterbury House in 1939, Elinor Carlisle is having a sandwich lunch with Nurse Jessie Hopkins and Mary Gerrard, Elinor's rival in love and illegitimate daughter of Elinor's late aunt Laura Welman. The three women eat a lunch of salmon paste sandwiches and Mary dies, apparently of morphine poisoning. Elinor, who bought and prepared the fish paste for the lunch, had both motive and means, is subsequently arrested and charged with murder, and stands trial. The Hearn case is then cited as being similar to this one. Dr Lord says:

'Counsel will make a song and dance about the sandwiches, too, saying all three ate them, therefore impossible to ensure that only one person should be poisoned. They said that in the Hearne [sic] case, you remember'.

'But actually it is very simple. You make your pile of sandwiches. In one of them is the poison. You hand the plate. In our state of civilization, it is a foregone conclusion that the person to whom the plate is offered will take the sandwich which is nearest to them'.[1]

Anyone who has ever offered someone known to them food from a plate will acknowledge the accuracy of Dr Lord's comment (the reader may care to try this). However, as we shall see, the defence did not only claim that the poisoner could not ensure that the intended victim was poisoned; but also that there was no poison in the sandwiches and that it was a case of food poisoning.

Note

Money values are expressed in the coinage of the time, the pre-decimal currency wherein 12 pence (abbreviated to d) made up a shilling (abbreviated to s) and 20 shillings were a pound, 21 shillings being a guinea.

Chapter 1

An unexpected death

O n Saturday 18 October 1930, 43-year-old Mrs Alice Maud Thomas fell ill. She had had an indoor picnic tea with her husband, William Henry Thomas, a farmer of Trenhorne Farm, Lewannick, Cornwall, two years her junior, and their mutual friend, whom they knew as Mrs Annie Hearn. That morning, Mrs Thomas had asked her husband to invite their friend and neighbour along as they often did, so he went to Trenhorne House, Mrs Hearn's home, to do so and she accepted. Thomas said, 'My wife proposes to go to Bude to take my mother back and would like you to come'.[1]

Mrs Hearn recalled:

'Mr Thomas came to my house about noon and informed me he was going to Bude with his mother. Mrs Thomas was going as well and asked if I would like to go. I said I would like to go very much, but I had not time to mention food, but as we had taken luncheon at other times, I got some sandwiches to take with me. I used tinned red salmon that I had previously purchased from Shuker and Reed's and I took some chocolate cake from my own house'.[2]

The coastal village of Bude was a popular bathing resort and small seaport on the north coast of Cornwall. Mrs Hearn later wrote of the place, 'Bude is quite a small place, but there are some very nice shops there. It was a great treat to look at all the pretty things in the windows'.[3] With the three on the trip had been Thomas's mother, Mrs Elizabeth Thomas (1860–1949) of 3 Falcon Terrace, Bude, who had been staying at the Thomas's farm, in order to drop her off at one Mrs Vickery's house, Hele Farm, which was nearby. Bude was about twenty-five miles from Lewannick. Thomas had driven them there in his saloon car, leaving at three that afternoon, and they arrived at Bude at four o'clock. Thomas went for a haircut, meeting the two ladies at John Henry Littlejohn's café on Northgate. The Thomases had been there before, but Mrs Hearn had not.[4]

They met at the café at five o'clock. They were served by Ivy Victoria Willshire (1899–1974). It was not a large café, and though busy in the summer was less so by October. It was not unusual for people to bring their own food into the cafe – though also making payments for goods from the café – and later Ivy had trouble remembering the three guests.[5] Miss Willshire later said 'It is quite a usual thing to bring sandwiches into the café… I couldn't say why it is'.[6]

Thomas asked the others, 'What are you going to have for tea?' Then, either Thomas or his wife ordered tea, cakes, and bread and butter. Thomas sat between the two ladies at a large square table which could seat ten. The ladies sat in the corners. They also had some tinned salmon sandwiches, which Mrs Hearn had prepared, wrapped in brown paper and brought with her. This was a surprise to the other two, according to Thomas, as no prior arrangement had been made for their neighbour to do this. Mrs Hearn stated:

'I said to Mr and Mrs Thomas that I had prepared some sandwiches and I placed the cake and the sandwiches, on the table between Mrs Thomas and myself and Mr Thomas. Mrs Thomas took the first, I took the second and Mr Thomas took the third, whilst Mrs Thomas took the fourth'.

This is the order that would have been expected. Thomas was not certain about the order of eating and later said 'I cannot say who took the first sandwich, whether I did or whether my wife did'. He thought there were six sandwiches but could not be certain, and he had forgotten about the cake. He thought they were small. Thomas thought it was unusual for Mrs Hearn to bring such food along with her when they all went out together. The sandwiches were made of white bread and were straight cut.[7]

Thomas did not taste anything out of the ordinary when eating his sandwich. They left, taking their wrapping papers, after being in the café for half an hour. Ivy Willshire made out the bill and Thomas paid it.[8]

Thomas then went for a stroll and the two women went to look at the shops. However, when walking down the street, he 'felt funny in my inside about a quarter of an hour after tea'. His solution was to go to the Globe Hotel and drink whisky. This seemed to do the trick, and he returned to his car at about 6.30pm then found the two ladies. According to him, Mrs Thomas told him, 'I have got a sweety taste in my mouth' and asked if there were any fruit shops in Bude.

Thomas found one and bought some bananas and gave some to his wife. Mrs Hearn did not remember any such complaint at this stage from Mrs Thomas, but agreed that the two ladies ate some fruit bought by Thomas. They left Bude at about 6.45pm.[9]

It was not an uneventful journey. Mrs Hearn later stated:

'When we were half way to Launceston, I noticed Mrs Thomas was leaning forward. I was sitting with her in the back seat. Mrs Thomas did not speak for some time and I thought she was trying to pick up something on the floor. I touched her and asked her "What is the matter?" and she replied "I am alright" but I was not satisfied and I looked forward and noticed that she was fumbling with the inside handle of the door. Mr Thomas then turned around and said to Mrs Thomas "Shall I stop the car?" Mrs Thomas said "No, it is alright". Mrs Thomas was then sick. Mr Thomas said "Shall we stop" and I said yes. Mr Thomas then pulled up, but before he could stop, Mrs Thomas got the door open. We assisted her out of the car. I looked after her'.

Thomas thought that this was at Whitstone at about 7.10–7.15pm. Thomas then said that Mrs Thomas stood on the grass. She was sick again. Mrs Hearn helped Mrs Thomas up. The latter vomited several times and they were unable to proceed for another half an hour. Mrs Hearn stated that 'After a time Mrs Thomas recovered and we drove to Launceston'. Mrs Thomas then sat in the front and Thomas drove as slowly as possible to avoid jolting her.[10]

They eventually arrived at Launceston at about 8pm. Thomas parked the car in the old sheep market and arranged to meet the ladies at 9pm as he had some business to conduct in the town.

Mrs Hearn recalled:

'Mr Thomas offered to get a doctor but Mrs Thomas said "No". Mr Thomas went about some business and Mrs Thomas and I went about the town. Mrs Thomas went into a fruit shop and bought some pears and then we went back to the car, where she was sick again. I was sitting in the car when Mr Thomas returned and Mrs Thomas was then at the lavatory'.

Thomas remembered things differently. When he returned to the car he could only see Mrs Hearn standing there. He asked where his wife was and was told that she was in a ladies' lavatory. She had been ill several times. Thomas whistled outside the lavatory and his wife came out. When he asked how she was, she replied, 'We will get right home'. Her husband suggested that they contact a doctor and she said 'I don't want any doctor'. 'Would you like any brandy?', the concerned husband asked. 'No, get me home, I will be better', she replied.[11]

According to Mrs Hearn, 'On the way home I think she got out again to be sick, and then Mrs Thomas got in the front seat as it was thought the jolting of the car made her worse'. They arrived back at the farm at 9.20pm. Thomas and Mrs Hearn put his wife to bed. Mrs Hearn put some hot water bottles in the sick woman's bed. Thomas then declared: 'I am going to get some brandy and get the doctor'. Mrs Thomas said firmly 'No, I don't want any doctor and I don't want any brandy. I shall be alright tomorrow'.

Thomas ignored her wishes and went to a nearby social club where he bought brandy and returned about ten minutes later to administer this to his wife. He then drove to Polyphant, two miles away, to the house of Dr Eric Graham Saunders (1887–1965) of Polyphant House, Lewannick. The doctor did not return with Thomas but followed him shortly afterwards in his own car.

Dr Saunders found that Mrs Thomas's pulse was rather rapid and she complained of severe cramps in her legs, though these disappeared after a few days. He added 'She had no temperature, her pulse was a bit rapid, and her abdomen was slightly tender. Otherwise, there was not much wrong with her'. He later said, 'I thought it was ptomaine poisoning. It flashed across my mind once that it might be arsenical poisoning. Some of the symptoms are common to both', but he thought it was the former, which is more common.[12] He gave instructions for nursing and feeding the sick woman. The diet prescribed was eggs and albumen water and Benger's (a liquid food aimed at children with stomach troubles). Kaolin was prescribed. The Thomases asked Mrs Hearn to stay at their house that evening so she could help. For the next ten days Mrs Hearn lived in and did all the cooking. She prepared different food for Mrs Thomas compared to that for Thomas and herself. Both shared nursing duties, but most of this was undertaken by Thomas. On 19 October Mrs Thomas told her husband that she did not feel at all well and Thomas asked what was in the sandwiches, 'tinned fish' replied Mrs Hearn.[13]

The doctor called the next day and found Mrs Thomas to be slightly better, but not by much. She had had more vomiting, diarrhoea and the leg cramps remained. Next day she was better physically but was agitated mentally. He called on 21 October and was told that she had vomited once that day. She also had diarrhoea, but the cramps were beginning to go. On 22 October she was not sleeping well and was mentally agitated but physically better. Next day she was still not sleeping but the cramps had gone. On 24 October there was tingling in the feet and vomiting. Next day she was much the same, but by the 26th the tingling had ceased. The doctor noted 'All the time she had the agitated condition. She had worried feelings'. On this day her husband moved her to another bedroom.[14]

On 27 October there seemed to be improvement, but there was tingling in Mrs Thomas's legs and hands. Her pulse was rapid and there had been vomiting. The doctor did not visit the next day, but on 29 October she seemed better. On 30 October the gastric symptoms had cleared up but there was pricking and tingling in the legs that was so painful that she could not stand. On 31 October and 1 November she was much the same. Apparently 'she complained more of her legs and to a certain extent of her hands that day. There was also shingles. She said her hands were very weak'. On this day the doctor prescribed bromide in 7½ grain doses. Earlier, apart from kaolin, he had prescribed a medicine containing rhubarb and bicarbonate of soda.[15]

Thomas seemed concerned about his wife and discussed her condition and treatment with the doctor. He said 'I don't want to spare any expense whatsoever. What about second advice?' but was assured it was unnecessary. He asked this again on 30 October and was told 'it seems better today, it is not needed'. 'What about that numbed feeling in my wife's legs?' 'That will come right again but it will take time'. 'I don't want to spare any expense whatever. I want my wife to get well. I don't want my wife to be a cripple'.[16]

During this time at least eight other local women came to the farm. One was Mrs Rosalind Parnell (1901–93) of Trenhorne Cottage, a neighbour who came in three times a week in the mornings to do the cleaning. Another was Mrs Emma Pearce, who came to make the butter on the farm. The others came in to see how Mrs Thomas was faring. Thomas did not think his wife was particularly worried, however. Mrs Anne Elizabeth Tucker (1873–1938), a widow living a quarter of a mile away and a good friend of Mrs Thomas, visited on alternate days, bringing grapes and jelly. She recalled Mrs Thomas vomiting and complaining of sickness and numbness in the limbs. She said Mrs Thomas spoke highly of Mrs Hearn. On 23 October Mrs Thomas changed her bedroom so that she was in the one that Mrs Hearn had been sleeping in, and so Mrs Hearn took her friend's room. Mrs Thomas was incapable of walking, so when she wanted to move her husband carried her about.[17] Thomas wrote to his mother two or three times during these days and told her of his wife's illness, though she did not visit, presumably because she thought the situation was under control.[18]

On 26 October Mrs Elizabeth Spear, another neighbour described as a smallholder, visited Mrs Thomas and 'she said that she was feeling better but her legs were still numb'.[19] Mrs Lucy Wadge (1869–1948), of Daisy Mount, Launceston, who was Thomas's aunt, was also a visitor, apparently on 29 October (but probably at least a day before), likely in the morning. When she arrived, she saw Thomas and Mrs Hearn in the kitchen and the former was drinking milk. Mrs Wadge said, 'I would like to see her while I am here'. Thomas went up to see his wife, for whom Mrs Hearn was preparing a beef or chicken mixture. On his return he apparently said to Mrs Hearn that she was too sick to want any food or drink, so Mrs Hearn went up with some tea to see her and apparently Mrs Thomas said 'no, I cannot be bothered', so she returned and told Mrs Wadge 'Mrs Thomas is very quiet now'. When Mrs Hearn was asked about keeping the visitor away, she answered 'Nothing had ever entered my mind'.[20]

Mrs Wadge told her niece, Kathleen Parsons (1902–84), about Mrs Thomas's illness at the cattle market and she told her mother, Mrs Tryphena Parsons (1865–1936), wife of Samuel Parsons (1858–1934), a retired farmer, who lived in Palmery House, Egloskerry, about five miles away, about her daughter's illness, so Mrs Parsons wrote to her married daughter on 28 October to say that she was coming over. Thomas, thinking that his mother-in-law might be able to help his wife, drove over on the next day. He saw Parsons and Miss Parsons and said simply 'Alice is not well' and added 'don't be frightened'. He then said to the two, 'I want either you or Kathleen to come with me'. He did not do so before because his wife did not want him to, as there had been family friction in past years. He wanted Mrs Parsons to come to the farm to help and he drove over to collect her in his car, arriving the following day on 29 October.[21]

Mrs Parsons, who had last seen her daughter at Launceston in September, went straight to see her as soon as she arrived at 4pm. She recalled 'We kissed when we met but she did not say how she was. She didn't look particularly ill'. She did not enquire as to her daughter's health, which seems strange, as that was why she was there, but this is what she said. The others told her of the sandwiches at Bude, the doctor's visits and that food poisoning was suspected.[22]

Mrs Parsons found that Mrs Hearn was doing the cooking in the house for Mrs Thomas, Thomas and herself. Thereafter Mrs Parsons prepared the food, but Mrs Hearn continued doing all the cooking. One change was that Mrs Parsons slept in the same room as her daughter. Thomas slept in the spare room.[23]

Mrs Thomas had remained in bed for several days. However, on about 30 October she felt well enough to get up. Mrs Parsons said 'She seemed to be bettering the whole time I was there'. However, the doctor, who visited most days, suggested that she be taken to Launceston Infirmary. She refused, although it is not known why. Mrs Hearn was doing all the cooking and was giving Mrs Thomas white of egg, biscuits and light food.[24]

Mrs Parsons said that her daughter bore all her pain without a murmur, that she was of a sweet disposition and had always been very healthy.[25] She also said: 'she was very weak and complained of severe sickness, she lost the strength in her arms and legs and never got up again. She made a number of statements in the course of her delirium'.[26]

On Saturday 1 November, Thomas thought his wife seemed better. She was sitting in various rooms in the house and was no longer confined to bed. On 2 November, Mrs Parsons brought her tea in the morning. Then, for Sunday dinner, Mrs Hearn prepared and cooked the food. It was roast mutton, roast potatoes and green vegetables. Mrs Parsons put one potato and some vegetables onto her daughter's plate and took it to the dining room. She also cut up the mutton for her daughter. She then fed her it with a spoon and Mrs Thomas ate about half of it. The remainder of the mutton was put in the oven in the kitchen. Mrs Parsons then had her dinner in the kitchen with the others and Thomas went to the kitchen and took the mutton out of the oven, telling Mrs Parsons, 'I will give it to her. You go on eating your own'. Returning to the dining room he laughed and showed an almost empty plate. 'I made her eat it,' he said. After the main course, Mrs Parsons served a pudding which she had made herself. Mrs Thomas ate some of this and seemed quite well afterwards. In the afternoon she had a snack and a drink of lemon juice that Mrs Parsons had made the night before, because her mouth was dry and her throat was burning.[27]

Later that day Thomas was busy on the farm. His wife was comfortable and he talked to Mrs Tucker about how his wife was improving. He returned at 9.15pm and found his wife in the dining room. He then carried her up to bed a little later and sat chatting to her. He then found out what had happened earlier that afternoon. Mrs Thomas had complained of a burning and dry sensation in her throat. Her mother gave her another lemon drink and she was sick. When she went to bed she asked her mother for some aspirin. Mrs Parsons gave her a tablet from a bottle that stood on the mantelpiece, which had been brought from Mrs Hearn's house a few days earlier. She gave her another later in the evening. She also had a bowl of porridge. But at night Mrs Thomas complained that she did not feel well and put this down to the two aspirins. Mrs Parsons slept in the same room as her daughter, as she had on previous nights, and recalled that her daughter was restless. At some point in the day she complained of having a 'sweety taste' in the mouth, as she had on 18 October.[28]

Thomas turned in at about 10.15pm. He and his wife had been sleeping in different rooms since her illness began. At about 11pm he heard a noise next door where his wife was. Entering the room, he saw Mrs Parsons with her daughter and Mrs Parsons said, 'These genaspirins have upset Alice, she is not so well'. His wife became quiet and Thomas returned to his room.[29]

Mrs Thomas grew worse and at four in the morning of Monday 3 November she cried out for her husband. She said 'This bed is streaming wet [her mother said that this was not the case] and the bed clothes are torn to pieces' and asked him to take her away. He carried her into his bed, where she remained quietly until 8 that morning. He then carried her back to her own bed. Her mother made her a poached egg with bread and butter for breakfast. Later in the morning she had a nosebleed which lasted a long time, from about 11am until 2pm, and it was very difficult to staunch. At 9.50am Thomas went to the doctor's surgery, but found he was out. He left a message to the effect that his wife was a lot worse. Mrs Parsons gave her daughter a glass of milk. Dr Saunders arrived at about 2pm and he stemmed the nosebleed. He advised that a specialist be called in and a trained hospital nurse employed.[30]

That evening Mrs Thomas grew worse. A nurse arrived and later, at the request of Dr Saunders, so did Dr William Alexander Lister (1897–1971), who was a consultant at Plymouth City Hospital. He found her in a bad way:

'Rambling and restless and completely delirious. She was sitting in bed supported by her husband. Muttering and crying out and unable to make any coherent statement. There was herpes around the mouth and also on the abdomen. Pulse and respiration were rapid and pulse was 120 and of good tension. The heart sounds were not of good quality, but there were no abnormal sounds to be heard. The lungs showed general fine crepitations'.

Lister thought this was generalised catarrh. The pupils were equal and of moderate size, neither dilated nor contracted. They responded to light but he could not see the optic disc because the patient was so restless. The muscles felt soft and wasted. Movement in the legs was absent and he could obtain no reflexes. This was severe and generalised peripheral neuritis. Dr Lister concluded:

'Taking the findings and the history of the case as given by Dr Saunders, I diagnosed that Mrs Thomas was suffering from arsenical poisoning and consequently arranged for her admission to the City hospital at Plymouth'.[31]

Lister thought that Mrs Thomas ought to be removed to hospital because:

'The reason of my advising the patient to be removed to Plymouth was that it looked odd that she should be the only person suffering, out of those in the house, and that it would be better for her if she were got away from those surroundings. I knew there were single wards in the City Hospital, so I took her there. I don't think it was in accordance with the rules'.[32]

Shortly afterwards Mrs Thomas was removed by ambulance to Plymouth Hospital. Dr Lister recommended that Dr Saunders gave her a 1/70th grain of hyoscine hypobromide so as to quieten the patient on her journey and to make it less difficult for the attendants. He then returned to the hospital to put the arrangements in motion, to have her in a side ward free from other patients, and to give instructions that suitable vessels be prepared to preserve her urine and faeces. They left the farm at a 11.45pm in a St John Ambulance. Thomas accompanied his wife but was not allowed in the room.[33]

At 1.20am Lister was told the patient had arrived and he went to the patient's bed. He found her quieter and he discussed with Dr Millicent Fox (1878–1961) of the City Hospital, residential medical officer there, what they should do. She advised stimulants in the form of injections, hot water bottles and fluids, strychnine if needed, and morphia if she was restless again. Thomas left the hospital at 2.15am.[34]

Dr Lister recalled his visit to the house and stated that Mrs Thomas was rambling, restless and completely delirious. She could not make any coherent statement. The doctor diagnosed arsenic poisoning. He thought that it was odd that she was the only person in the household who had suffered in such a manner, and so the best course of action would be to remove her from the scene of poisoning. Her condition was serious indeed and travelling to Plymouth to the main hospital would do her no good. However, he decided that this was the better of two evils and that it offered her a chance of life.[35] Dr Lister concluded that Mrs Thomas had been given a large dose of arsenic some time ago and then had been given a later dose of the same poison.[36]

Dr Fox recalled that Thomas was in an agitated condition and was very distressed about his wife's condition. She told him that his wife was being treated for ptomaine poisoning. Because she was being treated for arsenic poisoning, he was only allowed to see her through a hole into the wall of her room.[37]

Fox recalled, of Mrs Thomas, that 'She was delirious, unconscious, and she was throwing her arms and head about. She was clammy, her pupils were dilated. She had no reflexes…there was blood in her nostrils'. Her pulse was rapid and her temperature was 120 degrees Fahrenheit. Dr Fox saw her four times before 4.30am. At 7am the patient collapsed. At 9.30am Fox saw her again and 'She was in extremis. She was past any help'.[38] Meanwhile Thomas left the hospital and later said 'I spent part of the night in the street and part in Andrew's garage'.[39]

Mrs Thomas died at 9.45 in the morning of Tuesday 4 November. Thomas saw her and later related 'It was a shock to me to see the condition of the body of my wife'. He paid a woman to clean up his wife's face and then returned by train to Lewannick. The body was removed on the orders of the coroner to the public mortuary on Vauxhall Street. Thomas was allowed to see her the following day, accompanied by the coroner's officer and a policeman, and a post mortem was held shortly after her death. Her will, proved on 25 February 1931, left £110

10s 5d to her husband. On the evening of the death, Mrs Hearn returned to Trenhorne House and told Mrs Spear, 'They seem to think I poisoned her'.[40] Why she should have said this is not known. It is certainly the first time that this possibility was aired. For the next few days, Mrs Hearn continued to keep house for the widower.[41]

It was noted that Thomas 'seemed very agitated and told me his wife had been treated for ptomaine poisoning. Considering the fact that I had been told his wife was suffering from arsenical poisoning, I told Mr Thomas he could only see his wife through the window'.

Apparently Thomas was very distressed and seemed deeply concerned for his wife.[42] Mrs Hearn later said 'He was very much upset and did not seem to be his ordinary self'.[43]

Mrs Hearn wrote in 1931, 'Words cannot describe the strain of those last days, when we saw her terrible sufferings, but nothing that Mrs Parsons or Mr Thomas could do ever seemed to alleviate her anguish during those last hours'. She added 'When I lost Mrs Thomas, I lost one of the kindest friends I had ever known'. Two days after Mrs Thomas died, Mrs Hearn wrote to her surviving sister:

'Dearest Bessie,

Many thanks for your letter. Yes, I knew you would be worrying, but somehow I could not seem to get one off before. I was very busy with several things in between and kept thinking that Mrs Thomas would be better when I could have sent you some good news. But Bessie, I am sorry to say, she has not got better, and on Monday night they took her to Plymouth. The ambulance came about 11.30 at night. Mr Thomas went with them. That was an awful night, and it had been an awful day. She was getting worse all day – delirious and excited all the time. Mr Thomas was with her all day, she did not seem to know him a bit sometimes. Her mother has been here over a week, but nobody could do like him.

It does seem a terrible thing. I wish we had never gone to Bude. She died at 9.30 the next morning. Mr Thomas sent a wire from Plymouth. The funeral is on Saturday. I shall be here till then I expect, don't know after. Some of her relatives are coming I think. Perhaps when you write you will include a

message to Mr Thomas sending sympathy to him. Please excuse more now.
Your loving Annie.[44]

On 5 November Thomas mentioned to Mrs Hearn that there might have to be a post-mortem examination (which had already occurred).[45] On the evening of 6 November, the Thursday after Mrs Thomas's death, Mrs Hearn and Thomas had a conversation in the dining room. According to him, he told her that he had had a severe loss. They then talked about money, namely the sum of £38 (equivalent to several weeks' wages) that he had lent her on 17 December 1928. Could she write him an acknowledgement that he had lent her this, which she then did, 'I will give you an acknowledgement if you write a few words. I will sign it'. It read 'Trenhorne House, Lewannick, Launceston. I received the sum of £38 on loan from William Henry Thomas 17 December 1928. Sarah Ann'. She said she could pay it back when she had boarders in the house but could not have done that while her sister had been so ill (though this had been three months ago). She had previously offered to write an acknowledgement but he had told her it was unnecessary. Thomas was very upset, 'losing my wife was a big blow, a terrible worry', then said that he did not know what to do as regards his domestic arrangements (unsurprisingly so as his wife would have hitherto have seen to all these while he ran the farm), but told her that she would have to leave the farm after the inquest. He had had a terrible loss and incurred great expense. He said this with as much kindliness as possible. They did not discuss the cause of his wife's death as the inquest had yet to take place.[46]

Later that day, according to Mrs Hearn, 'He then appeared more abrupt in his manner and said to me "They are going to send some organs to the analyst to find out what it is. They will blame one of us. The blame will come heavier on you than me. People are saying so. The detectives may be here at any time. Whatever it is they will find it out".

'If people think like that I had better go to my own house'.

'Just as you please'.

Thomas denied that this conversation occurred.[47]

Mrs Hearn also said 'On one of these occasions, I suggested that if people talked like that, I had better go to my house. Mr Thomas said "Please yourself. I don't want you to go". I said 'Perhaps I had better stay until after the funeral".'

Thomas was less certain about the exact nature of the conversation, however, so either Mrs Hearn's memory was better or she was being inventive. This affected Mrs Hearn very much, so she claimed, 'With people outside saying and thinking things like that I was in an awful position'.[48]

In 1931 Mrs Hearn wrote:

'At that time I was very lonely after the death of my sister, and I had just lost a very good friend in Mrs Thomas. It seemed horrible to me that it should be thought that it was my food which was responsible for her death, but it did not strike me even then that it might not be a case of food poisoning'.[49]

A death notice was inserted in the local newspaper for Mrs Thomas. It read:

'THOMAS – at a Nursing Home, Plymouth, on November 4th, Alice, the beloved wife of William Henry Thomas of Trenhorne, Lewannick'.

This shows a degree of respect, but created the fiction of death in a nursing home rather than at the hospital.[50]

Saturday 8 November was the day of Mrs Thomas's funeral. Several family members arrived at Trenhorne Farm prior to the service. Among these were Percy Roy Parsons (1890–1948), a farmer and a brother of Mrs Thomas, from Tremaine Farm, with his wife Florence and sister Kathleen (apparently the first two came uninvited), as did Mrs Tucker. They were met there by a woman whom they did not know. This was Mrs Hearn, who seems, from what transpired, to have been seen as a social inferior and an outsider, and, being non-Cornish, as a foreigner. She took the other two women upstairs at the farm and chatted to them before coming down and waiting on them at table.

Mrs Hearn recalled:

'They were having lunch. I was preparing some things in the kitchen and taking them into the dining room... Some women were discussing Mrs Thomas' illness and naturally looked to me for information. I told them what I knew, and of course, I said the doctors thought it was food poisoning. I don't know if I mentioned sandwiches.'[51]

Parsons asked if the woman was Mrs Hearn and she identified herself. According to Parsons:

> 'I said something about I had made enquiries about my sister, and she said she believed she had been worrying over the harvest. She also made some remark about my sister looking rather unwell when she went to Bude. Then I believe I said "Then you went to Bude with them" and she said "Yes".'

He then asked her 'Where did you have something to eat?' but she could not remember exactly where it was. He then asked: 'What did you have to eat?'. Mrs Hearn replied 'Tea, and I think, cake and bread and butter and sandwiches'. Mrs Hearn was rather reluctant to mention the latter, but Parsons naturally assumed that all the food and drink had been supplied by the café.

Parsons's wife then said 'Where did the sandwiches come from?' and Mrs Hearn replied 'They came from here', or 'We took them with us'. Parsons turned to Mrs Thomas senior and said 'Did you help to make these sandwiches with my sister?' She replied 'Certainly not. Mrs Hearn made all the sandwiches and brought them with her'. Parsons said 'This looks serious. It must be looked into'. Mrs Hearn then left the room.[52]

Apparently Parsons first spoke to Mrs Hearn in an enquiring tone, but once he heard about the sandwiches, he began to shout at her. His words upset her very much.[53]

Parsons wondered if the death was a result of foul play. He thought it odd that his sister had been ill and yet his mother (who lived five miles away) had not been told until ten days later. He thought it strange that Mrs Hearn was the only woman in the house doing the housekeeping and nursing his sister. Another curious incident to him was that when Mrs Wadge came to the house both Thomas and then Mrs Hearn went upstairs and then came down to tell her that Mrs Thomas was too sick to see anyone. However, Parsons was biased. He was not on good terms with Thomas and had heard that 'Mr Thomas and Mrs Hearn were too friendly'. He also thought that his sister and her husband did not get on with each other because he often saw her out by herself and knew that they had rowed once (in two decades of married life).[54]

Parsons then asked Mrs Hearn where she bought the salmon from and she told him the name of the shop. He questioned her and remarked 'This must be cleared up'.[55] This was to have a powerful effect on her, which she recalled in writing two days later. That evening Mrs Hearn was, not surprisingly, given the accusations against her, very depressed and talked about life not being worth living.[56]

There was a large gathering at the funeral. Mrs Thomas was buried under a coroner's warrant in the churchyard of St Martin's, the parish church of Lewannick. Thomas was accompanied by a Miss Wilcox; it is unclear who she was and she is never alluded to again. Mrs Hannah Jane Gubbin (1893–1969), wife of a farmer at Petherwin and a younger sister of the deceased, attended and had a talk with the widower beforehand. She recalled that he had said: 'I wish to goodness sake that Alice hadn't gone to Bude. She didn't want to go. Only she is always home evenings quiet: I made her go'. He added 'I wish 'twas me instead of her'. Mrs Gubbin knew of Mrs Thomas's illness, but had thought nothing of it and the next news was that her sister was dead.[57]

Mrs Spear was also at the funeral and she recalled, about Mrs Hearn 'She seemed quite upset about something. I was with Mrs Hearn in church during the funeral service, and she seemed alright. She sang with the rest of us'. Apparently she had asked Mrs Spear to go with her to the funeral.[58]

According to the local newspaper, 'On Saturday, the 4th inst., quite a gloom was cast over the parish and district when it became known that Mrs Thomas… had passed away… The deceased was much beloved and will be greatly missed'. Before the funeral party left the farm, Mr Gimblett offered prayer. At the church the newly appointed vicar, the Rev Charles Harcourt Blofeld (1880–1938), officiated and one of the hymns sung was 'Jesu, Lover of my soul'. There were thirty-two members of the family and close friends, including parents, brothers and sisters, in-laws, uncles, aunts, and cousins, 147 others and nineteen wreaths. Mrs Hearn did not send a wreath, perhaps out of economy.[59]

Many family and friends came to the farmhouse after the funeral. Parsons related that he did not speak to Mrs Hearn on this occasion. Mrs Thomas stayed at her son's house for at least a month after the funeral, doubtless to cook and do the housework for him. She remembered that on the day after the funeral, Mrs Hearn made several references to Parsons as 'that horrid man'.[60]

The new gravestone in the churchyard read as follows:

IN LOVING MEMORY OF
ALICE MAUD
THE DEARLY LOVED WIFE OF
WILLIAM HENRY THOMAS
OF TRENHORNE
WHO DIED NOV. 4TH 1930
AGED 43 YEARS

Mrs Hearn later said: 'From the day of the funeral, I felt people were suspecting me of having poisoned Mrs Thomas'.[61] She continued:

'It appeared quite sure that Mr Thomas or me would have to suffer for it. I felt I could not face the ordeal. Mr Thomas told me we should have to attend the inquest and it appeared as if somebody would be charged with murder. I could not think of anybody but us two, and sooner than that. I thought I would go my own way and take my life'.[62]

If Mrs Hearn meant this, then she surely knew who the poisoner was. If it was not her then it must have been Thomas. Likewise, Thomas would have known this, too. One of them knew that they were innocent and so the other must be guilty. When such realisation came on the innocent is another question, as to which one was guilty. Or could it have been a joint venture, as was probably the case with Dr Crippen, his wife and secretary in 1910, when Crippen was in love with his secretary, Ethel le Neve, and his wife was murdered? To help decide, it is necessary to know more about the parties concerned.

Chapter 2

The characters in the story

We need to now examine the three principals in this case. There is far more evidence about Mrs Hearn and her family, though much of this was recounted by the woman herself in later years. How accurate the details are is another question; memories can go awry and the veracity of witnesses may well be questioned.

Mrs Hearn had been born Sarah Annie Everard on 2 June 1885 (she later claimed not to know her age and did not know that of her elder sister) at a house in Legsby Road in the village of Middle Rasen, Lincolnshire. Her parents were Robert Edward Everard (1853–1928), son of a farmer and himself a small farmer with ten acres of land in 1881, born in Leverton, Lincolnshire, and Betsy Everard, née Day (1847–1915), his wife of six years his senior and born in Scotter in the same county. They had married in 1875. Annie was the fifth of at least eight children born to the Everards, all of whom lived to adulthood. The others were Lydia Maria (known as Minnie), born in 1876, Betsy, (1878–1960), Robert William (1879–1969), Henry (1880–1962), Jesse Albert (1887–1973), Grace Mabel (1889–1917) known as Mabel, all born in Glentham except for Jesse and Grace who were born in Market Rasen, Lincolnshire. The last of the brood was Oliver Ronald (1891–1921), born in Snitterby in the same county.[1]

By 1885 the family had moved from Glentham to Middle Rasen, another small farming community in Lincolnshire. It was here that Annie was born. They were not there long, as by 1887 they had moved to Market Rasen, which was a market town about a mile eastwards. The Everards lived on Serpentine Street, where Everard was listed as a shopkeeper and carter.[2]

By 1891 the family were living in Snitterby, eleven miles to the north-west of Market Rasen. This was a far smaller place. There was a National school, which the Everard children of school age, including Annie, would have attended. By now Annie's father was a mere farm worker and the family took in two lodgers to make ends meet.[3]

Soon after the family moved again and Annie attended Welholme Road school, a new Grimsby council school.[4] She later recalled having to learn poetry off by heart, including Tennyson's *Memoriam*, 'That men may rise on stepping stones/Of their dead selves to higher things'.[5]

In 1893, Jesse, Henry and Annie attended the same school, but left on 6 April 1893 to go to the small parish of Farforth with Maidenwell. It may have been there on 18 May 1896 that a number of children, including Annie, were included in a report that stated that they 'do not attend [school] regularly at all and retard the progress of the class, in causing the teacher to go over the same work several times'. The 10-year-old Annie was not a diligent pupil.[6]

In a newspaper article written in 1933, Annie wrote a little about her childhood, claiming she was born on 2 June 1890. She wrote that her father had two accidents on his small farm when Annie was little. She also wrote that she 'tried to live a god fearing life, as my father taught us to live', adding 'When I was a little girl in Market Rasen, father, who was a very religious man, would never let us grumble at anything' and he told them 'There must be some reason for it'. She also remembered, 'I can see father sitting every morning in his life, reading to mother and us children a chapter out of the big family Bible, or saying one of his favourite hymns, "Oh God our help in ages past... And our eternal home"'.[7] In 1931 she claimed 'We were a happy, united family'.[8]

In 1901 the family was living at 21 Heneage Road, in the suburb of Clee in the town of Grimsby. Bessie no longer lived with her parents but the remainder of the children were still under the same roof, either at school or in employment. Their father was now a self-employed gardener. Annie had left school and is not noted as being in work.[9]

Minnie and Bessie had entered domestic service by 1891, but probably earlier. In about 1895 Minnie joined Bessie to help in her dressmaking business at Sutton-on-Sea, Lincolnshire. Robert and Henry, though, were doing rather better, being employed as clerks by 1901. By 1901, Minnie is recorded as having no occupation, which perhaps suggests that she was unwell and incapable of paid work. As we shall see, illness was her common lot. Her sister Annie, then aged fifteen, was also listed as having no occupation. Perhaps she was involved in unpaid caring or household duties or was between jobs.[10]

Annie later recalled living with her sister Bessie at Sutton-on-Sea when she was fifteen, but she returned home to nurse her sister Minnie, who was suffering from gastritis and gastric catarrah. Annie slept in the same room as her sister, who called her 'the little nurse'. Annie later wrote, 'I never did like nursing, but somehow ever since I was a little girl I have been forced by circumstance to nurse people. When it happened I made up my mind to do all I could for them and the doctors have always been pleased with me'.[11]

Many years later it was stated that the Everards were a middle-class family, though this does not seem to be the case. They are never recorded as having a servant, for example, and two of the daughters entered domestic service: 'The Everard farm was not very wealthy in resources, and inevitably, and at any early age, she became accustomed to hard work. On all sides it is testified that as a housewife, Annie Everard had few equals. She could cook and sew with the perfection of a natural instinct of domestic duty'.[12]

By 1911 the family was dispersed. Its head was still a jobbing employed gardener, and he and Betsy were living in Ulceby, a small village not far from their previous haunts, where they had been since about 1904. Only Oliver, their youngest child, remained with them in their eight-roomed house and he worked as an insurance clerk.[13]

The head of the household had a sister who was slightly older than him: Mary Ann Everard, born at Leverton on Christmas Day 1849 to William, a small farmer, and Maria Everard. She was the third of six children. She never married and commenced her working life as a servant. In 1871 and 1881 she was a parlour maid at the Vicarage, occupied by the Rev James Allan Smith, in Nottingham. However, she did rather better for herself as the years went by. From at least 1891–1911 she was a certified cookery teacher, being employed in 1891 at Paignton, Devon (employing one servant but also having a lodger), then by 1901 at The Hall, Ulceby, Lincolnshire (where she lived with her elderly father) and shortly afterwards, once he had died, in her own School of Cookery at 46 Harlow Moor Drive, Harrogate, Yorkshire, where she was Principal. She was also very active in the parish church of St Mary's.[14] Annie recalled:

'For a time I went to stay with my aunt at Usselby Hall, a very fine old house with huge rooms, in a little village outside Grimsby, and one thing which stands out in my mind is the fact that the little church there could have easily been put inside the dining room at Usselby Hall.

We were extremely fond of one another, and when she opened her school there she allowed me to assist her, so that I had all the advantages of studying under her, and thus became efficient as a teacher of the things which she taught there.

It was called The Harrogate Residential School of Cookery, Laundry and Domestic Science, and in addition she also taught dress cutting and fitting. She held diplomas for those arts, and had taught cookery in the schools of Keswick and Cockermouth, as well as lecturing for the Cumberland County Council, the Lincolnshire County School, and in Devonshire, Worcestershire, Lancashire, Durham and Westmorland, so that she was well fitted to embark on a school of her own.

Girls came from all parts of the country, and we were able to take six pupils who lived with us in addition to those who attended daily. It was there I learned so much about the domestic arts and sciences which proved of such service in later life.'

Annie later claimed 'It was my ambition to make a success of the business'. By 1911, Annie had dropped her first Christian name, Sarah. She was clearly on good terms with her aunt (known as Aunt Pollie) and was to remain close to her all the rest of her aunt's life, as we shall see.[15]

As for the remainder of the family, Oliver was married in 1915 to Gertrude Kathleen Barnard and they had two children. Bessie married Alfred Richardson Poskitt (1870–1953), a railway employee, in 1921. They lived in the West Riding of Yorkshire, at Rose Cottage in the village of Long Sandall, near Doncaster. Henry was a contractor's clerk in 1911, boarding with a family in Cleethorpes. He served in the Royal Navy from 1916–19 and married Elsie Smith in 1921. He was later a local government clerk and lived in Grimsby. By 1917 his brother Robert was living in Clapham, south London and was employed as an auditor. Oliver served with the Royal Garrison Artillery in the First World War and died of war-related illness on 19 March 1921.[16]

Jesse had emigrated across the Atlantic by 1908 to live in British Columbia on the west coast of Canada, and he later moved to California. The fates of Annie's other two sisters are of interest. Minnie was living with a cousin, Mary Hartley, a dressmaker, in her house at 286 Heneage Road, Grimsby, in 1911. She is recorded as having no occupation, as had been the case in 1901, which is another pointer to her frail health. She was not the only one in the family who was unwell. Her younger sister Mabel was an inpatient at the Mendip Hills Sanatorium at Hillgrove in Somerset, suffering from pulmonary tuberculosis.[17] Annie said of Mabel that she was, 'always rather a frail delicate girl, but we thought that as the years went on she would grow out of it. She was one of the loveliest girls I have ever seen, and she was as sweet and patient as she was beautiful'.[18]

Mabel was apparently greatly loved and rarely complained about her lot, bearing her illness bravely and smiling at her troubles. The vicar said 'if ever there was an angel on Earth, it was Mabel'. When she returned home, Annie claimed that she rigged up a telephone so that Mabel could communicate with her family, 'I have always been of a mechanical mind,' claimed Annie, though there is no further evidence of this.[19]

Apparently, in about 1912 the Everards: father and mother, and Minnie and Mabel at least, lived in Croft House, in the hamlet of Barn in the Wood, near Hathersage, Derbyshire 'in a most secluded part of the country between Grindleford Bridge and the little village of Hathersage'. Annie used to visit to nurse her sisters. Minnie, in 1916, went to Sheffield Infirmary as an inpatient suffering from stomach troubles (Bessie Everard was then living in Sheffield). She also suffered severe pains in her arms and legs and pins and needles in her hands. She was at the infirmary for several weeks and a stomach pump was used on her. On leaving, she was only a little better. In 1917 she went to Harrogate. She saw an eye specialist there.[20]

In 1931 Mrs Hearn claimed that:

'When my sister Minnie, my aunt and myself were living at Grindleford, in Derby, we used to play cards with a pack of ordinary playing cards from which the three of spades was missing.

When we played, one hand would be the one card short, so that when a spade was led the one with the missing three of spades would not lay a card, and in this way things were evened up.

One day I was standing waiting for a bus with my sister, when she pointed to a card lying face downwards in the road. It was a very wet day. 'Wouldn't it be funny if that was the three of spades?' she remarked to me and I agreed it would.

I turned the card over with my toe, and sure enough it was the three of spades. I picked it up and put it in my pocket'.[21]

Apparently, at this time, her mother learnt that two girls whom they knew from Grimsby had contracted tuberculosis and their parents were despairing. It was decided that they should join the Everards out in the country 'for a time, to see whether the fresh air and new surroundings would help them at all'. Annie wrote 'Mother was a dear soul and could never refuse anyone in trouble'. The girls came, and it seemed that they were improving, but when Mabel caught a chill which turned to pneumonia, they returned to Grimsby and died soon after. It is a pity that their names and dates of death are unknown. Annie wrote 'It was a tragedy which played on the minds of Mabel and my mother very considerably and from that time Mabel never seemed to recover'.[22]

While at Harrogate, Annie, so she said, met a young man, a commercial traveller, and they fell in love, but she had to tell him they could not marry because she needed to nurse her family members. In 1915, Annie received a telegram from her family that read: 'Come at once. Mother ill'. She went immediately. She learnt that her mother had been nursing Mabel, who was a consumptive and had returned from the sanatorium having been classed as incurable, and that Mrs Everard had caught influenza from her. Bad weather had accelerated this. Annie later wrote, 'Too late we realised that it would have been better to have the hut built nearer to the house so that Mother could have just slipped over whenever was necessary without going outdoors'. Bessie first thought to remedy this and paid for it to be done, 'I mention this just to show what a loving family we were'. A week after Annie's arrival, her mother was on her deathbed. She called Annie to her bedside, and said, 'Annie, I'm going now. Don't leave Mabel as long as she lives. She will need you. You have to take my place'. Annie later wrote 'That was a terrible blow to us all'. Mrs Everard was sixty-eight when she died on 18 November 1915. Her death certificate, signed by Dr Ethelbert Hearn, recorded that she died of hypostatic pneumonia, which she had suffered from for twenty-one days previously, and it resulted in cardiac failure. Contrary to Annie's later version of events, apparently Minnie was in attendance and informed the registrar of her mother's death four days later. Annie then lived with her sisters and widower father, nursing Minnie and Mabel. The former had another breakdown and was sleeping in an outdoor bedroom in the garden for fresh air. Annie called at Dr Hearn's for medicines. Dr Ethelbert Hearn (1865–1943) lived at Grindleford, and in 1930 wrote thus: 'I had been attending her sister who was desperately ill with tuberculosis and eventually died'.[23]

Mabel developed tuberculosis 'and as time went on grew worse and worse'. Annie was informed by letter and arrived from Harrogate. It was advised by a doctor that she live in the open air and to this end a hut was built for her at the bottom of the garden. Here she slept and lived for the most part, whatever the weather. She claimed that the doctor said Mabel would not live long, but survived:

> 'for two terrible years, during which she suffered the most awful agonies. And during that two years I stayed with her and nursed her, looking after the house, and looking after my father. And all the time she got steadily worse and worse. Her weakness became greater and greater, and she simply prayed she might be taken. "When you keep on going on and on, until you simply can't bear any more – what can you do?" she asked me in her weak, pathetic voice, and I could only shake my head. I could not speak, for had I done so I should have broken down.
>
> Then she expressed a wish to be confirmed before she died, and as she was too ill even to be carried to church, it was arranged that she should be confirmed at her home which had held so much tragedy for her.
>
> It was the Bishop Suffragan of Derby who carried out the pretty ceremony, and never was there a more patient, sweeter, subject of confirmation than my sister Mabel'.[24]

Mabel died in Annie's arms on 14 November 1917, apparently of pulmonary tuberculosis, which she had suffered from for ten years. In her last forty-two days she had also suffered from tubercular peritonitis and died from exhaustion. Again

Dr Hearn signed the death certificate. This time, the death certificate notes that Annie Everard was present at the death and it was she who told the registrar the news twelve days later.[25]

The remaining family members left after the death and their father moved to Sheffield where he married Mary Sargent in 1922. Not much was known about them at this time, but a resident said Annie was quiet and superior.[26] Another source, a Cornish woman, claimed that 'She is a strangely reserved woman. We have thought of her as a woman of great sorrows'. This was not surprising: four friends and family members had died in quick succession.[27] After Mabel's death in 1917, Minnie and Annie went to live with their aunt in Harrogate,[28] although one account has Annie staying with another aunt at Louth from 1917–19.[29] If this was so, this was probably Betsy Holland (1853–1926), a widow.

Annie claimed that she and Minnie went to Harrogate: 'I took some part, just as I had done before, in running the school. But my aunt during my absence had not been able to carry on quite so well, with the result that the school had gone down somewhat and was not the success it had been. I did all I could and worked night and day, trying to pull things together, but without success'.[30]

Annie also claimed that Mabel's death left 'Minnie prostrate with grief, and as an invalid, and myself a broken woman with Minnie a scared charge to look after and keep'. Earlier, Minnie had been so ill that she was unable to take a drop of water for six weeks, so that they thought she was dying and she replied 'I thought I'd gone that time'.[31]

Mrs Bessie Poskitt, a loyal sister, wrote in 1930:

'Mrs (Annie) Hearn is kind and unselfish to a degree. She has nursed many of her relations during their last illnesses and has frequently attracted the praise of the doctors. I do not think she liked nursing, but she was very good at adapting herself.

Her life had been a vale of sorrows.'[32]

Just after the end of the First World War, Annie's life apparently took a bizarre turn. There appeared in the Births, Marriages and Deaths column of a Harrogate newspaper the following announcement under Marriages (curiously misspelling Hearn in two different ways):

'HEARNE-EVERARD – on June 6 1919, at St. Andrew's church, London by the Reverend Fairfax, M.A., of Leonard Wilmot Hearn, M.D., son of F. Hearn, to Annie, daughter of Arthur Robert Everard of Sheffield and Harrogate.'

In the same column of the same issue, under Deaths, was:

'Herne, June 12 1919, suddenly at Bedford House, Southampton Row, London, Wilmot Hearn, M.D., recently returned from service in France'.[33]

These were a tissue of lies. Annie's father was Robert Edward not Arthur Robert and he never lived in Harrogate. There was not a London clergyman of the surname mentioned in 1919 and there is not a Bedford House in Southampton Row, London. The only Anglican Rev Fairfax at this time was Charles Henry Fairfax of Brailsford Rectory, Derbyshire, who died in July 1919 but once lived near Market Rasen, so the name may well have been known to Annie.[34] The name Hearn was that of the Grindleford doctor she had professional dealings with during the family's residence there c.1912–17. The only Dr Leonard Hearn's father's Christian name did not begin with F, for it was Ethelbert, and his middle name was Wilfred not Wilmot. And the man himself was alive and well, and unmarried.

However, in addition to these announcements, Annie also bought a postcard in Sheffield of the late Lieutenant Charles Stewart Vane Tempest, once of the Royal Flying Corps, which she pretended was a picture of her late husband. The young man's mother, Mrs Nigel Harrison, later said 'There is no justification for the use of my son's photograph by this woman of whom I am sure he has never heard'. He had been the son of her first marriage and died in a German prisoner-of-war camp in March 1917 of wounds inflicted at Ligny.[35]

No such marriage or death was ever recorded in any official documentation. Why Annie should invent such a story is not recorded. It has been suggested that she was disappointed about not being married and that by her early thirties she was definitely, to use the terminology of the time, 'on the shelf' and never likely to be wed, especially given the loss of male life in the recent war. So to compensate she invented a fantasy life in which she had been married to a war hero or a doctor who had also served in the conflict and was now conveniently dead. She talked to relatives about this as if it had actually happened. Naturally no one had ever met her 'husband', nor had they been present at a ceremony. Anyone can post a marriage/death announcement in the local press for a small fee and it will not be checked. According to her sister, Mrs Poskitt, Annie had married the doctor just after the war, in London, and her husband had collapsed during the ceremony and died three days later.[36] She thought they had met at Grindleford or Harrogate.[37] Apparently Annie gave Mrs Poskitt a news-cutting from the Harrogate newspaper about her alleged marriage.[38] From now on Annie will be known as Mrs Hearn, the name she had chosen for herself. This was the first, but not the last, of Mrs Hearn's lies.

However, this was not then known. Mrs Poskitt was taken in and later wrote 'This [the alleged death] I am sure hit my sister terribly although she was the kind who do not talk much of the things they feel most. I never saw the man she married'.[39] Likewise, in the autumn of 1919, shortly after the alleged death of Dr Hearn, Mrs Hearn and Minnie visited a cousin, a Mr H. Houlton of Mildmay Street, Lincoln, and told him about their loss. There had been an application for a war pension but the death was not due to war wounds.[40]

Annie told Dr Ethelbert Hearn too and he recalled in 1930, 'Some time later she returned to her home, and she called on me. The maid announced that Mrs Dr Leonard Hearn wanted to see me. I, of course, was astonished, because it was the name of my son. When I went into the waiting room imagine my further surprise when I discovered the caller was Miss Annie Everard. She said, seeing my astonishment "Yes, I am Mrs Dr Leonard Hearn but a different Hearn from your family". This was eleven years ago. She told me her husband had suffered during the war and had a bad heart'.[41] He added, 'I knew her as Miss Annie Everard, a little, slim, quiet, unassuming young woman.'[42] Mrs Hearn was clearly a deceitful woman.

Annie later claimed that it was shortly after 1917 that doctors recommended that Minnie live in Devon or Cornwall in order that her health would improve with the fresh air. Annie said that the doctors claimed her trouble was gastric in nature, but their methods failed to make her any better. Annie saw her sister's health worsening. Annie wrote, 'I was frantic with grief. On the one hand there was my aunt, who had been extremely good to me, needing my services to help her with the school. On the other hand, there was the news regarding my beloved sister Minnie. Unless I got her to the South of England she would die. I did not hesitate'.[43]

It is not certain when they travelled southwards and the evidence already given suggests that it was not until 1919 and that is the earliest year that they are definitely known to have been there, as shall be seen. They apparently took a bungalow in Hatherleigh, Devonshire, but things were not easy financially. Minnie enjoyed an annuity yielding £1 per week from one of her brothers, but there was little money, with expenses and doctor's bills to pay. Annie later claimed she often went hungry so her sister could eat. They also took in lodgers.[44] In 1919 they were living in Worle, a village near Weston-super-Mare, Somerset. Possibly they moved there on account of their sister Mabel being resident in the sanatorium in the same county and their aunt having once lived nearby. Perhaps it was to escape from Lincolnshire, or perhaps it was for health reasons as regards Miss Everard. Certainly this was later cited, as was business failure. Miss Poskitt wrote 'My sick sister Lydia went out there to be under Annie's care', and from then on these two sisters were inextricably linked.[45]

Less well known, and never mentioned in 1930–31 or since, was an incident which is a pointer to Mrs Hearn's character. She had her first known brush with the law over an alleged jewellery theft. The sisters were staying from 1 November to 16 December 1919 as paying lodgers at The Woodlands, Spring Hill, Worle, the home of the widowed Catherine Bullus (1845–1925) and her daughter, Minnie Henrietta Bullus (1869–1921), who took in lodgers. Apparently the former was mentally unstable or at least had poor memory. The sisters seemed 'quite respectable' and had been kind to their hosts.[46]

Shortly after 2 December, Miss Bullus showed the sisters a number of pieces of jewellery, including a gold watch, two mourning rings and two silver brooches, which were kept locked in a work box. When the sisters departed they were seen to have a green suitcase among their luggage. Miss Bullus soon realised that these, together with £5 in notes, handkerchiefs and some private letters, had disappeared. They were later found at Miss Everard's house in Harrogate, along with a letter from Mrs Hearn instructing her aunt to bury them.[47]

Miss Bullus informed PC Swatbridge of the theft, who then saw the accused sisters, who had clearly not travelled far. Knowing they did not have the goods, they invited him to search their rooms and belongings as this would be 'more satisfactory to all'. They suggested where he could search. They agreed that Miss Bullus had shown them the missing items. However, there was an investigation in Harrogate, in which DS Baldwin of the West Riding Constabulary was handed two parcels from Miss Mary Everard and he checked to find the missing items in them. Inspector Munro charged them with theft and Miss Everard replied, 'I know nothing whatever about it' and her sister said 'What I have to say I will say presently'.[48]

Mrs Hearn and her sister were brought before the Weston-super-Mare Magistrates' Court on 24 December 1919, accused of theft of the jewellery. A newspaper described the defendants as 'two sisters of genteel appearance, who deemed to feel their position acutely'. So much so that Mrs Hearn was apparently seized with a fainting fit and so the hearing was postponed, though whether this was real or pretence is another question. Both women were remanded in custody.[49]

The sisters next appeared before the same court on 31 December. Mrs Hearn was described as being forty-one and her sister thirty-six (they were really thirty-four and forty-five respectively). William John Wentworth Dickinson (1885–1952), a solicitor, defended the pair, whose alleged theft was valued at £61 15s. Miss Bullus gave evidence of their losses. She denied that her mother had given these items to the sisters as presents and said that Mrs Bullus did not have access to them in any case. Miss Mary Everard, 'an elderly lady of superior appearance and address' appeared as a witness. She attested that in mid–December 1919 she had received a parcel from one of her nieces. Then a second parcel arrived with a letter (now destroyed) from Mrs Hearn.[50] Superintendent Richardson then asked 'Were there certain instructions in the letters with reference to the parcels?' Miss Everard replied, 'I was asked to take care of them, and to put them in a safe place until she arrived home in the following week'.

The letter, which had been written in pencil, was indistinct and Mrs Hearn was ill at the time, but signed it with her pet name 'Tannie'. Miss Everard said that Mrs Hearn had lived with her for ten years and was her adopted daughter, an interesting statement which is never again mentioned; did she mean that after her sister-in-law died, leaving Mrs Hearn without a mother, she had assumed that position? It certainly suggests that her aunt had a great deal of affection for her niece, or assumed great responsibility for her, though the younger woman was thirty when her mother died, so was hardly a helpless child. The letter had said that the parcels should be buried in the garden, and the witness noted that there were handkerchiefs in one of them, but she did not examine them further. Mrs Hearn had said that the items had been left to her by an aunt and she would explain when she arrived in Harrogate. Miss Everard said Mrs Hearn had been used to handling large sums of money and was utterly trustworthy. 'Everything I have known of both of them has been most satisfactory'.

Frank Castle Froest (1857–1930), a magistrate, then asked if Miss Everard had complied with the request and buried them, to which the old lady said 'I simply could not. It was a pouring wet day and I am 70 years of age'.[51]

Dickinson said that there was no evidence against Minnie and so charges against her should be dropped at once. The magistrates agreed and she was dismissed. Her sister Mrs Hearn was asked to explain herself and she said: 'I am not guilty of stealing the goods. They were given to me by Mrs Bullus and I sent them to my aunt to look after. What I have to say I will say later at my trial'.

Mrs Hearn was committed for trial at the Quarter Sessions on 7 January. She was bailed for £50 of her own money and her aunt entered into a recognisance for a further £100. Dickinson said that Canon William Edward Haigh (1873–1932), vicar of Clifton, could be a further surety if required. Presumably the sisters knew this man.[52]

Mrs Hearn was brought before the Somerset Quarter Sessions on 7 January. She was described as being aged thirty-two, a cookery teacher and as 'a well dressed woman of superior education, and stated to be the widow of an army doctor'. She retold her married fantasy of 1919, and to good effect. She pleaded not guilty. Mr Wethered was the prosecutor. Mrs Hearn said that Miss Bullus gave the items to her and she sent them to her aunt to look after, remarking that Miss Bullus was sane and responsible and when the box was handed to her, as a gift, she did not know what it contained. Later, when she realised its contents, she became frightened and told her aunt to hide them. Mr Weatherby spoke for the defence. He said his client was a foolish woman but not a criminal. Mrs Hearn was found not guilty and so was discharged.[53]

It would seem that Mrs Hearn had had a fortunate escape from a short prison sentence. She clearly took the valuables and ephemera from her host's daughter and sent them to her beloved aunt for safe keeping. If she was innocent, why send them there and why ask that they be buried? And her claim about her host's mother, who was elderly and very forgetful at best, senile at worst, could never be disproved. Presumably the crime was a simple one motivated by greed or the need for money (neither sister is noted as being employed), though quite why personal correspondence was also stolen is a mystery. It shows that Mrs Hearn was cunning and deceitful while appearing respectable and kind. Whether this was a template for her future actions is a moot point. It is not known what, if any, part her sister played in this, but Mrs Hearn was the moving spirit behind it.

Probably Mrs Hearn's appearance counted much in her favour, as she was seemingly the respectable widow of an army doctor. Some women would have been found guilty on such evidence. It is unknown what the sisters' financial situation was, but the robbery, if indeed it was a robbery, was actuated by want. It is also unknown what part their aunt played in this, but clearly she was trusted by them. Her imagined marriage made Mrs Hearn seem more respectable and more of an object of sympathy and so more likely to escape imprisonment for theft, many women having lost husbands in the recent war or its aftermath.

Annie's aunt clearly had a great deal of time for Annie; on 1 September 1922, she wrote in her will, 'I give to my dear niece, Sarah Ann Hearn, known as Annie Hearn who was my assistant and partner for many years everything I possess'. The two got on very well indeed.[54]

Although Aunt Mary usually lived and worked in Harrogate, in 1921 she was living at 36 Woodstock Road, Oxford. She had a paying guest, Miss Kathleen Nuttall, a 22-year-old student from Keighley in Yorkshire.[55]

The sisters lived briefly in two rooms above a shop in Weston-super-Mare High Street, then moved to Devon; Miss Minnie Everard was by now suffering from gastric catarrh.[56]

By June 1921 the two sisters were living in three rooms in Bradford Manor, Brandis Corner, in Holsworthy, Devon. Miss Everard was described as the householder as she was the elder, but is not listed as having an occupation, presumably due to her illnesses. Mrs Hearn called herself Annie Hearn, a widow born in 1887. She was self-employed as a cook, presumably using the skills she had learnt and taught at her aunt's cookery school, and this was the sisters' main way to make ends meet.[57]

In later 1921 the sisters began to live in North Hill, a small village in Cornwall. Miss Everard was an invalid and was treated for dyspepsia from 1922.[58] In 1922 Dr Douglas Hugh Galbraith (1889-1959), and his partner Dr Charles Gordon Gibson (1865–1947), both of nearby Launceston, first treated Miss Everard for inflammation of the bowels and stomach, the former suspecting gastric ulcers. Her eyes troubled her and they bought her some glasses at Heath and Stoneman's in Plymouth. She also suffered from neuritis in the feet and Dr Hugh Hamilton

Serpell (1877–1925), of Lewannick, saw her about this. The sisters said that they had left the Midlands for Cornwall for her health. She also suffered from catarrh and constipation and took medicines from Shuker and Reed for this; cascara tablets.[59]

Dr Gibson recalled: 'I was treating her for stomach trouble mostly. My recollection is that I was told she had gastric ulcer, but when I came to examine her I found no definite evidence of gastric ulcer, but rather of chronic dyspepsia or indigestion and bowel trouble'. He and his partner saw her every week from November 1922 to 12 January 1925, and then not until 21 October 1925. 'At that time Miss Everard was still in North Hill Village and very poorly with similar digestive troubles and pains and the question was whether she was in fit state of health to be moved to Trenhorne. I saw her on October 21st and October 23rd'.

The various medicines Dr Gibson prescribed were a soothing stomach mixture on 21 October, and again 10 days later. Later he gave her a laxative for the bowels, and reverted to a prescription given back in 1922 for a stomach and bowel mixture. On 4 November Miss Everard was much better and he subsequently saw her walking about the place. He did not see her professionally until January 1930.[60]

As at Brandis Corner, Mrs Hearn had cooked food at home and sold it to people living nearby.[61] Mrs Poskitt wrote about Mrs Hearn, who had worked at her aunt's catering college: 'My sister was clever at cooking. She said when talking of giving up the home, I can always make my own living'.[62]

Priscilla Aunger, a 91-year-old carpenter's widow in poor circumstances, boarded with sisters and paid 30s a week. Mrs Poskitt described this as an act of charity: 'Annie also invited an old Cornish woman who would otherwise have had to go into a Guardians institution to stay with her which she did'.[63]

Priscilla Aunger was born Priscilla Willcocks in 1835 at Lanivet, Cornwall. Her father was variously an agricultural labourer, a bailiff and a grocer. In her twenties she was a schoolmistress and from at least 1861 she lived in North Hill, first with her parents and then with her husband, James Aunger, on her marriage in 1876. The couple had no children and her husband died in 1904. Priscilla was probably not well off by 1921 and she certainly did not leave a will.

The sisters lived in a two-storey cottage next door to the sexton, Richard Hocking, which was opposite the Anglican parish church, St Torney's. He recalled Mrs Hearn in 1931:

'She was a quiet sort of woman and kept much to herself. We never saw much of her. The only time she was in our house was when she opened a cake shop. We knew she had a good knowledge of cooking and about seven years ago she used her cottage as a shop. That was about two years before she left North Hill for Trenhorne. She came to North Hill about eight or nine years ago. Mrs Hearn came to tell us about the opening of her shop and asked if we would care to buy any cakes or pastries. But I told her we all baked them ourselves and could make them cheaper than she could sell them. The shop idea was not a success and she stopped it after a few months, as she had hardly any customers. As far as I knew she was in poor circumstances and never seemed to have much money. I don't think she had much when she went to Trenhorne. Mrs Aunger was a native of this parish and everyone knew her'.[64]

The sisters moved to near Lewannick, some miles to the north, on 27 October 1925, with the intention of setting up a boarding house there and presumably taking Mrs Aunger with them at some stage. They took the tenancy of half of Trenhorne House, part of the hamlet of Trenhorne and just to the south of the village of Lewannick. The house was also the residence of Mrs Elizabeth Spear and her daughter, who had been there since 1923, who kept four cows, though the two sections of the house were self-contained. The two-storey house was owned by a Thomas Nicholas Wenn, an auctioneer of Launceston, and he rented it unfurnished to the sisters. The back garden was very overgrown with weeds in December 1930. The sisters were not in a good financial state. Both the sisters and Mrs Spear had front gardens, but the back garden belonged solely to the sisters.[65]

In 1937 the property was described as having nine acres of land, five bedrooms, two reception rooms, a kitchen dairy, scullery and conservatory, and was 'very pleasantly situated' on the bus route to Launceston, five miles away. There is no reason to suppose it was any different in the previous decade when the sisters arrived there. To the south-west of the house were ruins and an old building.[66] However, it was not perfect, as Miss Everard wrote on 14 January 1930: 'All kitchen part and house awfully wet, floors awful, dining room very damp'.[67]

A more lengthy description made in 1930 was as follows:

'This is a semi-detached house about three quarters of a mile outside Lewannick. A glass porch runs along the front of the house and a weathered vine runs through the small conservatory. In front of the two houses which stand alone there is a lawn. Alongside the neighbouring house to that of Mrs Hearn is an orchard. The two houses overlook a rolling expanse of fields.

The front rooms of the house, which have bay windows, evidently had been used as a sitting room and a room at the side had evidently been used as a breakfast-room. It bore the marks of recent use. On a table near a basin with jug inside, two wooden boxes, and a small piece of paper.

The garden was untidy, although it was stated that gardening was one of Mrs Hearn's hobbies. In the garden were a few flower pots and an old pan. A wooden table and a chair stood in the grass.

Through the kitchen window could be seen a number of small photographs on the table, evidently the work of an amateur. A printed sheet of paper bore the headline *Christian Herald Prayer*. A basket and some clothing were also on the table. On the corner of a clothes horse at the other end of a kitchen was a woman's hat.'[68]

Dr Gibson took them from North Hill to Trenhorne in his car. Mrs Hearn later recalled of her invalid sister: 'She was so ill that she could not sit up in bed. It would have been impossible for her to have gone if the doctor did not take her'. She was wrapped around in a blanket when she got to Trenhorne.[69]

Mrs Hearn later recalled the move:

'I went over to Trenhorne taking with me a wire mattress and an overlay, and this I put down in the bedroom upon the floor, making as comfortable a bed as I could for Minnie under the circumstances. There was also an easy chair.

Then I beat her up some eggs in milk and had to leave her there whilst I went to and fro from one house to the other superintending the removal.

I was tired out when at length the task was finished, and I went to my neighbour, Mrs Spear, one of the dearest women who ever lived, for some milk, and she arranged to supply me with some milk in the future…

The first Sunday I was there she seemed so ill that I would cycle over to the doctor to get some medicine'.[70]

Mrs Hearn described how the sisters went out for walks on the moorland. Miss Everard would walk with a stick due to her infirmity. On one occasion, they saw flowers and Miss Everard went over to pick them, without any awareness of danger. Her stick began to sink into the bog and Mrs Hearn saved her sister's life.[71]

According to the local newspaper, 'Mrs Hearn lived a singularly quiet domestic life, her friends describing her as "first and foremost a home-loving woman; the kitchen always scrupulously clean, with shelves lined with shining pots and pans, was her great pride"'.[72]

Miss Everard's diary gives an insight into her sister's activities in 1930; as a semi-invalid she rarely left the house. According to her, Mrs Hearn was active in both house and garden. In the former, she made dresses, washed clothes, cleaned the place, baked and cooked. Outside she worked in the garden, planting various vegetables and fruit. She was occasionally ill and perhaps with all the domestic work it was not surprising that her sister wrote 'Annie is looking very pale and tired'.[73]

Meanwhile, the Thomases also lived in Trenhorne. William Thomas was born at St Germans on 22 August 1889 to William Henry Thomas (1844–1900), a farmer, and Elizabeth Ann (1860–?). He had an elder brother, Wilfred Thomas (1887–1962) and a younger brother, Frederick Thomas (1890–1952). They lived at Catchfield Farm. In 1901 he lived with his now widowed mother at that farm. On 14 April 1910 he was married to Alice Maud Parsons, who had been born in Tremaine, Cornwall and was baptised on 31 March 1887. She was the youngest of six children.[74]

A year later the newly-weds were resident at Church Farm, Tremaine, Egloskerry.[75] In May 1918 they took a lease on Trenhorne Farm in Lewannick, which was 102¾ acres. The farmhouse was a seventeenth-century two-storey building of seven rooms (on the ground floor were the kitchen, sitting room, dining room and dairy; on the first floor were five bedrooms). Lewannick was 12 miles north of Liskeard and five miles to the south-west of Launceston. It had a church, St Martin's, rebuilt in 1890, two Methodist chapels, a public library and a pub, the Archers' Arms. Most of the population were farmers. There were thirty listed in 1930 and nine had 150 or more acres, and the main crops were oats and turnips. There was also a garage, a dressmaker, a temperance hotel, a shoemaker, a carpenter, a blacksmith and a fishmonger. The population in 1921 was 456. In 1921 a war memorial had been unveiled in the village square. The Thomases' farm was to the south of the main village. The Thomases were childless. They employed one Leslie Albert Wilson, described as a farm hand, who lived on the premises. Thomas Pearce, born in 1899, of Altarnun, had also been employed there since 1921 (in that year he lived in the farmhouse), described as a horseman and farm worker and later his wife, Emma, came in on a daily basis to do the butter-making. In 1921 Beatrice Sandercock, aged twenty-one, was employed there as a servant.[76] There were, in 1931, forty-two breeding ewes, a ram, and usually between fifty and sixty lambs. In 1932 it was stated that there were also fourteen cows, twelve steers or heifers, thirteen summer calves, five pigs, a sow, 120 poultry and some rabbits.[77]

The farm and Trenhorne House are about 180 yards apart, or two shotgun lengths, as Thomas later put it. In 1930 Thomas was described as being 'A typical Cornish farmer, stockily built with dark hair turning grey on the temples'.[78] His wife was described by her mother thus, 'She enjoyed pretty good health, and never complained, although she was never very strong'. A friend of Mrs Thomas, Mrs Anne Elizabeth Tucker (1873–1938), remarked that the Thomases were 'Happy as a general rule', and Mrs Thomas had no complaint against Mrs Hearn. The Pearces also testified to the Thomases living together harmoniously.[79] However, there may have been a fault line in that Thomas remarked that he was not a teetotaller and his wife probably was, because on death it was written 'In her association with the United Methodist church at Congdon Shop [a hamlet near Trenhorne] she was a valued member'.[80]

The Thomases and their neighbours first became acquainted in the autumn of 1925 when Mrs Hearn came over to Trenhorne Farm for some butter. However, in 1931 Mrs Hearn thought it was when she went over to the farm in search of firewood and met Mrs Thomas and asked her if she could help. Mrs Thomas said that she would have to ask her husband, who was then out. That evening Thomas came to the house and was invited in. He saw Miss Everard on the sofa and 'in his shy and rather retiring manner he talked to her for a while'. He asked if there was anything they ever needed in Lewannick or Launceston, and he would get it for them. 'It was a kindly thing to do, and I was very grateful', Mrs Hearn recollected. Her sister wrote 'He is very nice indeed'.[81]

One of the conversations between Thomas and Mrs Hearn concerned gardening and weeds. Mrs Hearn did not mention the use of weed-killer. Some products containing arsenic were held at the farm. There was a small tin of Cooper's worm tablets on the kitchen shelf along with other farm cattle medicines. Thomas had used these occasionally for several years, but their last use was in 1928. He also had Cooper's sheep dip in the house for about five years. These were locked in his desk in the dining room. He had used it two years ago to clean his farm dogs.[82]

By 1926, there was a deepening of the sisters' friendship with the Thomases. This was when they said goodbye to the Thomases on an extended trip to Harrogate. On their return the next year, Mrs Thomas and Mrs Hearn became good friends and the latter also befriended Thomas, who would often visit Mrs Hearn without his wife and vice versa. Thomas, and/or his wife, would visit the sisters daily, though the evidence from her sister's diary of 1930 is that it was always Thomas, usually in the evenings and for about an hour. He later said 'I visited their house very often. During 1930 I should say I went there as a general rule everyday... My wife visited their house at times, occasionally... we have been together'. After all, they were neighbours. He would bring things like newspapers and dishes that his wife had cooked for the sisters, including cream and junkets. He said that his wife did not object to this because there was no cause for concern. Sometimes he would ask if there was anything he could buy for them when he visited Launceston and they would usually repay him. The four of them often went out for picnics and the food would be supplied by the two women. No one had ever been ill and quite possibly salmon sandwiches had been provided by Mrs Hearn. Thomas would take the sisters for drives in his car, sometimes with his wife and sometimes not. There were picnics at Downderry and Cheesewring. Sometimes the sisters were taken out individually. Once Thomas drove Miss Everard and her sister Miss Poskitt as far as Plymouth. They always called each other by their titles and surnames on all occasions.[83]

In 1931 Mrs Hearn recalled that she and her sister often played cards with the Thomases:

'on occasions Mr and Mrs Thomas would come over and play cards with Minnie and me. Strangely enough, it became a standing joke that when we were playing in this way it generally happened that either Mr Thomas or myself would have the three of spades in our hands, and although Mr Thomas knew nothing whatever of the story of this fateful card, he has often remarked: "Well, who's got the three of spades? If I haven't got it, I suppose Mrs Hearn has" and more often than not it was so'.[84]

Mrs Hearn's later recollections of the Thomases were a little different to those as outlined above. According to her published reminiscences in 1933, she asked Mrs Spear where she could buy some firewood and was told that the Thomases would oblige, telling Mrs Hearn that 'He is a very nice man and a good neighbour'. She went to the farm and met Mrs Thomas, whom she described as 'a smiling woman with an apron. Her figure was well made. Her face was pleasant but rather pale... I liked Mrs Thomas. A kind hearted farmer's wife.' She later wrote of her, 'Mrs Thomas looked a lonely woman and I felt very sorry for her. In time I liked her and will always cherish her memory. She was one of those thoroughly genuine women whom one meets more often in the country than the town. I believe Mrs Thomas liked me from the first. I am sure of it and she showed it in many ways... the only friend I had in that lonely part of the world except Mrs Spear'.

Mrs Thomas told Mrs Hearn that her husband would be along with the firewood. He arrived later that evening and was described by Mrs Hearn thus, 'a man of medium height and good build'. She later wrote that after 1926, 'Mr Thomas was now a regular visitor to Trenhorne House. He came about three times a week, generally in the evening. But not to see me [this was contradicted by her sister, as we shall see]. Let me say here and now that from first to last Mr Thomas and I were nothing to each other except friends. He was a big hearted man who when he came would go up and sit with Minnie. He visited her and talked with her, not because he had any affection for her or me, but because it was in his nature to help anyone who was in trouble'.

Likewise Mrs Spear said, 'Mr Thomas is such a kind man and willing to help people that his motive might be misconstrued... He would do a kindness for any neighbour'. She told how Thomas would often use his car to fetch a doctor for an ill neighbour.[85]

As to his wife, Mrs Hearn remarked:

'Mrs Thomas came not so frequently. She had her work to do. But it was Mrs Thomas, who, good soul that she was, and free from jealousy, sent her husband down from Trenhorne Farm with junkets and other delicacies she made for my poor sister.

She knew that at times I wanted to go to Launceston to see the doctor or buy things for Minnie. He used to call and take me in his car… To him I was always Mrs Hearn. To be frank I liked him as a big brother. When I used to see him coming up the drive with his dog at his heels, I used to be happy because he broke up the loneliness of our lives'.[86]

Miss Everard's diary records frequent occasions when Thomas arrived, always by himself, at the sisters' home. On New Year's Day 1930 he called round with his dog, while on another occasion he found them in the garden and asked if he could buy anything for them at Launceston as he was driving there. On another day she wrote 'Mr Thomas came in brought ½lb sponge finger bits from Launceston. We asked him'. On another occasion she recorded:

'Mr Thomas called about 2pm. Would we like to go to Launceston. He had work to do first, not ready until nearly 4pm and well went. It was a very nice outing. Sun came out nicely. Bessie was delighted with view. She thought it wonderful, then we went to Pictures, not bad in its way, but a war picture. We would rather have had something else. First time we had been. We got a packet choc. (no tea). Home at 8.30'.

Miss Everard also recorded working in the garden with her sisters:

'we all in garden. I did not do so much. Weeding bit on top border, etc. They have got some digging done and potatoes and some shallots planted, and we now have broad beans put in for garden. We all very tired'.

When Mrs Poskitt, who was visiting, went to leave, Thomas drove her and her sisters to the railway station in his car.[87]

The overall impression is that it was Thomas who was the sisters' friend more so than his wife, given the number of his visits there and none of hers; certainly not in 1930.[88]

Furthermore, Minnie's diary casts a very different light on the relationship and shows that her sister's later writings were lies. Of the 180 days from 1 January 1930 to 30 June 1930, Thomas visited the two sisters on 120 of them, occasionally twice a day. On 1 January Minnie wrote that Thomas visited 'to see how Annie is'. On twenty-eight of these visits he brought something with him for them; newspapers seven times, flowers thrice, medicine once and foodstuffs otherwise (cream from the farm on eight occasions). He also came round on six occasions to ask if they wanted anything from Launceston as he could drive over to collect them. It is also significant that Minnie wrote in her diary on 27 February, 'Mr Thomas has not called, how very strange that it always happens so. He has *never once* called when she has been out'. The 'she' referred to is Mrs Hearn, of course. This in direct contradiction to her sister's later statements. It is also worth noting that Mrs Hearn and Thomas sometimes went out to Launceston together; they went to a concert at Coad's Farm together on 24 January, not returning until 11pm, for example. In June Miss Everard wrote that Mrs Hearn and Thomas sat on the rug in the garden together for part of his trip in the afternoon, and two days later he was there to 'chat to Annie', suggesting a degree of intimacy. Never once in the six months of the diary does Mrs Thomas ever visit the sisters. Miss Everard once wrote 'Mrs Thomas has not been here for a long time, but she didn't seem to want bothering'. Yet in direct contradiction to this, Mrs Hearn in her published reminiscences gushes over how friendly she and Mrs Thomas were. Likewise, Thomas's visits often lasted an hour. However, in her published autobiographical writings, Mrs Hearn glossed over this and said he just stopped to chat for a minute or two or stayed to play cards for a few minutes of an evening. Yet the evidence of the diary clearly indicates otherwise. Miss Everard also liked Thomas, writing 'how kind of him' on one occasion and sometimes noting when he did not call.[89]

This evidence suggests that there might have been more to Mrs Hearn's and Thomas's friendship than first appeared. As we shall see, both strenuously denied any suggestion of an affair. This cuts both ways. It is entirely possible for a married man and a single woman to enjoy a purely platonic friendship, whatever others usually say and think to the contrary. But on the other hand, in this instance, it does seem excessive for them to have seen each other on an almost daily basis; these visits were not reciprocated and the sisters never, in the six month period of the diary, visited Trenhorne Farm, despite Mrs Hearn's later insistence on her being good friends with Mrs Thomas. The exact relationship between the two will never be known, but there is certainly the possibility that it might have been seen by one or even both of them to have been more than friendship, even though nothing may have been expressed explicitly and no known untoward physical behaviour occurred.

These, then, were the characters in the drama that was about to make headline news throughout Britain: relatively humble, ordinary folk in a fairly isolated and rural Cornish village. Their actions and their personalities were to be of great interest to those outside their immediate circle and we shall now turn to what may well have been the beginning of the immediate crisis, but only became of wider interest after the death of Mrs Thomas.

Chapter 3

The investigation begins

W e now return to the situation as it stood after Mrs Thomas's death. Thomas had suggested to Mrs Hearn that there would be an investigation into his wife's demise and he was right. Five hours after the death of Mrs Thomas, Dr Eric Wordley (1887–1961), pathologist at the South Devon and East Cornwall Hospital, had made a post-mortem examination of the body by order of James Alfred Pearce (1863–1945), the Plymouth coroner. Edward Thomas Adams, the coroner's officer, was present. Externally the body was well nourished. All that seemed abnormal was the wasting of the calves. There were no marks of violence and nothing abnormal in the mouth. The whole of the intestinal canal showed inflammation. There was some congestion of the lung but nothing abnormal. The spleen was not enlarged. Heart, liver and kidneys were of fatty appearance. There was no food in the stomach. The intestines were empty except for a black offensive fluid. There was no obvious cause of death, so the doctor removed several organs for chemical examination if Pearce deemed this necessary. He made several tests in the blood for bacilli. There was no bacterial infection.[1]

Death had been caused by the failure of the heart muscles. He could find no natural cause of death. He therefore suspected a toxic substance. It was not phosphorus poisoning, however, despite a later suggestion by the defence that it might have been.[2]

On 6 November, two days after Mrs Thomas's death, Mr Thomas Tickle (1872-1960), the county analyst for Devon, was given the internal organs from Mrs Thomas's body to examine. He found a total of 0.85 of a grain of arsenic in them (arsenic appears naturally in the body but in a far, far lesser amount than this). However, he could not give a time when the poison would have been ingested, because he had already been told the relevant dates of Mrs Thomas's sickness and death and was therefore influenced by this report. He thought that the arsenic used might be weed-killer (a prime source of arsenic, easily purchased and equally easy to explain away by anyone with a garden and used by poisoners) but could not exclude sheep-dip, commonly used on sheep farms such as Thomas's.[3]

A death certificate was issued by Pearce on 8 November, which read 'Arsenical poisoning due to homicide, but there's not sufficient evidence to show by whom or by what means arsenic was administered'.

Sir Bernard Henry Spilsbury (1877–1947), a noted pathologist of the day, observed in a lecture about arsenical poisoning that it had been known about for thousands of years, 'probably one of the earliest [poisons] to be discovered'. He added 'The frequency with which arsenic has been employed for homicidal purposes is due to its almost complete lack of taste, the ready administration in solid form, a solution in medicine, in food in drink and the small quantity required to produce a fatal result', and observed that its symptoms could be confused with those of acute gastroenteritis.[4]

A contemporary textbook on poisons noted that arsenic attacked the gastrointestinal tract and kidneys and affected the skin and hair of the victim. Symptoms of poisoning occurred between half an hour and an hour after ingestion. Initial symptoms included a great thirst, a dry and itchy mouth and throat, difficulty in swallowing, abdominal pain and diarrhoea. Later symptoms included headaches, dizziness, pain in the limbs, cold in the extremities, an irregular pulse, convulsions and even coma. Between 0.1 and 0.3 of a grain could be fatal (i.e. far less than had been found in Mrs Thomas). The liver was the main organ attacked; but the heart, lungs, kidneys and spleen could also be affected.[5] It is worth remembering this for what follows.

Given that death was due to arsenic, inspections of poison books, which buyers had to sign to purchase it, held by chemists and others in the locality, took place. The fact that Mrs Hearn had bought weed-killer in 1926 was noted. So too, was the fact that in November 1923, Mrs Elizabeth Uglow (1897–1986) of Tressorest Farm, Warpstow, a sister of Mrs Thomas, had bought a quarter of a pound of weed-killer. None, however, was found at Trenhorne Farm.[6] Mrs Thomas's death was looking suspiciously like murder and an inquest was almost certain to be held.

We now return to the situation at Trenhorne Farm following the funeral of Mrs Thomas. Mrs Hearn's position was becoming increasingly difficult, even though the Parsons presumably left late on 8 November, while Thomas's mother remained with her widower son at the farm. On 10 November Thomas left in the afternoon to go to Launceston and when he returned, just before tea time, Mrs

Hearn was not there, having returned to her own house at 3pm. Mrs Thomas had heard her say that day that her 'life wasn't worth living'. Mother and son had tea and then she suggested to him that he should call for her and ask her back for tea. He then called at her house to ask whether she wanted to have tea together, ringing the door bell, but no one answered. The house was all locked up. After talking to his mother and neighbours about this, it was suggested that Mrs Hearn might be unwell and so he reported it to Sergeant Frederick Charles Trebilcock (1885–1955) of the Cornish Constabulary, who had over twenty years' experience, was based at Launceston police station, and had attended Mrs Thomas's funeral.[7]

Trebilcock returned to the house with Thomas and they looked through the windows, but could see no sign of her.[8] On that same day, Sir Hugh Bateman Prothero Smith (1872–1961), the chief constable, notified Superintendent William Morley Pill (1886–1940) of the Launceston division of the Cornish Constabulary that he was to be in charge of the case. Pill had been a policeman since 1905, working as a constable in Launceston until 1907 when he transferred to Marhamchurch and Bude, where he remained until 1911. He was then at St Kew Highway and St Dennis. In 1919 he was a sergeant at St Ives and in 1924 he was an inspector at Stratton. In August 1930 he became superintendent of the Launceston division, replacing Superintendent Basher. As an inspector he had had some experience of murder cases, including that of the death of the aged Richard Roadley of Titson in March 1928 when William Maynard was suspected and Pill had been accused of using 'third degree methods' to intimidate suspects.[9] He was asked to confer with Pearce. As with many of the smaller county forces there was no separate detective division.

A clue to Mrs Hearn's fate came the following day. On 11 November Thomas received a letter from Mrs Hearn which was possibly suggestive of suicide. It read as follows:

'Dear Mr Thomas,

I am going out if I can. I cannot forget that awful man [Parsons] and the things that he said. I am *innocent, innocent*. But she is dead and it was my lunch she ate. I cannot bear it. When I am dead they will be sure I am guilty and you at least will be clear. May your dead wife's presence guard and comfort you still.

Yours,

A.H.

P.S. My life is not a great thing somehow now dear Minnie is gone. Will you send my love to Bessie and tell her not to worry about me? I will be alright. My conscience is clear. I am giving instructions to Wenn about selling things and hope you will be paid in full. It is all I can do now'.[10]

It is interesting that Mrs Hearn gave the food eaten at Bude as being the cause of Mrs Thomas's death. The meal there certainly resulted in Mrs Thomas being ill, but it was not then clear that it was the principal cause of her death. Thomas immediately showed the letter to the police. Fearing suicide, they were concerned about Annie's safety, so Thomas and Trebilcock entered the farm house using the key they found outside it, but could not find the missing woman.[11]

Three years later Mrs Hearn explained why she disappeared and began her account after she returned to Trenhorne Farm on 10 November:

'My mind was in a turmoil when I went. With every step I took I grew panicky. After all, I was only a lone woman with no one to advise me.

The more I thought about it the more frightened I became. Not because I was guilty of anything but because of the suspicion that might fall upon me.

My mind went out to my only living sister, Bunny. I tried to think what she might feel if I were mixed up in a case. What a disgrace it would be for her. Would she not wish I had died rather than hear that I was in the hands of the police on an awful charge – murder? I thought she would.

This decided my mind. I decided I could not face it.

I shall never forget my thoughts as I walked into my own little garden in which Minnie and I had spent so many happy hours. Should I see it again? Should I ever work in there again?

I let myself in at the back door. There was no time to be lost. But before I went there was one thing I had to do'.[12]

Apparently Annie had less than £2 in loose cash, and a gold sovereign that her sister Mabel had given her and that she kept as a souvenir.[13]

On 12 November, Trebilcock told Pill about Mrs Hearn's disappearance. Pill told the police at Liskeard and Looe about this, as well as his superior. There were searches of Trenhorne House on both 14 and 20 November. Pill had no power, presumably lacking a magistrate's warrant, to do so, but did it at his own risk. No clue to her whereabouts could be found there. However, they did find a red-backed book which was the diary of Miss Everard.[14] The diary was in a drawer of a small table standing between the window and the fireplace of the drawing room occupied by Mrs Hearn and it was brought to Pill's attention on 13 November.[15] The diary has already been cited and will be again in Chapter 5, as it cast considerable light on events at the house between January and July 1930. Thomas claimed that he did not realise his wife had died from arsenic poisoning until Pill told him so on 14 November; up to then he thought it was food poisoning.[16]

The police also started questioning anyone who might be able to shed light on Mrs Thomas's death. They presumably began by questioning Thomas. One of the leads he provided was to the café in Bude and Inspector Norrish interviewed Ivy Willshire on 16 November. It was later put to the witness that the police had suggested certain answers to her, but she denied this.[17]

Mrs Hearn's initial steps on leaving home were easy to trace after a number of witnesses came forward. Before she had left Trenhorne Farm on 10 November, she instructed Wenn, her landlord, to sell her furniture. She cashed a cheque for 21 shillings and then, wearing a check coat and carrying a small bag, went to the post office at Coads Green at five past four. Hector Albert Ollett (1888–1943), sub-postmaster of Coads Green, was there and recalled that she entered the shop and 'Mrs Hearn was speaking to Mrs [Ada] Ollett [1884–1977] about going to Looe. She asked about buses and then she wanted to know if she could have a car'. She wanted to travel to Looe, on the south coast. Ollett said that Mr Morcom was away but he could take her there. He said it would cost 18s and she agreed. She paid him by cheque and they left at 4.15pm and she seemed quite normal. On the way they had a little conversation, mainly about the sunset and the view from Caradon Hill at that time.[18]

Once they had left the Liskeard-Torpoint road, Ollett asked his passenger exactly where she wanted to be dropped. 'By the [railway] station' she said, but Ollett told her it would be very difficult turning there, so he suggested stopping by the bridge. She agreed that would do just as well; the bridge united West Looe with East Looe. They arrived at Looe at five past five.[19]

Apparently, in September 1929 Mrs Hearn had visited Looe to meet some friends of hers from the north of England who were staying there.[20] Thus Looe was not wholly unknown to her.

Edgar Tomms (1887–1940), a Looe fisherman, recalled colliding with a woman on the night of Mrs Hearn's disappearance and it was presumed it was her. He apologised but received no reply.[21] He said 'I was returning from my boats on the beach when I touched against the lady who was a stranger in the district. I apologised but she did not reply and hurried away'.[22] Tomms was, presumably, the last person known to have seen her, if see her he did. Mrs Hearn's whereabouts were unknown, even whether she was alive or dead, and at first the latter seemed more likely, especially after the letter received by Thomas. A few traces of what might have been the missing woman were later found. A black and white coat was found on the cliffs at Looe by Mrs Kathleen Alice Jones, a 23-year-old housewife of East Looe, on the afternoon of Wednesday 12 November.[23] She removed the buttons and buckle to give to a Mrs Pengelly and then replaced it.[24]

Thomas Worth, a Looe dairyman, recalled: 'I noticed the coat at about breakfast time on Tuesday morning. It was only twelve hours after Mrs Hearn disappeared. It was lying stretched out over some bramble and I thought "That's a nice coat to be lying out here". Each morning of the week as I passed it it was there. I read about it being found by the police [16 November] so I told what I knew'. The coat was identified as that being worn by Mrs Hearn on the day she disappeared.[25]

A woman's soft black hat, matching that seen on Mrs Hearn, was found on Millendreath beach three miles from Looe. It was half concealed under a hedge, half a mile from the nearest house, and was noticed by a rabbit catcher. It was half a mile from where the coat had been found.[26]

The theory of suicide from the cliffs and the body being washed out to sea was discounted by experienced fishermen, with one telling a journalist, 'For one thing if she had fallen from the cliff near to where her coat had been found, her body would have struck the rocks and remained on the beach. Then we have had some winds for the last ten days which means that a body would have washed up almost at once. Two people have been drowned here recently and both were washed up here within a couple of days.'[27]

There was a great deal of speculation as to where Mrs Hearn might be and many newspapers throughout the country covered the story. Firstly, could she be dead?[28] The majority view seems to have been that she was alive, however. There were rumours that she might be in Scotland or in London. She was also allegedly seen in a Bristol church. Given her cookery background it was thought that she might be working in a kitchen somewhere, which seems reasonable. She was referred to as 'the missing witness' and as a friend of the late Mrs Thomas.[29] Some in the press thought that Mrs Hearn was suffering from memory loss because of her overwork and sleepless nights while nursing Mrs Thomas.[30]

There was even the possibility that she might have gone abroad using a cross-Channel ferry, so ports were belatedly watched.[31] However, she had never been abroad before, had no known language skills, little money and no known acquaintances there, so this must have seemed unlikely, but was presumably only raised because of the cross-Channel ports on the south coast.

Someone of indeterminate sex (described as being a 'man-woman') was sighted at the edge of Bodmin, by the Bodmin railway station, wearing a long fawn coat and flannel trousers on 25 November and police searched woods near there. Mrs Baker, the wife of a chauffeur employed on the Lanhydrock estate, saw the person walking in an uncertain manner, and on seeing her, they hastened their pace and disappeared from sight. She told reporters:

'I was washing in an outhouse by the side of the road when I heard someone coming along. Although I don't usually take any notice of footsteps, as many people pass my house going up and down the lane, during the day, I stopped and looked out of the door and saw a strange person going down the road towards the wood.

The person had a fawn coat and a trilby hat, and she was wearing grey flannel trousers. The latter I could see quite plainly by the fact that her coat was unbuttoned. She appeared to be uncertain in her movements and she was going along at a jogging pace. All the time she was walking she was looking to the right and left of her, and sometimes looking back, as if she was afraid of being seen.

I watched her for a few minutes but she turned around her and saw me and immediately she quickened her pace, buttoned her coat and disappeared down the road as fast as she could.

A few minutes later, Mr William Cole, coachman at Lanhydrock, came along and I told him about the strange woman I had seen. He said he would go along and see what it was, but returned later, saying that he had seen no one.

The woman, in my opinion, must have got over the hedge and made her way across the woods in the direction of the main Liskeard Road. She was about five foot in height, and I knew she was a woman by her appearance. Her shoes were down at the heel and she gave me the impression that she was exhausted, although she quickened her pace when she saw me'.[32]

There was another sighting on the Liskeard–Bodmin Road. Harry Ball, a delivery man, was stopped as he was driving, but he refused a lift. At Fenton Pits, five miles away, a Mrs Stephens saw a similar sight, 'The woman seemed afraid of something and constantly watched either side of the road and behind her as if afraid of being seen. She appeared to be tired, and went on, and I saw nothing more of her'.

There was a small outhouse where the police believed the woman may have slept on the Saturday night. The boss of the delivery man said:

'My man was driving in the neighbourhood of Lanhydrock when he was stopped by a woman who appeared to be uncertain in her remarks, but she asked him to give her a lift along the road towards Bodmin Road Station. The woman, he said, was dressed in a fawn coat and had on grey flannel trousers but she was wearing no hat. He had no doubt that she was a woman. He refused to give her a lift, being under instruction not to give people lifts. Ball was at this time quite oblivious of the fact that a strange woman had been seen in other parts of the neighbourhood. From her hands and also her face he was certain she was not a tramp. About half a mile further a policeman stopped him and asked him if he had seen a strange person and he gave a description of the woman he had seen and the policeman set off in pursuit but was unable to trace her'.

The wooded terrain made the search doubly difficult.[33]

Apparently, however, after all this fuss, the person seen was one Roger Charles Lewis Kennaway (1910–1995), an officer from the Duke of Cornwall's Light Infantry who was running as part of a training exercise and was based in the nearby barracks.[34]

There were other sightings. A strange woman was seen at a house in Portwinkle asking for food.[35] Brownqueen woods were searched as was the coast as far as Fowey. Lack of food would force the woman to seek aid in a village. Vehicle drivers were asked to keep a look out and policemen were posted on lonely roads. Police swept moorlands.[36] A woman was also seen on Plymouth Hoe, smoking a cigarette, and on a railway carriage from Looe to Liskeard a guard, one Menhennick, saw, at 6.15pm on 10 November, a woman in a mackintosh and a boy's cap, later changing to a black velour hat.[37] An employee of the Co-operative Society at Liskeard drew this figure to his attention, remarking, 'Who is that woman dressed as a boy?' She was a short, thin woman standing by an open window. The train on which she travelled eventually arrived at Liskeard, but the signalman who collected tickets there did not recall her and nor did anyone else.[38]

Given that Annie had asked Ollett to drop her by the railway station, this would have seemed a clue worth following up. Anyone wanting to be dropped off at a railway station usually wants to catch a train. It is also suggestive that she wanted to travel away from Cornwall and evidence that she did not intend to hurl herself over the cliffs, despite speculation that she had done so or was planning to do so.

James Dymond of Penton Pits, a farm labourer, stated that he had seen, on 23 November, a stranger whom he addressed but heard no reply. The stranger seemed embarrassed and 'He stooped to tie his shoe lace and then took the opposite direction to that which he saw I was going. He looked a funny man. He had a pale face, light hair and a gait that made him look like a woman. He seemed to resent the attention that he attracted'.[39]

There was even a theory that Mrs Hearn might be in Manchester. Women's hostels and lodging houses in the city and Salford were combed and friends and acquaintances in the city were questioned. Carlisle and Preston were other possible destinations.[40]

Police Sergeant Dooney of Looe and his constables searched the district between Seaton and Polruan on 21 November, while Sergeant Hawkens of St

Germans searched Downderry and Hessenford. The banks of the River Looe were combed, especially as it reached Millendreath, where the hat was found.[41] On the same day, police searched deserted bungalows on Downderry hillside. These were used in the summer by holidaymakers but were very isolated in the winter months.[42]

The police information was that Mrs Hearn was a doctor's widow, the doctor having once practised near Sheffield. A man of that name was identified as a Dr Leonard Wilfred Hearn (1892–1966) of Nottingham, but he knew nothing of her. His father, also a doctor and now retired, was Dr Ethelbert Hearn and he related the strange story of Mrs Hearn's alleged marriage as already told in Chapter 2.

The police thought that Mrs Hearn was probably still alive and the chief constable of Cornwall had the following notice produced for distribution at police stations in Devonshire and Cornwall:

'Missing from home from November 10. Susan (Anne) Hearn, widow, aged 40 to 44, height five feet 2 in. to 3 in., light brown hair, short sallow complexion, thin build. Last heard of at Looe at 5pm on November 10. Believed to be the widow of a doctor who practised in Sheffield.

Maiden name Everard.

She once assisted at a cookery school at Harrogate. She has a sister at Doncaster and other relatives at Grimsby. Believed to have had little money when she left.

Desire to interview her in the connection of the death of Alice Maud Thomas who died on November 4, and who it has been ascertained, died from the effects of arsenical poisoning.[43]

In the meantime, Mrs Poskitt wrote to Thomas to pass on her sympathy about his wife's death and to ask if he had any news of her sister. He replied thus:

'I received your letter a few days since, but am unable to tell you anything concerning Mrs Hearn. I understand the police have written to you.

Yours sincerely

WH THOMAS[44]

In missing person enquiries, it is common to contact friends and relations. In Mrs Hearn's case this was a fairly small circle. Reporters also tracked down Mrs Hearn's sister, Mrs Poskitt, of Rose Cottage, Long Sandall, near Doncaster. She had written to her brother Henry, in Grimsby, in case he had any news. She said that when her sister was employed at the cookery school she had a favourite pupil called Jean who was now married and living near Manchester, and so she might have visited her, but she did not know the woman's surname. She told the journalist:

'I wrote her a letter which would have reached her on the day she disappeared, but I don't know whether she received it. She has had a tremendous lot of worry and strain with deaths and sickness, and her health has been undermined. She has been a brick, and has gone through what many a man would not want to face.

I don't think my sister is in Yorkshire. She would have come straight to me if she was. I cannot think how it is that I have not heard from her in some way. It was a great break to her when her invalid sister died in Cornwall.[45]

I have not heard anything from my sister for seven days, and have only just heard of her disappearance. Her last letter was rather a sad one, in which she spoke of the loss of her friend. It was written just before the funeral.

My sister did not mention coming up to Yorkshire. I cannot reckon it up. It has upset me very much. We used to write to each other frequently.

My sister used to live in Harrogate until about three years ago and had a house in Cornwall at the same time. Three years ago she gave up the school of cookery which she carried on with her aunt, Miss Everard, at Harrogate.

I think that if she had come this way my home would have been the first place she would have made for. I am at a loss to account for her disappearance'.[46]

Mrs Poskitt's opinion of her sister was very high. She also told of her sister's early life. 'She went to school at Grimsby. It was a good school, the Welholme Road School. She was there until she was about 16 and was at home afterwards until she went with her aunt to Harrogate'. Mrs Poskitt said that their father married twice (married Mary Sargent in Sheffield in 1922) and that Minnie was the invalid who was nursed by Annie. Mabel died at Grindleford in about 1917 from tuberculosis, Jesse was in British Columbia/California for a good many years, Oliver died in the war [actually three years later], Henry was a clerk in Grimsby and Robert lived in London. She also said 'What motive or object could she have in saying she was married if she was not?' She went on:

'The first time I saw her after her marriage I did not like to say very much. She told me a little about it. Since then we have been separated and when we have met there have been so many things to go into and talk about that little was said about the marriage.

She showed a photograph of Dr Hearn as a young man in uniform taken in Sheffield [clearly the late RFC officer]. I have no more idea as to what has become of my sister than you have. I want her to be found. She has always been such a good girl that it pains me beyond measure that people should be thinking there is anything wrong'.

Mrs Forrester from Harrogate recalled Mrs Hearn returning as a widow and telling of her husband who had been wounded and a prisoner during the war.[47]

Mrs Poskitt said that 'As far as I know Mr and Mrs Thomas and my sister are the best of friends. In some indirect and unfortunate way she seems to have become in some trouble. But she has the best intentions in the world,' and had told her 'I wish we had never gone to Bude'.[48]

In early December 1930, another relation, Mr Houlton, said that he thought Annie was dead.[49] She was said to be 'good looking with bobbed hair'.[50]

Mrs Hearn's brother Henry said that he had last seen her about ten years ago and had not heard of her for many years. He thought she was a woman of strong character so was unlikely to be a suicide, but that she had undergone much strain due to illness and loss of friends so might have had a breakdown.[51]

A schoolfriend of Mrs Hearn's was found near Manchester. She was in a state of collapse as she had been expecting to see her friend on a visit that weekend. She was to have been collected by a car in London and taken to Manchester, where she planned to live. The unnamed friend said 'Mrs Hearn was a woman who gave up the best part of her life doing good for others. Then three months ago her sister Lucy [Minnie] died despite the most tender nursing by Mrs Hearn. And now Mrs Thomas,' said the woman's mother. Mrs Hearn had been friends with her daughter since their schooldays twenty-five years earlier.[52]

Others who knew Mrs Hearn in her early days gave information to the press. The family had left Ulceby during the First World War. Her brother in Grimsby said he knew nothing about his sister's movements. Residents of Ulceby recalled Mrs Hearn as being a pleasant young woman but somewhat reserved, 'She has not altered greatly in appearance and if she appeared in this part of the country she would be readily recognised'.[53]

The official investigation also took the form of a coroner's inquest, to which we shall now turn. It was held as fruitless enquiries were being made for the whereabouts of the chief witness. However, Mrs Hearn could not have travelled far. She had limited resources and would either have to use public transport or walk. Yet there were no definitive sightings. It was a mystery which added to that of Mrs Thomas's death.

It is possible that the investigation was already flawed. The Cornish Constabulary, whose jurisdiction the deaths occurred in, did not have a detective division. It was customary in such cases for a county force to apply to the expertise, experience and resources of Scotland Yard, who could and did supply such, as occurred in the investigation of the murder of Irene Munro in Eastbourne in 1920. That the Cornish Chief Constable decided against that course of action was perhaps a show of confidence or arrogance and it might well have led to a flawed investigation.

Chapter 4

The inquest

P earce, the Plymouth coroner, convened an inquest at the Western Law Courts at Plymouth Guildhall on 24 November at 10.15am. Those also present included Prothero Smith and Mr George Graham Wilson (1888– 1968), a solicitor of Launceston who represented Thomas.[1] Interest in the inquest was so great that police had to guard the outer doors to stop a crowd entering. It was reported fully in the press and for the first time gave the general public an outline of events leading up to the death of Mrs Thomas, although the most important witness was missing. Pearce told the jury that they were there to ascertain the cause of death and if possible to state who was responsible.

Pearce said: 'In this case, you are concerned with the enquiry into the death of Alice Maud Thomas, wife of William Henry Thomas of Trenhorne Farm, Lewannick.'[2] He opened the case by adding that on 4 November he was informed of Mrs Thomas's death and he had ordered Dr Wordley to investigate by undertaking a post-mortem examination, the results of which would be revealed at the inquest.

Thomas was the first witness and he confirmed the identity of his wife. He then gave a lengthy account of what had occurred between 18 October and 4 November, as we saw in Chapter 1, as well as outlining the relationships between him, his wife and Mrs Hearn. He was asked about his wife's finances, but could only say she had some War Bonds and money invested in a housing scheme, not much more than £100. They ran their finances separately, he explained. He was then asked about the poisons on the farm.

'Have you ever obtained arsenic from any chemist?'

'Never in my life'.

'Have you ever had any sheep dip on your premises?'

'Yes sir'.

'Cooper's yellow powder?'

'Yes sir'.

'How long ago did you buy it?'

'Well, I cannot tell exactly when I purchased it. I should say five or six years ago, or it may have been longer'.

'When did you use the last lot of it?'

'I should say somewhere about two years ago'.

'Had you some rat poison?'

'Yes, a tin of Harrison's rat poison'.

'Where was it kept?'

'Locked in my desk in the dining room'.

'And two tins of Cooper's worm tablets?'

'They were kept on the shelf in the kitchen with various things used on the farm'.

'Now as regard to Mrs Hearn, did your wife ever object to her going to your house at all?'

'No sir, never'.

'Were they very great friends?'

'Well, I cannot say very great, but ordinary friends'.

This contradicted Annie's claims that the two women were close.

'You and Mrs Thomas were friends with her sister Miss Everard, when she was alive?'

'Yes'

'I believe you used to pass on newspapers to them?'

'Yes'.

'And if you were going to town?'

'I would call and see if they wanted anything'.

'Had you ever given your wife cause to be jealous about Mrs Hearn?'

'Never sir'.

'Was your association with Mrs Hearn a perfectly friendly one?'

'Yes'.

There was then some discussion about the £38 Thomas had lent Mrs Hearn in December 1928. Apparently a friend in Harrogate had lent Annie some money; the friend had then died and her son demanded repayment. Mrs Hearn did not have the money and so Thomas offered to loan it to her.

'Taking your mind back to Bude, did Mrs Hearn complain of feeling sick at all on that day?'

'No, not to me'.

'When you saw Dr Saunders, did you yourself say that you had been feeling rather funny?'

'I can't be sure'.

Thomas answered 'quietly and clearly' in what must have been a 'trying ordeal'.[3]

Mrs Elizabeth Thomas was next to speak and recalled that her daughter-in-law had no animosity towards Mrs Hearn to her knowledge. She 'gave her testimony clearly and without hesitation', but when dealing with the death of her daughter-in-law, 'it was obvious that she was very much attached, she all but broke down, but with marked willpower overcame her emotion and resumed her story'. George Matthew, a Launceston grocer, stated that in early August 1926 Mrs Hearn had bought weed-killer from him. Mrs Spear was asked about Mrs Hearn's use of weed-killer.

'Have you ever seen Mrs Hearn use weed-killer in the front garden?'

'No'.

'Might she have used weed-killer in the back garden without your knowledge?'

'Yes, she never said anything about using it'.

On the night of Mrs Thomas's death, Mrs Hearn asked Mrs Spear for hot water, so she could wash some cups.

'Did you not think that rather extraordinary because she had not been to her house for some time?'

'Not at all. She said she had used the cups when she was last home'.

'Did you give her some hot water?'

'Yes. I don't know if she washed up any cups'.

Mayburne Pearce, a solicitor representing the police, then asked a rather interesting question.

'How many people have died in Mrs Hearn's house since you lived there?'

'Three. A very old lady, Mrs Aunger, Mrs Hearn's aunt and Mrs Everard'.

'What has been the nature of their illness – has it been sickness and diarrhoea?'

'I think there was sickness'.

Pearce then shut down this line of reasoning, perhaps deeming it irrelevant to the main enquiry he was pursuing as coroner, which was to focus on the death of Mrs Thomas only and in any case all three had apparently died of natural causes and had been certified as such, as he said, 'We must bear in mind that these deaths were duly certified by a medical practitioner in each case'.

Dr Saunders then gave evidence as to Mrs Thomas's health and his initial diagnosis, as noted in Chapter 1. Then came Mr Tickle.

'From such preliminary analysis, can you say what the minimum number of grains in the body would be?'

'I cannot put it in any other terms but the minimum. There must have been a substantial quantity but how much I cannot say'.

'Would there have been sufficient to cause death?'

'Yes'.

'Can you definitely say in this case there must have been a fatal dose in the organs you have examined?'

'There can be no question about that'.

'Will you be sure of that when you have completed your analysis?'

'Yes'.

The inquest was then adjourned, it being 7pm, until Wednesday 26 November.[4]

Two days later, the first to give evidence was Mrs Parsons. She described how she came to the farm as her daughter was unwell. She talked of the Sunday lunch during which her daughter was unwell and the trip to the hospital.[5] Mrs Parsons gave evidence of her daughter's poor health and of her visit to Trenhorne Farm on 29 October after a request from Thomas, asking for her or another of her daughters.

Pearce asked: 'Did Mrs Hearn interfere at all?', to which Mrs Parsons replied that 'She might have prepared a cup of tea'. Mrs Parsons then spoke of what happened on the days of her visit and especially on 2 November. Pearce asked, 'How were you and Mrs Hearn getting on all this time?'. 'Quite all right,' replied Mrs Parsons. One of her sons then spoke of his suspicions against Mrs Hearn. Pearce asked, 'I take it the families were not all on friendly terms?' The son replied 'Well, she never came to my house and I never went to hers. No, that's wrong. She came to my house about four years ago but never since'.

Parsons talked of attending the funeral and confronting Mrs Hearn about his sister's death. Pearce confirmed, 'She made no secret about the sandwiches?' 'No, but I noticed she was rather reluctant. There was a pause between bread and butter and sandwiches'. Parsons had assumed that the sandwiches were from the tea shop, but his mother said otherwise. Pearce asked what happened next.

'Mrs Thomas (senior) entered the room. Mrs Hearn had made me believe the sandwiches were made in that house, and I turned to Mrs Thomas and said "Did you help to make these sandwiches?" She said "Certainly not. Mrs Hearn made them and brought them with her"'.

'What did you say next?'

'I believe I said "This looks serious and must be looked into". She then left the room'.

'Your statement varies a little from that which you made 10 days ago. Was it not that Mr Thomas came into the room and nothing further was said.'"

'It might have been that'.

'What did you mean to infer? That the sandwiches might have been tainted by the meat, or whatever was in them, having gone bad? Did you mean to infer that somebody poisoned her?'

'I had my suspicions sir'.

'That somebody had wilfully poisoned her?'

'I had my suspicions that there had been foul play'.

'What made you suspicious of foul play?'

'Several things, I knew my sister had been ill 10 days and not even my mother had been informed'.

'Anything else?'

'This Mrs Hearn had been the only woman in the house the whole time doing the house work and attending my sister'.

'And what else?'

'When my aunt [Mrs Wadge] called to see her, Mr Thomas and Mrs Hearn went upstairs and came downstairs to say she was too unwell to be seen. Yet my mother had not been informed'.

A juryman asked:

'Is there anything at the back of your mind which you have not told us? What really is your suspicion?'

'To put it plainly, that Mr Thomas and Mrs Hearn were too friendly'.

Pearce stated: 'That is only hearsay evidence'.[6]
    Wilson, representing Thomas, then questioned Parsons.

'Do you know that loose talk of this description is often responsible for upsets in families and worries to people?'

'I do'.

'In spite of that, you are willing to give consideration to the first bit of gossip you hear about someone connected with you?'

'I did not believe it to begin with'.

'Did a relation of yours die some years ago – an aunt or an uncle?'

'Yes'.

'Was there some money to divide among yourselves, including your branch of the family?'

'Yes, that was three or four years ago'.

'Did you hear any question as to whether your branch of the family was to share the money?'

'Yes'.

'Did not that cause a certain amount of friction between members of the family?'

'Not between our family but between other uncles and aunts, but not between us as brothers and sisters'.[7]

Mrs Tucker of Congdon Shop was Mrs Thomas's second cousin and her best friend and stated that Mrs Thomas had never complained about Mrs Hearn and was happy with her husband. Pearce asked, 'Did you understand that the friendship with Mrs Hearn had grown after Miss Everard died?' She replied:

'Yes. Mrs Thomas told me that they must do everything they could for her as she was lonely and would be leaving on Lady day [25 March]'.

'And Miss Everard was friendly with Mr and Mrs Thomas, too?'

'Yes, just as friendly. They did everything out of kindness for them'.

'Mrs Tucker said that Mr Thomas used his car late at night to fetch doctors for neighbours'.

Wilson asked, 'Is Mr Thomas always willing to help people in trouble, and consequently sometimes rather leaves himself open to the unkind tongue which puts a wrong interpretation on his acts?' Mrs Tucker replied 'Yes'.

Dr Lister then spoke about his visit to Mrs Thomas on 2 November. He described Mrs Thomas's state on 3 November and her being sent to the hospital.

'What was the object of removing Mrs Thomas to Plymouth?'

'It seemed odd that she should have been the only person in the family afflicted with these symptoms. It looked as if the poison had not been administered by chance, and I thought a change of scene would be advisable'.

'Do you think the journey that night would hasten her death?'

'No it would not. It was a choice of two evils. She was in such a serious condition that she would probably die, but a chance of saving her was removal to Plymouth'.

Lister was then asked about the cause of death.

'Had Dr Saunders explained very fully the symptoms as he found them from the first and as they progressed?'

'Yes'

'Was it from that and the condition of the patient when you saw her that you came to the conclusion that death was probably due to arsenical poisoning?'

'Yes'.

The foreman of the jury asked, 'Can you distinguish whether it was acute arsenical poisoning or chronic? She had had a large dose administered, possibly in a short period, or within some hours or days?' Lister replied:

'At the beginning she had had a big dose which made her vomit. The question is whether she had another dose subsequently. Personally I think she had. I think if she had another dose on the Sunday, one would have expected more vomiting and diarrhoea, but I don't see why she should have suddenly got worse unless she had had some more given her. I think that two thirds of a grain in the liver is a lot to be left after the initial dose of a fortnight before'.[8]

Dr Fox talked of the admission to hospital and said that Thomas looked distressed about his wife's condition, but was only allowed to see her through an internal window. Dr Wordley talked of his examination of the body five hours after death. He said the intestines were slightly inflamed, that there was fatty degeneration of the heart, liver and kidneys, but the body was of a healthy woman. He could not find an obvious cause of death and he removed organs for chemical examination. There was no sign of bacterial infection.

'Having found there was no evidence of bacilli, did you then come to the conclusion that death must have been through arsenical poisoning?'

'Do you mean before I have heard the evidence of the analyst?'

'Did you yourself come to the conclusion from your examination before you had heard Mr Tickle's evidence that the only solution of the matter must be arsenical poisoning?'

'I would rather say by far the most probable explanation. Bearing in mind the clinical history of the case and my findings post mortem and my examinations at a later date before I had heard the analyst's evidence. I had then no doubt that the cause of death was arsenical poisoning'.

'What have you to say about the sections?'

'The sections I made of the kidney, spleen and liver all showed cloudy swelling. There was necrosis in the liver, and the kidney showed intense fatty degeneration – all rather important changes'.

'Do you consider that death could have been due to the first dose of poisoning, assuming it was taken on October 18?'

'No, I do not think so myself. I think there was too much arsenic in the liver to suggest it had been taken 17 days previously. Actually you would not find 3 grains in the liver within 24 hours, however great the dose would be. Within a few weeks there would hardly be any trace. Where there is evidence of two-thirds of a grain it is more than would be present if the last dose was 17 days previously'.

'Which means if she had only one dose on October 18, you would not expect to find two thirds of a grain in the liver 17 days after and the patient still alive?'

'No'.

'How much arsenic do you consider to be a fatal dose?'

'It is usually given as two grains being a fatal dose, but the average adult would be unlucky to die from two grains and many cases are known where more than two grains have been taken and the patient has lived'.[9]

'If this case had been diagnosed as arsenical poisoning earlier, would there have been a chance of this woman surviving?'

'Yes, if the first dose was not repeated. But I suppose arsenic poisoning is never diagnosed until the end'.

'Have you ever doubted that the cause of death was arsenical poisoning?'

'No doubt at all'.
The jury foreman then said:

'Can you assume for how long the poisoning has been going on?'

'It is impossible to assume'.

'Was there any sign of ptomaine poisoning?'

'There is no such thing as ptomaine poisoning. The term is popularly used to describe food poisoning. The symptoms in this case are identical with those of food poisoning up to a point'.

It is perhaps worth noting that food poisoning comes about by eating contaminated food and when it occurs it usually afflicts all those who have eaten that dish, such as a private household. In this case, all three who went to the teashop in Bude had eaten the same food. Thus if it had been food poisoning, all three would have been affected, which was not the case.

Superintendent Pill was the next witness and he reported finding that Mrs Hearn bought weed-killer in 1926 and that there was arsenic at Trenhorne Farm. A juryman asked:

'Did I understand you to say you made a thorough search of Mrs Hearn's house?'

'We have no right to search there'.

'Will you obtain the right?'

'The position is that the most important witness is missing. We have no reason to believe that she has done what she said she was going to do in the letter'.[10]

Pearce then gave a lengthy speech to those assembled and it is worth relating because it provides a useful contemporary analysis of the case to date. He told the jury that their task was to ascertain cause of death and this he suggested was arsenic poisoning. All the doctors agreed on this.

'If you are satisfied from the evidence placed before you by Mr Tickle, Dr Wordley and Dr Lister that death could have arisen from no other cause than arsenical poisoning, if you are satisfied by the medical and analytical evidence that there can be no doubt whatever that the death of the woman was due to arsenical poisoning, that will be sufficient for the purpose of the inquest.

If you are so satisfied, the next point for you to consider is how and when the arsenic got into the body of the woman.

Poisoning by arsenic can only get into the body by one of three ways, it might be accidental, suicidal or homicidal – it must be either one or the other.

Could Mrs Thomas have taken this arsenic accidentally? Is there any evidence to suggest that arsenic might have been consumed at Bude, and have got there by some accident; or have been in any of the food she consumed at home after she left Bude in any accidental way? Is it possible? Is there any evidence supporting that theory?

If not, is there any evidence that it was suicidal; that Mrs Thomas had somehow obtained arsenic and mixed it with some food she herself was taking with a view to taking her own life? If so, what would her motive be for doing so?

She seemed to be living a very comfortable life at Trenhorne Farm. There seemed to be no evidence of any jealousy between her and Mrs Hearn, according to the evidence. And we have this fact – if it is a case of suicide it could not possibly have happened after she had left Bude because she was too ill to do anything at all. If it was suicidal, it must have been taken at Bude, and she must have known what she was doing?

I think we can eliminate the accidental and the suicidal.

If it was homicidal, who then killed Mrs Alice Thomas? Was it Mr Thomas? If not he, was it Mrs Annie Hearn? Or did both of them conspire together to bring about her death? Or was it some other person or persons not known?

Let us examine the case as it affects Mr Thomas. He had been married 20 years and according to the evidence, had lived happily with his wife during that time. There is no evidence, or at any event, any substantial evidence, to the contrary. Had he any arsenic in the house?

The evidence showed that there was none. He had had some sheep dip, some time ago, but this apparently, was used about two years ago, and although full enquiries had been made, no evidence of the purchase of any article containing arsenic could be found other than the sheep dip. You have heard the evidence of Mr Pill, about the tablets, but they were one of the ordinary drugs found in farm houses.

The evidence seems to show that the deceased woman was just as friendly with Mrs Hearn as her husband was, and there was absolutely no evidence to show Mr Thomas had formed a guilty association with Mrs Hearn.

If there had been such an association, it might well be conceived that it would be a motive for getting his wife out of the way so that he might marry Mrs Hearn. Can you say that there is any evidence that such a motive existed? For undoubtedly there must have been a motive underlying the actions of the person instrumental to the death of Mrs Thomas.

Take his course of conduct from the time he knew his wife was ill. On arriving at Launceston, he wanted to fetch brandy and for her to see a doctor. From Launceston to Trenhorne he had his wife sit by his side in the front of the car while he drove the car in the darkness as well as he could with one hand and held his wife with the other.

Immediately after they reached home and after putting his wife to bed, he fetched brandy and proceeded to Polyphant to summon the doctor.

During the whole of the subsequent illness, he showed concern for his wife's condition, and remained with her as frequently as farm duties permitted, finally accompanying her to hospital in Plymouth, where he wanted to remain by her side. This in the circumstances, could not be permitted.

Were all these actions compatible with a guilty conscience? It is for you to judge. Was he indiscreet? Undoubtedly he was, in the matter of the loan of £38 to Mrs Hearn, which he kept from his wife's knowledge and which I expect, he now regrets having done.

He might also have been indiscreet in having Mrs Hearn as a frequent visitor to the house, as such visits might, and undoubtedly did, give rise to gossip among the neighbours, who might not have been aware that Mrs Thomas was just as friendly with Mrs Hearn as he was himself.

He certainly was also indiscreet in not having informed his wife's mother of her daughter's illness until a considerable time after the illness commenced.

But being indiscreet is far from being criminal, and we have it in evidence that after the funeral, Mr Thomas told Mrs Hearn plainly that he required an acknowledgement from her for the £38 and that the future was so uncertain for him he would not be requiring her services after a short time. If there was in his mind any thought of marrying her, why bother about an acknowledgement for the money?

Those, therefore, are the facts as they concern the actions of Mr Thomas from the beginning to the end of this case as they appear to me, but it is entirely for you to say whether you think him guilty in poisoning his wife or of being the accomplice of any other person in poisoning her.

Now we come to Mrs Annie Hearn. Was it she who poisoned Mrs Alice Maud Thomas? Let us examine certain phases of the case, which may appear to support this theory.

First of all she undoubtedly prepared the sandwiches which were eaten at Bude on Saturday 18 October. We do not know of what substance the sandwiches were made, except that Mr Thomas understood they were fish sandwiches and afterwards heard from Mrs Hearn it was tinned salmon.

The fact, however, remains that Mrs Thomas' illness, commenced soon after the eating of those sandwiches.

Then secondly, Mrs Hearn was in the farmhouse from the time Mrs Thomas was taken ill until she was removed to Plymouth, and up to the time Mrs Parsons arrived there on October 29 she undoubtedly did all the cooking and therefore had ample opportunity of mixing poison with Mrs Thomas' food and Mrs Parsons has told us this morning that she practically did all the cooking after (Mrs Parsons arrived).

Then thirdly there is the undoubted fact that in August 1926, she obtained some Cooper's weed-killer from a Launceston firm of chemists, and it has been stated in evidence that such weed-killer contains practically all arsenic.

There would also be a probable motive if she had formed in her mind the expectation that if Mr Thomas were a widower, there would be a chance of his asking her in due course to be his wife. These circumstances are, therefore, those which appear to be those supporting the assumption that Mrs Hearn was the murderer of Mrs Thomas, if she was at all.

Firstly, the sandwiches; secondly the cooking; thirdly the purchase of the weed-killer; and fourthly, the possibility of becoming the second Mrs

Thomas, and they seem to be the only grounds some or one of which would account for the poisoning of Mrs Thomas by Mrs Hearn.

Now let us look at the other side of the question. First, take the question of the sandwiches. We have been informed by the café assistant that it is not at all an unusual thing for customers to bring food with them.

The sandwiches were apparently packed in one parcel and consisted of two layers, as stated in the evidence of the assistant. There is absolutely no evidence at all that Mrs Hearn acted in such a way as to indicate to Mrs Thomas the particular sandwich or sandwiches which she wished her to take.

Mrs Hearn had a sandwich as well as the others, and there is no evidence that the sandwiches contained any arsenic.

Then to the cooking. Is there any evidence whatever of the mixing of any poison by Mrs Hearn of the food which she had cooked whilst she was staying in the farmhouse? True, the opportunity was there, but can it safely be said that Mrs Hearn took advantage of the opportunity?

Then, as to the purchase of the weed-killer in 1926, is there any evidence to rebut the argument that this was used up to destroy the weeds in Mrs Hearn's back garden, which has been stated to have been full of weed?' At all events, there is no evidence of the possession of this.

Lastly, as to the marriage motive. Nothing in the evidence shows any ground for this having been the supposed motive, and I have dealt with this phase in discussing the motives in regard to Mr Thomas.

Then there was the letter to Thomas by Mrs Hearn. There were puzzling elements there, argued the coroner:

'Why should Mrs Hearn jump to the conclusion that Mrs Thomas had been poisoned? Nothing had been said by any person about Mrs Thomas being poisoned except what Mr Parsons himself had said and he knew nothing except what had been told him by Mrs Hearn herself.

As far as we know he was the only person who made any suggestion of poisoning at all, and it is not likely that Mrs Hearn knew anything of the result of the post mortem examination.

Therefore it had not been revealed, so it does seem very strange that she should have jumped to the conclusion that Mrs Alice Thomas had been poisoned.

A remark of Mr Parsons, of course, might have made her think that it was an accusation against her, and that as we colloquially say, the cap fitted.

She might have been frightened about what he had said about the poison and determined either to go away and destroy herself, or hide herself, we do not know which'.[11]

Pearce saw no reason to delay the inquest's conclusion. If the jury was happy with the verdict of arsenical poisoning, that was sufficient. He added that if this was a case of murder, then who was the murderer? Could it be Thomas? If not, was it Mrs Hearn? Or was it a conspiracy between the two? Or was it another person?[12] If Thomas were innocent, there seemed no likelihood that Mrs Hearn was guilty. She was on very good terms with the deceased. There was no evidence that Thomas and Mrs Hearn 'had fallen into guilty association'. If this was not the case then Thomas might have killed his wife in order to marry Mrs Hearn. Yet he had shown the utmost care and concern for his wife and this did not tally with him being a poisoner.[13]

The jury discussed the matter for half an hour and then found, as announced by Admiral Morshead, their chairman, that the 'cause of death was arsenical poisoning. It was homicidal, but there was not sufficient evidence to show by whom, or by what means, arsenic was administered'. This would not prevent the police from pursuing further enquiries and bringing the culprit to justice if sufficient evidence could be found.[14]

Thomas gave a statement after the inquest:

'I think the jury returned the only possible verdict, and I am satisfied with it. I have not only lost my wife, but now am under a cloud, though am perfectly innocent. The inquest has been perfectly fair and impartial. I did everything I could to help the police, and I shall continue to do so until the mystery is cleared up. One day we will know the truth'.[15]

After the inquest Pill instituted enquiries among poison registers in Cornwall in order to ascertain who had purchased arsenic, especially anyone in Launceston. All he could find that was relevant was a purchase of a tin of Cooper's weed-killer from a chemist in Launceston. The name of the purchaser was in a letter affixed to the register page. When opened, the name was revealed as 'Mr Hearn'. There were enquiries in Bude about cases of food poisoning but none could be found.[16]

The investigation, though, was to widen after the inquest, when doctors Gibson and Galbraith decided to contact the police about suspicions they now had about previous deaths at Trenhorne Farm. Their depositions were sent to the department of the public prosecutor to decide whether exhumations should occur.[17]

Journalists were interested in the case and none more so than Bernard O'Connell, who wrote for the Sunday newspaper *The Empire News*. He wrote a chapter about the case in his memoirs. He reported that locals were convinced of Mrs Hearn's guilt and that there was a rumour about her being involved with Thomas, of which 'there was not a vestige of truth' wrote O'Donnell. He confessed that 'things certainly looked black against Mrs Hearn'.[18]

Chapter 5

Earlier deaths

It has already been stated that there were three deaths at Trenhorne House while Mrs Hearn lived there from 1925–30. Death certainly seemed to follow Mrs Hearn around. It has already been noted that in Grindleford Bridge from 1915–17 she nursed both her mother and her sister Grace Mabel until their deaths, as well as having two unnamed guests from Grimsby die after their visits to her. There were others more recently, however. After Mrs Thomas's demise, there began to be suspicions about the deaths of the three other women whom Mrs Hearn had lived with in Lewannick.

Firstly, there was the elderly lady whom the Everard sisters had taken in while in North Hill and who came with them to Trenhorne. Priscilla Aunger died on 24 February 1926 of senile decay, aged 91 and was buried in North Hill churchyard on Friday 5 March. Dr Thomas Ewart Ashley (1886–1963) issued the death certificate. At 91 her death was hardly unexpected.[1]

The local newspaper reported the death. 'There passed away at Trenhorne House, Congdon Shop, on the 24th, one of the oldest inhabitants of North Hill'. Apparently Miss Aunger had been a member of the North Hill Methodist chapel and attended as often as possible, but 'she had been in failing health for some time'. The report also noted 'Deceased had been under the kind care of Mrs A. Hearn for some considerable time'. Neither Mrs Hearn, nor her sister or her aunt, are recorded as being among the few mourners.[2]

Writing later about the case, Oldridge noted that Mrs Hearn informed the doctor of this death, and that the doctor might not have even seen the body, and probably did not attend Miss Aunger in the time before her death. Furthermore, the doctor had a complex private life and his mind may not have been on what was apparently the very routine death of an old woman.[3]

Then there was Miss Mary Everard. Mrs Poskitt wrote: 'Auntie also visited her from Harrogate several times and on her last visit four or five years ago [1926 or 1925] was taken ill'.[4] Mrs Hearn claimed in 1933 that she visited her aunt in

Harrogate in 1924–25 and found that the 75-year-old was struggling to make ends meet. She suggested her aunt spend a month at Trenhorne House (so clearly the visit took place no earlier than late October 1925, when they arrived there). It may have been December 1925–February 1926, as the local newspaper noted in 1926 that she had arrived in Cornwall 'last winter'. Whether her stay overlapped with Mrs Aunger is unknown.[5]

It is not known when Miss Mary Everard became ill and what her symptoms were, though Mrs Spear said, four years later, 'She was not here long before she died'.[6] Mrs Hearn claimed that she had a severe stroke and was unable to speak. She called a doctor and a nurse, who confirmed the stroke. Annie later wrote 'Her death upset me very much. Aunt Pollie and I had spent many years of our lives together. We were very fond of each other'.[7] It may be mere coincidence that on 27 July 1926, Mrs Hearn had written to Messrs MacDougall and Robinson, in Barnsley, for a pound tin of weed-killer and enclosed the price, which was two shillings. Mrs Hearn later said that this was at her aunt's behest. On 28 July they replied:

'We have to thank you for your order of 1lb tin of powder weedkiller, but in view of the recent revision of the poison laws, we are unable to supply this direct and are sending the tin to Messrs Shuker and Reed, chemists of Launceston, with the request that they hand over the weed-killer to you'.[8]

On 29 July Mrs Hearn wrote:

'To Messrs Shuker,

Dear Sir,

The weed-killer referred to is in the enclosed letter. I should be glad if you would send it on to me at Congdonshop by Reid the baker, as you will not be delivering goods here for another fortnight.

McDougall's powder weed-killer has been recommended to me as a sure help to put in order a neglected portion of my garden. Which is quite enclosed. If there should be any restrictions about sending it out instead of "handing over" will you kindly send me a small quantity of another which you can recommend for the purpose.

Yours truly,

A. Hearn'[9]

This weed-killer was 70% arsenic and in the one pound tin there would be about 4,000 grains, only two of which were needed to kill someone.[10] Why Mrs Hearn should want to buy this poison from a shop in Barnsley (not far from where her sister lived) is unknown, but one possibility is that she did not want it known locally that she had purchased it, and did not want to sign the poison register, though she was obliged to do so at the Launceston chemist.

Two weeks after the purchase of the arsenic, on 15 August 1926, Miss Mary Everard died at Trenhorne Farm of cerebral embolism, according to the death certificate that was issued by Dr Galbraith. This is when a blood clot travels to block the supply of blood to the brain and causes a stroke. Mrs Poskitt wrote 'In this case too Annie nursed her devotedly until her death'.[11]

The funeral took place at the parish church in Lewannick. Mrs Hearn, Mrs Thomas and Mrs Spear were among the mourners. Thomas was not there and it was stated that 'Miss Everard was unable to attend', presumably due to illness. There were floral tributes from Trenhorne and Harrogate.[12] No one, in print at least, noted that there had been a fatality earlier that year at the same address.

Miss Mary Everard left her few assets, valued at £117 16s, to Mrs Hearn. In her will of 3 September 1922 she wrote 'everything I possess I give to my niece Sarah Annie Hearn, except my mother's picture' and that was for her sister Betsy Holland. However, as Betsy died before her sister, perhaps the picture went to Mrs Hearn too. Mary also asked that her niece erect a tombstone in the churchyard for her; this was never done.[13] Mrs Hearn recalled, however, 'I did not benefit from Aunt Pollie's death... In fact I was slightly out of pocket'. This was because there were debts to pay.[14] Miss Everard was seventy-six years old and so, as with Mrs Aunger, her death was hardly unsurprising. The money inherited was not large but may well have been very useful to pay bills and everyday expenditure.

Mrs Poskitt wrote 'After Aunties' death Annie and Lydia went over to Harrogate to put the cookery business in order'. This entailed a lot of work as things had been left in a very unsettled condition:

'Annie's job was really to wind up the business but it took her about two years to carry through. During this time I went over to see my sisters a number of times, and I very much regretted it when they went back to Cornwall'.[15]

In late 1926, therefore, Mrs Hearn went to Harrogate. Her sister came with her, at least for a time, and they stayed for about a year, returning on 12 December 1927. Miss Minnie Everard's health was still bad. 'She was better in summer and worse in winter, but there was very little in it… During the years we had been in Cornwall she was losing ground. She had been ill and she never seemed to get back'.[16] 'She was very kind to her. They were very kind to each other', Thomas recalled.[17]

Miss Cotton of Harrogate remembered Mrs Hearn and was far from complimentary about her:

'The house in which I had a dining room flat had a large kitchen in which a sort of cookery school was held. Soon after I took my rooms Miss Everard, the aunt, left the house in charge of the occupiers of the flats to go to spend the winter in Cornwall with her nieces. From Cornwall, Miss Everard wrote to me saying she was very poorly, Mrs Hearn having accidentally spilled some boiling water on her feet. Mrs Hearn wrote later saying her aunt had died suddenly and she was shortly returning to Harlow Moor Drive with her sister.

The tenants in another flat who had been there considerably longer than I had were at Scarborough at the time. I telegraphed to them as I did not want to have the responsibility of looking after the house and they returned at once. When Mrs Hearn arrived later and found I had telegraphed she was indignant with me, without explaining why.

Mrs Hearn turned all the tenants out at a week's notice and started on her own as a cookery school, but it was not successful and soon everything was packed up and removed to Cornwall'.[18]

One wonders whether there was anything sinister in Mrs Hearn's spilling boiling water on her aunt's feet. It was not an incident mentioned by the former's loyal sister Mrs Poskitt. It may have been an accident but perhaps it was not.

After Miss Mary Everard's death, Mrs Hearn had a removal firm take what was now her furniture from Harrogate to Trenhorne. Neighbours saw her as a reserved woman. She did not discuss her private affairs with others and lived in poor circumstances.[19] The sisters were not well off at all. They were not noted as having been in work. Miss Minnie Everard almost certainly could not do so. Their brother in Grimsby often gave them sums of money. In December 1928, as noted already, Annie had had to borrow £38 from her neighbour, Thomas, to meet a demand for cash by the son of a late Harrogate creditor who wanted his money back. In 1929 Henry Everard, a brother, gave them about £50. They made a little money from lodgers, such as a Mr Roberts, who allegedly stayed until the end of January 1930, though Miss Everard's diary does not confirm this.[20] Furthermore, the sisters' father, now living in Sheffield, fell ill and went to live with his son in 70 Earl Street, Grimsby, where Mrs Hearn nursed him until he died on 30 March 1928, aged seventy-six. The death certificate noted that he died of hypostatic congestion. Henry Everard was present at his father's death and informed the registrar the same day. The death certificate notes 'no PM', which perhaps suggests that the death was sudden or unexpected and that the suggestion that there be a post mortem was made. Why, we don't know, but the idea cannot have been pushed hard.[21]

Then there was Annie's sister, Miss Minnie Everard, a rather different case because she was younger, at fifty-four years old in 1930, although she had been in bad health for decades. Far more is known about her death and from a variety of sources. However, in this year, as Mrs Hearn later said, 'she got worse'. Before there had been constipation and vomiting but no diarrhoea, and no doctor had been called from 1925 until January 1930.[22]

From 1 January 1930 Miss Minnie Everard began to keep a diary. A transcript of the original exists, presumably typed by a police or court official. It is the only source of evidence about these months which was written at the time of events; most of the evidence later produced was by people recalling events of the previous year. From the very start, she recorded her almost daily physical suffering and despair, writing 'I do not feel at all well, my nose prickly and headache'. On Friday 2 January she wrote, 'I have had rather a bad night; a lot of indigestion

&c. seemed to have a good deal of inflammation of the inside. Bad headaches during the night and this morning'. Dr Gibson visited her on 4 January, as he was at the house to see other patients. She was able to walk about. Dr Galbraith was later called. He later recalled: 'She was in bed and complaining of abdominal discomfort and pain. That is all I can remember. I believe she had been sick'.

He then examined her, but found:

'Very little. I examined her mostly with the idea of finding some surgical disturbance, but I found nothing requiring surgical interference. She had apparently some slight feverishness. Beyond that I cannot remember more'.

He thought that it might be colitis and he prescribed a mixture containing kaolin and temperature-reducing drugs. He did not call again for some weeks.[23]

Dr Galbraith visited again on 17 January 1930. This time he told Miss Everard's relatives that the complaint was a chill on the stomach, but this was not a diagnosis. He was actually treating her for an ulcerated stomach. He gave her a solution composed of china clay that was as effective as bismuth but much cheaper. This medicine would counteract the acid in her stomach.[24]

However, the diary does not note these visits and instead reports that Dr Galbraith visited on 19 January when he prescribed salts and milk to neutralise the stomach acid.[25]

Dr Gibson did not see Miss Everard again until 24 January, though he later thought it was not until 12 April. On 24 January he took her blood pressure and ascribed her headaches, pains and fainting to be 'due to the change', presumably meaning the menopause. On 6 January Minnie had had a 'rather a bad night'. Ten days later there were further health concerns noted, 'I feel very uncomfortable inside; heart a bit upset too'. On the next day, 17 January, matters were no better, 'I kept getting worse last night as time went on, worse and worse. Very bad indeed, a lot of pain, and finally sick. I went off altogether for the first time in my life'.[26]

On 18 January, she wrote 'I had a very bad night. Face and head very bad, also feeling very bad inside. Very feverish, a lot of pain in body'. On 20 January she had a 'bad stomach', on the 21st 'neuritis pain' and on 22nd she wrote 'Tongue still very white'.[27]

However, by the end of the month Minnie seemed to be staging a recovery, for she wrote on 27 January, 'Last night is the best night that I have had'. However, on 30 January she reported 'eye trouble'.[28] Almost every diary entry includes a reference to ill health. In January her symptoms included: a prickly nose (twice), headaches (eight times), a chill, shivering, indigestion (four times), great pain in the stomach and body (five times), inflammation of the stomach and bowels (twice), an upset heart (thrice), sickness, fainting (twice), an acidic stomach, pain all over the body and in the face and head, heat (twice), pain in the back and legs, a white tongue, neuritis (twice) and wind (twice). She suffered from pain at night as well as during the day, but it was not wholly unrelieved as there is no reference to it from 8–12 January. Quinine was used on at least two occasions to ameliorate the pain.[29]

It was not all doom and gloom. Minnie read *Nicholas Nickleby* and her sister made her soup and also gave her Benger's food to eat. There were letters written and received, including one from their sister Mrs Poskitt on 25 January, and of course the almost daily visits from Thomas. Very occasionally there was also Mrs Spear, as on 19 January. Mrs Hearn was sometimes ill: on 1 January she looked faint and a little sick and on 17 January she wrote 'Annie sad looked like death'.[30]

There was initially no respite from Minnie's health worries as February began. On 1 February she was unable to digest food, and the next day she could eat poached eggs but was then in pain for hours and Thomas had to help her upstairs to bed. To summarise her symptoms over the first two weeks of February: pain in the body and head (twice), nose and throat very bad, hard to breathe (once), bad headaches (five times), indigestion, cold and uncomfortable body. On 13 February she did not come downstairs at all.[31]

However, on 15 February things improved somewhat. Not only was Minnie not unwell for a time, but there was the delightful news that Bessie (Mrs Poskitt) was to visit them. Furthermore, on 16 February Thomas brought flowers when he visited and Mrs Hearn read the Bible to her ailing sister, the passage being 'Show me a penny'. In anticipation of the sisterly visit 'Annie busy doing things'. Mrs Poskitt took the train from Doncaster to Plymouth and then changed for Launceston, the nearest railway station; the whole fare cost £1 17s 10d.[32]

Mrs Poskitt arrived on 17 February and stayed for one month, leaving on 17 March. Miss Everard wrote of her arrival, 'Oh we are pleased to see her. We can hardly believe she is here. It is wonderful'. Miss Everard complained about her gastric trouble, which Mrs Poskitt knew had troubled her for many years. Sometimes she was better and sometimes not. When later asked about when her sister was in pain, she replied: 'Generally after tea. She got more tea and there was numbings in the limbs. My sister used to rub her legs and arms many times'.

Miss Everard was often up and about, but as an invalid she did very little housework. She was able to do a little cooking, alongside Mrs Hearn, and there were two or three occasions when she spent several days in bed.[33]

There was more good news on 18 February. The sisters' brother, Henry, sent them a letter and £7 which was owing from their uncle's will. Miss Everard wrote 'It does seem wonderful this money comes just now. Surely our Heavenly Father is taking care of us', which casts a light on their precarious financial situation as well as her strong Christian faith.[34]

However, Minnie's health was not always good as the month wore on. Her breathing was 'so bad' on 19 February and on the 22nd her nose and throat were 'worse'. Her throat was very bad on 24 February. On eating Benger's, grapes and mashed potatoes on 26 February she suffered indigestion and next day she wrote 'not felt at all well' and also had a headache.[35]

The next month did not begin too badly. Miss Everard records a meal of shallots, potatoes and broad beans. There was a good sermon at church and she later read *Martin Chuzzlewit*. The garden received attention with the sisters digging and weeding on 4 March and Mrs Hearn and Mrs Poskitt were baking the next day. However, on 5 March Miss Everard had a bad night and on the next day endured pain in the stomach and wind. There was more woe, with her writing on 7 March, 'I got a nasty shock when I found how little money we have. I thought we had several pounds more… I ought to trust more especially now with all these wonderful evidences of our Heavenly Father's care'. Later that day Thomas drove them over to the Launceston Picture Theatre and she recorded 'not bad in its way, but a war picture. We would have preferred something else'. This seems to have been her only day out in this six-month period.[36]

Minnie's health problems persisted. On 9 March she was 'not feeling at all well', with pain in the body. Next day there was a headache and a shaking hand. She passed a lot of blood on the 12 March. There was a bad night with both chills and heat. At the end of her visit, on 17 March, Mrs Poskitt was driven back to Launceston railway station by Thomas.[37] Minnie's health continued to be consistently poor in the second half of the month. From 17 to 28 March the symptoms were as follows: very cold, headache (twice), pain in the shoulders and back, faintness (twice), prickly nose and throat (twice), passing blood (twice).[38]

However, in late March Minnie took a new turn for the worse, writing on the 29th, 'Still bad, when I get up especially. I keep feeling worse and worse. So very faint. I fainted right away before I got to bed and soon I was sick'. On this day, or rather night, Dr Galbraith was requested to visit and so he did and found her complaining of intestinal discomfort of the stomach and bowels. 'She did not seem to me to be very bad when I saw her,' he said, but he assumed that there must have been a sudden attack for there to be such concern about her. She complained of sickness and vomiting but did not suggest a cause. He prescribed a powder to soothe the stomach. On 30 March there was much the same, 'I had a very bad night. Lot of pain in the stomach and top of the body'. Thomas was called in by Mrs Hearn and they found her sister in a fainting condition. They took her up to her bed.[39]

There was a bad fainting attack in March and Mrs Hearn told Mrs Poskitt, 'It was very much the same as the other, only with a very bad sick and faint part, and didn't last so long'.[40] She did not know why this happened.

Stomach pains and neuritis pains persisted during April. On 1 April Minnie wrote 'Had a lot of pain. Head rather bad. I feel so bad altogether'. She was in pain for the next three days as well, in her body and in her hips, thighs, legs and shoulders. After having had porridge and soup on 4 April she felt sick. From 5–11 April her symptoms were as follows: bad stomach (thrice), sickness (thrice), faint (twice), uncomfortable, discomfort in the stomach and bowels (twice), and a white tongue. On 8 April she wrote, steadfast to her faith, 'Oh I do wish things would get a bit better. I am praying and trusting for it'. There were occasionally times when she felt a little better.[41]

Doctors Galbraith and Gibson concluded that Minnie was suffering from inflammation of the intestines. Galbraith called again on 4 April (or so he later said; the diary does not record the visit) and found her symptoms much the same. She was depressed and complained about her bowels. Dr Gibson visited her on 12 April at 11.30am. In his opinion: 'My own view was that it was the old dyspepsia trouble. I gather she was getting nausea when she had food – that she felt she was going to be sick rather than she was sick.'

As in 1925 he prescribed her a stomach mixture with a preparation to aid the digestion, which should have had a soothing effect.[42] This was bismuth and aromatic pepsin and liquid takadivstase.[43] She commented on his visit 'He was very nice. Says I may have Marmite, stomach tonic and anti-fainting medicine'. On that day she had no food between 2 and 11pm and felt worse.[44]

However, the visit and the prescriptions made little if any difference. On the day after Dr Gibson's visit, she recorded feeling faint and was pained in her stomach and bowels: 'felt very bad indeed for several hours'. This led to her writing the following 'I pray that I may be restored to health for a while longer, but I seemed to come near the Eternal, and I seemed to feel that it might not be so terrible as I feared, I have so dreaded the last illness, but I think my heart will give in and not let me suffer so terribly after all. I thank God for this comfort'. The next day was less bad and so was the next. However, on 16 April she felt weak and faint and had a bad night on 17 April. Her stomach felt painful on 20 and 22 April. On 23 April 'The pains had been bad today' and she felt sick.[45]

Gibson saw her again on 19 April. Miss Everard told him that she could not take the medicine and he noted that she had had hardly any of it. She told him it upset her. He advised her to try it for another week, taking smaller doses. He visited a week later and Miss Everard told him she had not been able to take any of it. He then made a change in the ingredients and she could take half doses.[46] Or so he said; the diary does not record this visit. Instead, her litany of pain continued. On 24 April there was a nasty taste in her mouth and pain in her stomach. On 25 April she recorded a very bad night of bowel pain and more bad taste in the mouth; the bowel pain continued the next day.[47]

On 26 April Dr Gibson visited and gave the same medicine but digitalis was included instead of liquid takadivstase.[48] She wrote that the doctor told her that she could eat small amounts every two hours: chicken mince, beef tea and pieces of fish. She wrote 'I am so awfully thirsty all the time'. On the next four days she had a dry and nasty mouth, felt in pain and thirsty, was weak and sinking and on 30 April had pains in the body and was eating Benger's only.[49]

On 14 April Mrs Hearn called at the sub-post office at Lewannick. Walter Martin, the sub-postmaster, recalled her calling about National Savings and producing a form for the repayment of them. It was probably signed by Miss Everard and witnessed by Mrs Spear. These were paid out on 19 April, to the value of £32 14s, quite possibly being needed to pay medical bills.[50] On 25 April Mrs Hearn wrote to Mrs Poskitt, 'I am sorry to say Minnie is not much better… she has a lot of pain and feels sick'. [51]

Annie wrote another two letters that month. On a Wednesday in early April she wrote:

'Our Dearest Bessie,

I am just finishing this letter for Minnie. I think she has answered your letter. We are very pleased with the parsley roots. It is looking well and taking root nicely. You will be wondering how we are. Minnie had a rather bad attack a week last Saturday. It was very much the same as the other only the *very* bad sick and the faint part did not *last so long.* We have not seen anything of Mr Thomas for several days and he has just come in with some papers. Minnie was feeling rather bad, but she got much worse, very faint and very bad. She wanted to get upstairs if possible. We helped her up, but before we could get to the bed, she fainted right away. We lifted her on to the bed and afterwards she was sick. He went downstairs and brought some hot water to drink and stayed a bit. After he had gone we thought we would like the doctor and Marian went to Lewannick and phoned. He was here at 10.20. He said he would send some powder, thought it would be more good than medicine. Mr Thomas went for it on Saturday afternoon. Well, she's a bit better, but it's so awfully slow, first one little drawback and then another. Still in bed of course. We hope she will improve more. We don't want you to worry. We are hoping for better things for all of us. Well, goodbye our Bessie for just now. Best love, don't worry.

Help is still "the best dog in the world". He comes up to me sometimes and lies down real still, for quite a long time sometimes'.[52]

The other letter was dated 25 April:

'I am sorry to say that Minnie is not much better. In fact, she is not able to take anything but Benger's food, and has been really bad with a lot of pain and feeling… There seems nothing to do but wait until the stomach takes food. But will she have strength to wait? The doctor is coming tonight. We are all in our Father's hands. Mrs Spear came in one day, brought her Testament, read the 14th of St. John and made a very nice prayer'.[53]

At least when the new month began Miss Everard could feel glad of the weather, 'Another lovely day'. However, her previous night was 'not very good', with a nasty sensation in the stomach and pain and discomfort throughout the day. On 2 May her sister was not looking well: 'Annie is looking very much run down. I am very sorry'. Miss Everard was sick and suffered pain in the bowels. Thomas visited; they chatted and prayed together. Dr Gibson called at 8pm and thought that her condition was worsening and brought her an effervescing mixture to be taken two or three times a day. Mrs Hearn suggested her sister go to Launceston hospital.[54]

Miss Everard's diary for that day read: 'I feel very bad – feel like being sick every minute'. Two days later, she wrote, 'I am so awfully weak and stomach still so bad. I get weaker and fainter every day'. She felt weaker and thinner, with more sickness, stomach pains, thirsty and having little sleep. On 6 May she saw Dr Arthur Budd (1879–1937), the third partner in the three-doctor practice at Launceston, but 'he was simply horrid'.[55]

On 8 May Miss Everard was taken suddenly ill and so her sister called on Mrs Spear between 5 and 6pm, telling her that her sister's condition was a lot worse. Her throat burnt, she felt faint, with cramp all over, stomach pain and she wrote 'I was bad and seemed like to die if I get much worse'. Mrs Spear came with Mrs Hearn to the sick woman's bedroom and recalled that Miss Everard told her, 'That medicine is too strong for me. *It is poisoning me.* [author's emphasis] I have had a full dose of it. I can feel it creeping all over my hands and my feet are numbed. I only had part doses before this time'. Mrs Hearn explained to the neighbour, 'It was an emergency medicine to be taken when Miss Everard was in much pain'.[56] Dr Galbraith visited on the evening of 8 May by special request. Apart from Miss Everard's usual complaints about abdominal pain she said words similar to 'as though she was going'. Minnie wrote of the doctor 'he not at all nice'. She then wrote 'Then later, about 10 or so I was sick again, four separate times. I felt so faint and ill and every time I moved, if only to speak, I was sick. Bad until nearly 1'.[57]

Miss Everard wrote of her symptoms on that same day, 'Hands and arms all prickles and then began to feel stiff and legs cracked. No proper use of them. Then got it in the legs, pain in the stomach and all over... Oh I was awfully bad. It seems as if I were poisoned'. How significant is this last phrase, taken in conjunction with that already cited by Mrs Spear? She never again used it in her diary and so whether or not she had any further suspicion about the cause of her condition but did not commit it to paper is impossible to answer. This diary entry corresponds with the sentiment she is said to have made in the last paragraph,

'It is poisoning me' with regard to the 'special medicine' given. Both doctors attested that they never prescribed a medicine such as Miss Everard described. They never prescribed any 'emergency' medicine. Apparently Mrs Spear, who called Dr Gibson on one occasion, claimed that when Miss Everard described her symptoms, the doctor treated them lightly.[58] The question must be what was this special medicine and who prepared it; the suggestion must be that it was anything but beneficial and that it was put together by the one nearest to her and most trusted by her; her sister.

Dr Gibson returned on the 9th and it was then that Miss Everard made a further dramatic declaration. 'She said she felt she was being poisoned'. This ties in with the diary entry of the previous day and Mrs Spear's recollection and is the only known occasion on which she confided this suspicion to a doctor and he did not act upon it. This poison was allegedly in the medicine allegedly prescribed by his partner. Mrs Hearn, who was always in the room at the time of these visits (as a caring sister or as a controlling poisoner), exclaimed, 'How could she say such a thing?' The doctor suggested that she could go to Launceston Infirmary, but she refused. He did not see her again.[59] Minnie wrote of him 'he was horrid' after suffering from diarrhoea. She added that the doctor:

'said I was not bad at all last night, only silly and hysterical. That was an awful lie, it was because, we said, the medicine brought it. He wouldn't have that at all. Then he asked me abt going into hospital, and we said no. Seemed quite cross and very soon went. I have never known a doctor so half as horrid. My word, I would not like to be at his tender mercies. Surely we can do as we like. It upset us a lot'.[60]

It is not known why Minnie refused to go to the hospital. Perhaps she hoped against hope that she would be better cared for by her sister, rather than trusting those she did not know. Perhaps it was her antipathy towards Dr Galbraith. The reason can never be known with certainty. However, Annie's part in this is peculiar to say the least. She had witnessed increasing and incessant suffering on her sister's part and despite all her efforts had been unable to help her. The normal response to a loved one who is *in extremis*, medically speaking, and whom one is unable to help, is to seek help elsewhere. Annie did not, and again the question must be asked. Why?

That night, as on at least one previous occasion, Mrs Hearn asked Mrs Spear to come to her sister's room to pray for her. Mrs Hearn explained that 'She did not feel at all well, and she had not been to a service for some time, and she would like to have a little prayer'.

Mrs Spear came in but there was little conversation about Minnie's illness. Mrs Spear read a chapter from the Bible and said a prayer. On other occasions she would read from a hymnal. The first time she read from the Bible it was from the Gospel of St John, chapter 14, beginning with 'Let not your heart be troubled'. They all joined in with saying amen. These were regular events, though did not occur every evening.[61]

There were improvements on the next day, though Miss Everard felt pain in the shoulders and arms. She was sleeping better by 10 May. The pains did not go away, but were at a far lower threshold. Stomach pains persisted on 12 and 13 May. But on 14 May Minnie was sick and suffered even more from stomach pains, writing 'I feel very bad and so very weak. Although I am very weak, I murmur not and merely cry every time I move'. Next day was no physically better. On 14 and 15 May Mrs Spear came to pray with them.[62]

Dr Gibson made several more visits that month, on 12, 19, 24 and 26 May. He prescribed the effervescing liquid on 20 May. He saw her on 23 May and prescribed a laxative on 30 June but did not see Miss Everard that day.[63] However, the diary only records the visit of 23 May when 'He was quite nice', in contrast to Dr Galbraith. Minnie was unwell at nights and her stomach was in pain for much of the time. Diary entries read 'I moan a lot and nearly cry every time I do anything or get out', and after having cocoa on 18 May, 'Oh I did feel bad after it, so very sick and lot of pain. Oh, it was awful, for hours. Prayed about it. Stomach bad' and on 21 May 'did not feel very well after it' (a meal of fish and lettuce).[64]

On 26 May Miss Everard wrote, 'Oh dear, I have felt bad today. I cannot think what has brought this attack on, unless salts and do not know what else to take, must have my bowels cleared'. She suffered from more sickness and stomach pains throughout. She lacked an appetite and felt uncomfortable. She even recorded her sister being unwell on 27 May. [65]

On 30 May Mrs Hearn and Thomas went into Launceston to cash Miss Everard's £30 worth of War Savings Certificates; presumably the money was needed to pay bills, including the medical fees for Miss Everard's illness. She was awake all that night with stomach pains and Thomas asked the doctor to send her pills. Stomach pains and sickness persisted on the last day of the month.[66]

For Miss Everard, the next month saw further instances of vomiting and sickness. On 1 June she was awake for most of the night with pains in the shoulder, arms and stomach. Mrs Spear came around every day in June, and Miss Everard complained much of vomiting though Mrs Spear never saw her being sick. She also complained about pain in the legs and shoulders. She could not move unless her sister moved her and Mrs Hearn often rubbed her legs for her, but she could move her arms alright. Minnie wrote 'Annie has had to spend a good deal of time with me. I am sorry. She cannot get on with much. She washed my back'.[67]

Throughout the month there was much of the same suffering for Minnie. On 7 June she wrote 'I didn't know what to do… I prayed abt it a lot'. On 10 June she wrote 'never had so much pain for so long' and on the next day 'Oh it was a long long night for us both'. Other symptoms included being sick often, pain in the left shoulder, pain in the bowels and stomach, faintness, and a white tongue. She also had a lack of appetite.[68]

Meanwhile, Mrs Hearn wrote to her sister on 12 June and part of the letter survives:

'Thank you for your two dear sympathetic letters. We have kept wanting to write to you, but somehow the time has been full up with things. Minnie is still very bad, we kept saying we must write to Bessie & then we have not done it. We do hope you are feeling a little better than you were & that things are as smooth as it is possible under the circumstances.

We heard from Mrs Brent that they would come on June 16th. I suspect they will pay something for the time that they should have been here, she has not yet written to say time of arrival or anything, we are expecting to hear…

It is very disappointing for poor Minnie, we have thought several times she seemed improving then she has gone back again, sometimes it has been with taking salts or something. Last week when the weather was so warm & fine, I helped her downstairs & on to Mabel's chair outside into the sunshine two or three times, but she has been very bad since, such a lot of pain & we think it must be that she got a chill although she was careful and well bundled up. The pain is easier now, but she has been so sick & could not take anything that she is very weak. We are doing our best we don't seem to know what else to do the doctors don't seem any good much. It is good growing weather, you wouldn't know our garden. It is all grown up with one thing or another, weeds chiefly. It has had to be neglected awful, you did me a good job at the strawberry bed & I have managed to keep that all right, they are coming on well, but not ripe yet, we have some…

Her very best love, & may God bless and help you and open a door to things for you very soon.

The enclosed little note explains itself, would you like us to send you a copy of it to the Vicar at St. Mary's, if you would do the same & what would be the right address. You know about that new house of the Jacksons had don't you, it was such a nice place.

Best love from us both to our Bessie (From Annie)'.[69]

On 24 June Minnie's diary reads, 'I feel very bad this morning. I was very sick and had pains more or else all over. My legs and feet are very bad and very prickly. I felt easier in the afternoon and evening. Nothing tastes right. I cannot take anything much'.[70] Next day she wrote 'I had a very bad day today, sick oh so many times'.[71]

From then on, the diary entries become much shorter. On 25 June Minnie wrote 'I have had a very bad day today, sick over so many times, straining awful, nothing on stomach except bile now and then. Oh I have had a lot of pain'. On 26 June she wrote, 'Very bad today, oh, so sick many times. It was a very long night. Very sick until the morning. Nothing to eat'. There were no entries on 27 and 28 June. The next few days' entries were then lumped together, several days in each entry. Dr Gibson called on 4 July and found that her condition was getting worse. He stated:

'I found Miss Everard had certainly lost ground seriously. She was thinner, not taking food well, and getting in a grave state. I remember very clearly examining her that day with great care to see if there was any sign of a malignant growth or cancer anywhere in that neighbourhood. She was very thin, and to that extent, easy to be examined and I could not satisfy myself there was any sign of malignant disease – no lump in the liver or anything of that sort. I could find nothing more than I found before. She was suffering from want of nourishment'.

He added that she was able to turn herself in bed and complained of pains in the abdomen and arms.[72]

The diary entries for July are very much shorter and read as follows:

1 July

Sick all time. Tongue coated very much

[There was no entry on the next day.]

3 July

Tongue began to clear a bit it has been awful. Heart not quite so fast. Dr Gibson called abt 6.30. We sent postcard yesterday.

[There were no entries on 4–6 July.]

7 July

Received letter from Bessie.

8 July

Wrote to Bessie.

9 July

Wrote Mrs Brent. Broad beans cooked.

10 July

Dr did not call.

11 July

Letter from Bessie also from Mrs Tatham.

This was the last entry in Minnie's diary and she clearly was too weak even to write a few words, which had been the case until the end of June.[73]

Mrs Hearn wrote on 13 July to Mrs Poskitt:

'Minnie, was, of course, very bad, not in such bad pain or anything, except now and then pains in the body and sometimes very bad pains in the legs and the feet, a sort of neuritis, and cannot move them except what I do for her, a prickly sensation, like asleep, and also her sight was bad, and could not see the other side of the room clearly and that when she looked at the window it was all yellow.

She did want to go. It was really awful she had to wait so long'.[74]

Dr Gibson was asked to call again on 18 July and came. He later described what he saw:

'She had gone down very markedly indeed and was still thinner and more emaciated and seemed unconscious. She was very heavy and gave the impression of the question of head symptoms. So on that occasion, I examined her eyes with the ophthalmoscope to see if there was any kind of brain trouble, but found no sign of optic neuritis. I formed the opinion that she was dying'.

He told Mrs Hearn that her sister was near death.[75] Three days later, he stated:

'I got a message to see Miss Everard on the Monday with the message that she was in great pain. My recollection is that I took out with me a bottle of medicine I cannot absolutely remember if I took it out with me, but I have no notes that it was sent out in any other way, and I have a recollection that I took it out with me because she was in pain'.

On his arrival he found 'She had very severe pain. Her condition was pitiable and was in the last extreme of weakness, I could not hear what she said. She tried to whisper'.[76]

Gibson visited Minnie again on 21 July and found that she was suffering from acute stomach pains. He gave her some medicine, hoping that it would help her. It did not and she died in the night. Mrs Hearn was present when she died and she reported the death the next day. All this time, Mrs Hearn had nursed and fed her sister. She seemed efficient and devoted to her, so Thomas and Mrs Spear claimed.[77] Thomas said 'I should say Mrs Hearn was devoted to Minnie'.[78]

Mrs Hearn's version of Minnie's death, which she wrote in 1933, is a little different. She claimed then that Mrs Spear said to her, 'Oh do come. Minnie is terribly ill'. Mrs Hearn arrived in her sister's bedroom and Minnie said 'Oh Annie, I feel so bad'. Mrs Hearn gave Minnie medicine from the 'emergency bottle' and said 'Drink this dear, it will make you better'. She then called the doctor who arrived and saw that her sister was in great pain. She recollected 'For ten minutes after the doctor left her she lay with her eyes shut. Then all of a sudden she moved in my arms and I knew the end had come'. She then called to the Thomases to come, 'Oh do come and help me' and her neighbours did so.[79]

Just before her death, in the last one or two days, Mrs Spear, who helped lay her out after death, noted that Miss Everard was wracked by pain and completely unable to move.[80]

The doctor later said, 'I came to the conclusion that she died from chronic gastric catarrh and I added to my certificate colitis because she had certainly had bowel symptoms as well as stomach symptoms'. The death certificate was written accordingly. It was issued on 29 July; no post-mortem was deemed necessary.[81]

On 21 July Mary Jane Hoskin of Lewannick came to the farm at Mrs Hearn's behest to perform the last rites. Richard Alford, undertaker and carpenter, was called upon to make an oak coffin and he lowered Minnie in and screwed the lid down on the day before the funeral. The plaque on the lid read 'Lydia M. Everard Born February 22nd 1882. Died July 21st 1930'. The coffin was buried four feet six inches deep.[82] Thomas was later asked about Mrs Hearn's reaction to her sister's death and he replied 'She seemed a bit upset about it'.[83] The year of Minnie's birth on the coffin plaque was incorrect by six years. It is presumed that the funeral (on 24 July) at the parish church was a low-key event and attended by few; unlike with Mrs Aunger and Miss Mary Everard, the local newspaper did not report it and as with Miss Mary Everard no death notice was inserted into the local newspaper.

An analysis of Minnie Everard's symptoms in relation to the symptoms of arsenic poisoning makes it clear that the symptoms were indeed those of arsenic poisoning and that the doctors did not recognise them.

Minnie Everard's symptoms[84]	Arsenic poisoning[85]
Vomiting (being sick)	Vomiting
Nausea (feeling sick)	Nausea
Indigestion, sometimes constipation, 'water move' at one point	Diarrhoea
Abdominal pain	Abdominal pain
Tachycardia (heart beating fast)	Tachycardia
'Nasty' taste in mouth	Metallic taste in mouth
Headache	Headache
Gastrointestinal bleeding (passed a lot of blood)	Gastrointestinal bleeding
Sore throat	Sore throat
Neuritis pains, neuralgia, prickly nose, numbness of legs and feet, arms and hands 'all prickles'	Numbness in hands and feet, 'pins and needles' sensation (peripheral neuropathy)
Dizziness	Dizziness
Tired, weak	Fatigue
Poor sleep on many occasions	Insomnia

Apart from the information garnered from the diary, other pertinent evidence was found when Minnie's body was exhumed, as we shall see in a later chapter.

All three women at Trenhorne Farm had apparently been considered to have died of natural causes and had been buried without any fuss. No post-mortems or inquests were felt necessary. Presumably there was nothing obviously wrong with Mrs Aunger and the elder Miss Everard except old age, and doctors had been regularly attending the long ailing younger Miss Everard. However, following the death of Mrs Thomas on 4 November 1930 suspicions arose and so, on 9 December, the corpses of the two Misses Everard were exhumed by order of the Home Office and their internal organs were sent for analysis.[86]

Mrs Poskitt later wrote of her sister's dilemma:

'Last July Lydia died. I should have liked to have gone over to nurse her when I heard she was ill, but Cornwall is a long way away and I left it in Annie's capable hands.

This last tragedy made her think of giving up the house and returning north which I would have liked her to have done. And it was while she was still more or less undecided that Mrs Thomas fell ill. Having nothing else to occupy her attention Annie thought that she should give her nursing experience for the benefit of Mrs Thomas and her help was accepted.'[87]

Mrs Poskitt saw the deaths as tragedies for her sister, but others saw them in a rather more sinister light, especially after Mrs Thomas's death. Drs Gibson and Galbraith certainly became suspicious after reading about Mrs Thomas's inquest in the press and so reported the earlier deaths to the police.[88]

Mrs Hearn wrote a lengthy letter thus to Bessie on their sister's death:

'My dearest Bessie,

What a long time it must seem to you before you get a real letter. I am so sorry. Well I will begin somewhere at the beginning. Tuesday 13th July Minnie was of course very bad but not in such bad pain or anything except now and then pain in body, and sometimes very bad pain in legs and feet, sort of neuritis and she had no use in them, couldn't move them except when I did for her and a bad prickly sensation in them a bit like asleep, also her sight was bad could not see the other side of the room clearly and said when she looked out of the window it was all pale yellow mist. Mr Thomas came in a bit in afternoon. We had the wireless on in evening for a service and afterwards Mrs Spear came in last thing for perhaps an hour, finished with nice prayer (she had come in like that every night for I should think 3 weeks altogether) it would have been a nice day if only poor Minnie had not been so bad – she was very uncomfortable and of course couldn't speak much and looked unlike herself. Keep getting worse and weaker all that week and more pain as time went on. Oh she *did* want to go, it really was awful she had to wait so long. We always thought Minnie's heart was a bit weak, but it seemed the strongest thing about her at the last. You see there was nothing actually to make her die except weakness. She really died of starvation and it seemed as if the heart would keep on beating little beats hardly enough breath with for ever. Doctor came on Friday, he said she was dying then might last a few days. He was very nice and gentle etc. he looked at her eyes – she couldn't see at all and had not been able to for some days, she couldn't see when he flashed a bright light on them – he said it was neuritis of the eye nerves. She was seeming a bit more comfortable then and quieter, and we thought she would go on to the end, there was nothing he could do really, he said to me it was no use trying to do anything, or give her anything that might bother her, best let her go as quietly as possible. Sat. was a bad day and Sunday pain was bad and we hardly knew what or where but she was in great distress and of course awfully sore etc. with lying, they told me there were no real sores though I had thought once the skin was through in just one place. She was much weaker and helpless than either Mother or Mabel got and she was thinner too. On Monday everything was worse and could hardly breathe it was terribly hard work to get enough – of course we were all expecting the release to come any minute almost, but about noon I couldn't stand it any longer and they phoned for doctor – he was out of round and didn't get here until about 10 at night. Mrs Spear and me had been sat watching helplessly for about 2 hours what we thought was the very last – then he came, and I gave her a dose of med. by teaspoon and in a minute or two she was easier and in 5 minutes asleep. He stayed about ½ an hour and said if she woke with pain give her another dose. He said I have put every four hours on the bottle, but if she is in pain, give her every two – regulate it entirely by the pain or even sooner. Oh what we are studying is to give her an easy passing. I don't think she will last through the night. He went. Mrs Spear came up again. I told her, she went down and told Mr T. who was in kitchen. Mrs Sp. came up again, and I ran down speak to him. I had not been upstairs 5 minutes when Minnie just quietly stopped breathing. Mrs Sp was sitting by her. I said She hasn't gone but she had – as still and quiet as anything. I ran down to Thomas, he had just got undressed but not in bed. He fetched Mrs Hoskin and I did not go upstairs again. I slept at Spears that night. The funeral was on Thursday. Mr Wadge took bearers in his car (he was one himself) and Mr T. took his wife, Mrs S and me. Mrs Hoskins had tea for bearers at her home in Lewannick as some of the bearers belonged there. I went home with Mrs Thomas, stayed until 20 to 10 because Spears were going out in evening, then came to Spears. I am still sleeping there for a few nights longer, they have visitors next Friday and I am expecting someone too but I'll tell you all about those things next time, I am expecting to hear.

Yesterday I went to Launceston got a coat 25/- it is a black and white tweed. I didn't want a mack, and a hat and black gloves and a pair of black cotton stockings. I have a pair or two of silk ones to mend a little bit. I have made frock and shall just wear it straight out it will last as long as I want it. Then there is a black and white silk one of M Maud's: I am going to alter a bit soon.

Well Bessie darling I know it will make you sad to read all this but darling its over and don't worry about me at all. I shall be alright somehow – something will open up. Minnie wanted me to keep on here if I could, but of course one cannot be sure of anything. I would like to if I can pay my way but funds are lower than Minnie knew – anyway, I shall not do anything in a hurry – only I mean I *can* earn my living in a post if I can't here so we won't worry. I can't realise things and yet sometimes I do very much. One thing is sure dear Minnie cannot be hurt again and I am all right, things don't hurt me like they did her. This is all just about me etc. Bessie, I *do* hope you are not having one of the *bad* times just now. Minnie and me talked about you often, she said she knew you would wish to go with her and perhaps it isn't a long good-bye after all. She said she would be looking for you. She couldn't write anything but she knew that you would know just how she felt about you and one can't put these things not words anyhow. I have not written to tell Henry yet. I am going to next and post with this tomorrow. I am not going out today at all – I am wondering what you are doing. It is nearly 5, I am going to get some tea now – I have hardly been anywhere but kitchen lately but have come in front room today to write. Now I am going in kitchen to boil kettle and shall perhaps bring my tea here.

I hardly know how to finish but Bessie dear think of yourself and do best for yourself that you can in every little way. I am looking after myself too, we want you know. Minnie said so so many times.

Your loving Annie.

Dr said Minnie's stomach etc. were prematurely worn out through cataarhal inflammation or Colitis'.[89]

Annie also wrote, at about the same time, to a Miss Slack of Dobholme, Froway, Sheffield:

'Dear Miss Slack,

I am writing to tell you very sad news, sad that is for me, but glad I am sure for our dear Minnie. I am afraid it will come as a shock to know that she has gone to join our other loved ones – she passed away on Monday night July 21st at about 10.45. I ought to have written to you sooner but there have been so many things to see about and letters to write and only me for everything, and I am tired out too with it all. You know dear Miss Slack what it is to see our dear ones suffer and suffer in spite of all ones efforts still suffering badly. I cannot yet realise that poor dear Minnie is free from pain and comfortable, but I am trying to. The funeral was on Thursday 24th here at Lewannick. She had been very ill all the summer but we kept hoping for improvement. She could not take any food without great pain and often sickness. There she got she could take nothing at all even water. She was 4 weeks and a few days with nothing and for a long time before that she had very little she was thinner than dear Mabel and weaker, could not lift her hand, and hardly speak. Yet she was in pain bad pain. The last 2 nights were awful. The doctor said her stomach and bowels were prematurely worn out through chronic cataarhal inflammation also at the last she suffered from neuritis all over. Earlier on she talked a lot of you and your people told me to send you her love. We were so pleased she saw you that last time, she has talked of that visit many times and of Eric.

I hope I shall see you again sometime. I would very much like to. We would *so much* have like to have had you down here for a bit but Minnie and me.

I hardly know yet what I shall do; but I shall not decide in a hurry. I have someone coming next Friday to stay a month or 6 weeks. She has stayed with me before, so it will be company for a time as well as a help.

I hope you are all keeping fairly well and things are going well with you. With love to all

Yours very sincerely

Annie.[90]

Mrs Hearn wrote further about her experiences after her sister's death in 1933: 'Mrs Thomas, good soul, tried to comfort me and wanted me to stay with her. But I wanted to be near Minnie, so I went back and spent the night with Mrs Spear. I felt as I lay in bed waiting for the doctor'.

A journalist visited the graves of the two Misses Everard shortly after Mrs Thomas's funeral and noted: 'The graves were overgrown with long grass, and looked as if they had not been tended for some time'.[91]

Were the Trenhorne Farm deaths what are now called serial killings, where someone kills several people over a period of time, often years, using a similar method and for similar reasons, only evident in retrospect? Or was it merely a coincidence, as the deaths of the aged and/or unwell are unsurprising? In any case, the possible charges against Mrs Hearn were accumulating.

Chapter 6

The discovery of Mrs Hearn

Meanwhile, the other major question was the whereabouts of Mrs Hearn. A new, but inconclusive, clue was found. The black patent shoe found on 1 December by a policeman at Mendreath Beach, between Looe and Torpoint, partly covered by shingle, might have belonged to Mrs Hearn. It was in a sea-soaked condition and when shown to those in Launceston who knew her they were not certain it was hers. One thought it resembled a shoe she wore a day or two before she went missing. If it was it suggested that she was indeed dead.[1]

Following a conference at Bodmin between Prothero Smith and his superintendents and after discussion with Mrs Hearn's friends and relatives, a new description was published a week later, stressing Mrs Hearn's habit of jerking her head from side to side when speaking.[2] The full description of Mrs Hearn on 30 November was as follows:

'Mrs Hearn is 45 years of age and is 5ft 2 or 3in in height, with grey eyes, brown shingled hair, and sallow complexion. She is of medium build. She is believed to have some artificial teeth in the upper jaw, and there is a noticeable defect in one of the teeth at the front. She walks briskly, carries her head slightly to the left, and when in conversation has a habit of looking away from the person she is addressing.

She is well spoken and speaks with a north country accent. She is rather of a reserved disposition. A photograph which has been published was probably taken some years ago, but it is still good of her lower facial features. Her eyes have of late been of a softer disposition.

When last seen at Looe on November 10 she was seen wearing a black dress, a shabby black beaver hat with fur crown and narrow brim, a black and white check three-quarter length coat, black shoes and light-coloured stockings. She was carrying a rush smoke coloured hand basket, but had no luggage'.[3]

By early December there was press speculation that Mrs Hearn was dead, as she had not been seen definitely by anyone.[4] Her cousin, Mr Houlton of Lincoln, shared this view.[5]

Also in December a reporter asked Thomas about his late wife and he replied:

'I would rather not say anything about the matter at all. You know what my position is and how I feel about my poor dear wife's death. I would rather not discuss the matter, which is to me a very painful matter. You appreciate how difficult it is for me.

I was cut up about seeing my wife's photograph in the papers. It is not very nice, for you know how some people talk about things of that sort. I have had all sorts of reporters from all over the kingdom coming to my house all over the time, and I must say that they have been very civil and gentlemanly, and when I have told them what I have told you, that I would rather not discuss the matter, they have gone away and not troubled me'.

Mrs Tucker, Mrs Thomas's second cousin, had the following to say:

'She never said very much to anybody about her private affairs. I have heard Miss Lydia Everard speak of her sister's husband, but did not explain whether she had ever met him.

We thought at first after Mrs Hearn's disappearance that she was dead, but we do not know what to think these days. I do not think she has gone far away if she is alive, because she did not seem to have much money and was in reduced circumstances. We hope this affair will be cleared up for Mr Thomas' sake'.[6]

There was great speculation about a possible exhumation. Graham White, a solicitor acting for Thomas, wrote to the Home Secretary on 28 November, requesting an exhumation of both Mary and Minnie Everard, and to check on the purchase of weed-killer on 30 July 1926. Three days later White was advised to apply to the county coroner, Dr William Fookes Thompson (1859–1932) of Launceston. If the coroner agreed to the request, it could go ahead, 'We respectfully urge you that you give these matters your consideration' and on 5 December the coroner agreed and it took place among the rain and wind on Tuesday 9 December. There were no tombstones for either and they were in a quiet corner of the churchyard, uncared for and only slightly raised earth marked their presence. Mrs Thomas's grave was to the left of the main entrance, about 40 yards away. A thin layer of snow lay on the ground. James Wilson, the sexton, opened the graves. When the coffins were removed after six feet of earth was dug up, at 1pm, they were put in a wooden structure covered by a tarpaulin. Joseph Harper, a carpenter, was present at the exhumation and noticed that the coffins were watertight; no water had leaked in from the soil. The bodies were well preserved.[7] The police, the pathologist and the vicar were then summoned. The police were present to deal with any onlookers, but there was no need. A carter passed with his waggon with barely a glance at the rising mound of earth. Cerebral embolism had been the cause of death on the death certificate of Miss Mary Everard, while her niece's certificate gave chronic gastric catarrh and colitis as the cause of death. Once they had been exhumed, Dr Wordley examined them, as did Home Office pathologist Dr Gerald Roche Lynch (1889–1957).[8] This was done by artificial light, and organs were removed and put into jars by Sergeant Albert Richards and sent to the Home Office the next day by train. The bodies were then reburied.[9]

This was a very peculiar procedure. Post-mortem preliminaries usually take place in a mortuary where conditions are far more conducive to such investigation, rather than in the open air on a cold and windy day. By choosing to save time, the investigators were taking a risk that their actions might well be challenged in open court.

Dr Lynch was senior official analyst to the Home Office from 1928–1954 and director of the department of Chemical Pathology at St Mary's Hospital Medical School. He had recently been involved in the inconclusive multiple arsenic poisoning case in Croydon of 1928–29. The Lord Chief Justice Lord Goddard said of him, 'He has become one of the most useful witnesses I have ever known since I have become a judge and even before'.[10] Dr Sydney Smith (1882–1969), a leading pathologist, was less effusive and wrote that he was:

'a quiet unassuming man of considerable eminence. Although never as famous as Spilsbury – with whom he often appeared for the Crown, Lynch was firmly established as the leading analyst in the public mind. He was neither as brilliant nor as stubborn as Spilsbury, but he shared in his dislike of admitting an error'.[11]

On 12 December, in London, Dr Lynch examined the organs from the nine jars. Miss Everard junior's body had been examined in the coffin. It was that of a short woman, about 5ft 4in tall, but only about six stone in weight, and her corpse was in a good state of preservation, though six months dead. It was greatly emaciated in all the organs. There was inflammation of the stomach and intestines. The heart was small. The liver and kidneys could not be tested as they had decomposed. There were 62 parts per million of arsenic in the body. The hair contained arsenic, as did the skin and nails. The actual quantity found in the body was 0.77 of a grain.[12] It was presumed that the four-year-old corpse of Miss Everard senior would yield far less evidence due to decomposition, and so the decision was taken not to proceed with an examination of her body. However, since it was thought that her niece might well have been poisoned, her death was treated as being suspicious. Certainly all the signs of arsenic poisoning were there.

No application was made to exhume the corpse of Priscilla Aunger in North Hill and none was deemed likely. Again, with her corpse being even older than that of the elder Miss Everard, the chance of there being any evidence remaining was minimal, and perhaps her death was seen as being entirely natural.[13]

To help find Mrs Hearn the *Daily Mail* offered a reward: 'to facilitate and expedite the task of the police in clearing up the Cornish arsenic mystery, *The Daily Mail* has decided to offer a reward of £500 for the discovery of Mrs Annie Hearn, the missing witness'. The money would go to 'the first person who gives either conclusive evidence of the decease of Mrs Annie Hearn or information which will enable her to be interviewed by the police'.[14]

One possible clue was from Mrs Beattie in Ashton in Mersey, who had advertised in a Shropshire newspaper for a cook. She had a reply from a woman in Callington, Cornwall, and wondered if it could be Mrs Hearn. She gave the letter to the police, but with no success.[15]

There was an alleged sighting of the missing woman in St Budeaux churchyard, but the woman was not Mrs Hearn. Letters to the police arrived about sightings and were followed up.[16] A Harrogate man travelling from Manchester to Liverpool by train on the evening of 28 November was convinced he had seen her, though when he addressed her, she denied it.[17] A woman from Nottingham who stayed two nights in the YWCA at Lincoln High Street was misidentified as Mrs Hearn and when police found her they were able to satisfy themselves that she was not the missing woman.[18]

Near the end of December, a journalist, wondering where she was, spoke to fishermen who told him:

'As far as we fishermen are concerned, it ain't worth it [the reward]. Cornwall be a purty big place and we doan even know that she be in Cornwall. If you ask me she be dead and we all think why should we waste our days looking for the likes of 'er, cos we baint be likely to find her and we can be better employed.'

Another fisherman said that if the body was at sea, sea creatures, such as crabs and sea lice, would have eaten it all away by now. Superintendent Drew also thought that the Looe tide could well have taken the body out to sea and so it would never be found.[19]

On 2 January the body of a woman aged between forty and fifty was found washed up at Weymouth Pier by a boatman. She had bobbed hair, wore glasses and had a ring on her finger. Many thought it was Mrs Hearn. However, Major Gustavus Phelps Symes (1856–1938), the Weymouth coroner, ascertained it was one Mrs Kingsman. This did not stop speculation about whether Mrs Hearn had a double identity so could escape detection so easily.[20] Police searched Garnethill in Glasgow for the her too, but to no avail.[21] There were also enquiries made in London by Scotland Yard, especially at houses where cooks had been recently employed, due to Mrs Hearn's known skill with cookery.[22]

In the midst of all this speculation, Herbert Cecil Powell (1887–1961), an architect living at Brooksby, Hesketh Road, in Torquay (married to Emma, born in 1883), came forward with major news. The previous year they had placed an advert in the *Torbay Herald and Express* for a cook general.[23] The advert, in the 12 November situations vacant columns on page two, read: 'Wanted General: good references are essential; sleep in' and the applicants were to apply to Box 1805 at the newspaper office.[24]

Powell had received the following letter from a Mrs Faithfull, from an address in Church Road, Ellacombe (a working-class part of Torquay), in response:

'Dear madam,

In reply to your advertisement for capable general, plain cooking, good home, I am seeking some such post, but have had no previous experience as a general servant. I am 39 years of age. My husband died two years ago. Afterwards I kept rooms for a time, but could not make them pay. I am now in rooms in Torquay and would like to get a post in a private family where I would do my best to give satisfaction. It is the "comfortable home" [the advert did not stipulate this] in your advertisement which appeals to me.

I enclose a copy of letter of recommendation from a doctor and his wife who had rooms with me last winter. I can come and see you any time you arrange & give any further particulars'.

The letter of recommendation was from a Dr and Mrs Watson and read as follows:

'The Larches

Heavitree

Exeter

1 March 1930

My wife and I have stayed with Mrs Faithfull at the above address for several months and have been most comfortable. She is an excellent cook and we have much pleasure in recommending her rooms. We are sorry to go.

Dr and Mrs B. Watson, late Mannamead, Plymouth'.[25]

Powell was impressed by the letter and met the applicant. He and his wife interviewed her on 13 November, appointed her and paid her at the end of each month. She told them she was Mrs Annie Faithfull (possibly the name was chosen from the character in the Christian classic by John Bunyan, *The Pilgrim's Progress*; Mrs Hearn told of a Christian background and had Christian literature in her house), a widow aged thirty-nine, and began work on the following Tuesday, 18 November.[26]

Had he checked the reference or even the 1930 *Medical Directory*, Powell would have found that the only Dr B. Watson listed was not a Plymouth man, but was Dr Bernard Gretton Watson of Birmingham.[27] The reference was faked. Like most people, Powell was trusting. It is interesting to note that Mrs Hearn chose to retain part of her real name when concocting an assumed one; this is quite common among those who change their names.

Powell thought that the new servant was highly satisfactory. She was told that she would have to do more than housekeeping, but was happy to do so provided she did not need to wear a uniform. She was a good worker and seemed well educated. She was quiet and attended church every Sunday.[28] However, he wondered if there was any story behind her. He said nothing to her because of his wife's delicate health.[29] As an avid reader of *The Daily Mail*, he thought she seemed to resemble the photographs of Mrs Hearn in the press (which his new servant cut out from newspapers), and he also saw a parcel addressed to a Mrs Dennis at his house, but wanted to avoid publicity due to his wife.[30]

In detail, Mrs Hearn's undoing was the result of decisions she took during a shopping expedition. On 1 January 1931 she went the shops for the clothes sales and went to Messrs Williams and Cox and saw a coat she liked and wanted to buy. It was a dark coat of a red/wine colour, with trim and a brown coney collar and cuffs. The shop assistant later recalled that she was 'a very quiet unobtrusive woman with an exact idea of what she wanted'. However, after paying a deposit of 14s 6d she did not take it away but wanted it shortened. She gave her address but gave the false name of Mrs Dennis. The coat was delivered to Brooksby on 3 January and the porter was met at the door by Mrs Hearn. However, she then found the coat needed changing again, so she returned it to the shop. However, when it was brought back to Brooksby Powell's son, John Arden Powell (1912– c.2007), answered the door and said that no one of the name of Dennis lived there. However, the porter was adamant that it was the correct address and so Powell junior received it and told his father. Powell senior tasked Mrs Hearn with it and she admitted that Dennis was the name of her first husband and that she had given it in error and on realising this thought there was no need to change it because the coat would be sent to the correct address. Powell was not convinced.[31]

On 10 January 1931, Powell was in conversation with a friend, Mr Edward Henry Sermon (1870–1955) JP, mayor of Torquay in 1929–30. He was wondering whether his new servant was the woman sought by the police. On that evening he told the police his suspicions, speaking to Superintendent Arthur Edward Martin (1885–1975) of the Devon Constabulary, based in Torquay. Two days later, on 12 January, Mrs Hearn was sent to the shops with the plan that the police would trail her. However, she left the house by the back door and went to Marychurch rather than leaving by the main road, and she took the Meadfoot bus to return home, eluding the police. It was then that she was spotted by a plain-clothes police inspector in the evening on a bus after having been out shopping. DS Milford of Torquay and Trebilcock of Lewannick, who knew Mrs Hearn, had been employed in Hesketh Road outside Powell's house that day, arriving at Torquay at 4.45pm. Two hours later a woman alighted from the bus nearby and started walking to the house. Trebilcock approached her and said: 'Excuse me, can you tell me where Albany House is?' She replied, 'I beg your pardon' and he repeated the question.

'No, I don't know'.

'I think I know you. You are Mrs Hearn of Lewannick'.

'No, my name is Dennis. I don't know you'.

'I am the sergeant from Lewannick and I know you as Mrs Hearn of Trenhorne House Lewannick, and I want you to come with me to Torquay Police Station'.[32]

This led to further conversation. DS Milford now joined in, saying 'You have been definitely identified as Mrs Hearn. You must go to the police station with Sergeant Trebilcock as he has something to say to you'. The three went to the police station by car where they met Martin. It was then that the woman agreed that she was Mrs Hearn. Mrs Hearn later recalled the scene:

'The first thing that happened at Torquay station was that someone told me in a kindly way to sit down and gave me a cup of tea.

It did not seem so terrible.

Superintendent Martin of Torquay was the first to talk to me. He talked quite nicely, asking me if I really was Mrs Hearn.

"Oh yes" I said "There is no use in denying it any longer. And while I am at it, I may as well admit that I got my situation my using a false reference".

He nodded.

"Oh well, don't worry about that sort of thing. You just make yourself comfortable until Superintendent Pill comes. He is on his way from Launceston by car".

When I heard the name of this officer I started to tremble.

Whenever I had gone into the library or whenever I picked up a paper at home the one name that seemed to be written in larger type, to me at least, was the name of Superintendent Pill.

The officer had charge of the case. His name filled me with terrors beyond description.

Often at night I used to lie awake trying to picture him. Once I could see him in my dreams.

A terrible man!

Late that night they told me he had arrived. I was still trembling.

Presently he came into the room with a nice looking woman – his wife.

Then I managed to muster up courage and look at his eyes.

At that moment I experienced a pleasant thrill of surprise.

Here was the man I had feared so much and somehow I liked him. He did not look a terrible man. To me he looked right from the start the sort of man whose only desire was to get at the real truth. I had nothing to fear from him'.[33]

Pill arrived at Torquay at 11.20pm, talked to Martin, cautioned Mrs Hearn and then charged her with the murder of Mrs Thomas. She initially made no reply.[34]

In the meantime, the police had made a few pertinent discoveries among Mrs Hearn's possessions at Brooksby, including a third-class railway ticket from Liskeard to Plymouth, dated 10 November 1930, the day of her disappearance, as well as a number of invoices, including one for a mackintosh bought on 11 November for 13s 11d.[35]

Later that night, between 11.40 and 11.45, in the presence of Martin, Inspector Smith and a matron, Pill made this statement to Mrs Hearn:

'I have been given to understand, Mrs Hearn, that you went to Bude with Mr and Mrs Thomas and Mrs Thomas senior, back in October, and that Mrs Thomas was taken suddenly ill. I thought that you might like to give some explanation'.

She replied: 'Yes I would like to make my statement'. She then became extremely talkative, often corrected her previous statements, and spoke for nearly two hours, from 12.15am to 2.15am and began by giving an account of the day. After talking about the invitation to lunch she said:

'I have been cautioned by Superintendent Pill, who has informed me that he had come to Torquay to see me. The Superintendent informed as that enquiries have been made with a view to tracing me, and also told me that the cause of the death of Mrs Alice Thomas had not been cleared up yet.

I wish to say that on the day we went to Bude, Mr Thomas came to my house at about noon and informed me that he was going to Bude with his mother. Mrs Thomas was going as well and asked if I would like to go. I said I would like to go very much. I did not have time to mention food, but as we had taken lunch at other times, I cut some sandwiches to take with me. I used tin salmon that I had previously purchased from Shuker and Reed's; I also took some chocolate cake from my own house, it was my own make. Mrs Thomas and I ate some of that and the remainder I brought back to Trenhorne Farm.

While at Bude Mrs Thomas and I were together the whole of the time excepting a few minutes when Mrs Thomas went to look for a cloakroom.

When we were at the café, I said to Mr and Mrs Thomas "I had brought some sandwiches with me" and I placed a packet containing the cake and I think six sandwiches on the table between Mrs Thomas and myself. Mrs Thomas took the first sandwich, I took the second and Mr Thomas took the third, and Mrs Thomas took the fourth.

I remember hearing Mrs Thomas ask Mr Thomas to get some fruit. He got some bananas, I had one and Mrs Thomas had two.

I did not hear her complain of anything. Then we were half way to Launceston, I noticed Mrs Thomas was leaning forward. I was sitting with her in the back seat. I was on the right hand side besides Mr Thomas. Mrs Thomas did not speak for some time. I thought she was trying to pick up something from the floor. She remained in that position for some moments. I touched her on the shoulder and asked her "What is the matter? and she replied "No, it is alright" but I was not satisfied. On looking closer I noticed she was fumbling with the inside handle of the door on her side of the car. Mr Thomas then turned around and said "What is the matter? Shall I stop?" Mrs Thomas said "No, it is alright". Mrs Thomas was then sick, and I said "Yes, stop". Mr Thomas then pulled up, but before he stopped, Mrs Thomas had got the door open. He assisted her out of the car: she appeared pretty bad. I looked after her and Mr Thomas was pulling grass and cleaning the car. After a time Mrs Thomas recovered and we drove on to Launceston. Mr Thomas offered to get a doctor. Mrs Thomas said "No". Mr Thomas went about some business. Mrs Thomas and I went about the town. Mrs Thomas went into a fruit shop and bought some pears. I know she ate one. Then we went back to the car, where she was sick and bad again. I went to the lavatory with her the first time and then she went in alone. I was sitting in the car when Mr Thomas returned. Mrs Thomas was then in the lavatory.

On the way home, I think she got out again to be sick. On getting into the car again, Mrs Thomas got in the front seat as it was thought the jolting of the car made her worse.

On returning to Trenhorne Farm, I was asked to stay there to assist in the house work and to look after Mrs Thomas.

When Mrs Parsons came, she took over the nursing of Mrs Thomas, and prepared her food with the exception of the last day or two, when Mrs Thomas partook a little solid food.

On the Sunday before Mrs Thomas was taken away, I prepared roast mutton for dinner. I have read in the newspapers that I might have carved Mrs Thomas' portion. I did not carve it I did not help the gravy or anything. I remember Mrs Thomas complaining that a junket that Mrs Parsons made was too sweet. She did not complain of the meals I prepared.

Mr Thomas appeared to be very grateful to me for my help up to the time when he returned from Plymouth after Mrs Thomas's death. He then appeared more abrupt in his manner towards me. On occasions he said to me "They are going to send some organs to be analysed. They will find out what it is. They will blame one of us. The blame will come heavier on you than me; people are saying so. A detective might be here at any time. Whatever there is they will find it out".[36] On one of these occasions, I suggested that if people thought like that, I had better go to my house. Mr Thomas said "Please yourself. Go if you like. I don't want you to go". I said "Well, perhaps I had better stay until after the funeral".

On the day of the funeral, as I read it in the newspaper, I was supposed to have had a row with Mr Parsons. That isn't right. It wasn't a row. He asked me if the sandwiches were made at the restaurant. I said "No, here", meaning my house not Bude. He said "Did Mrs Thomas make them?" I replied, "No, I made them". He said "Here". I replied "No, at home".

At that moment, Mrs Thomas senior entered the room and Mr Parsons asked her a question. In reply, she said, "Mrs Hearn brought them from her house".

From the day of the funeral, I felt people were suspecting me of having poisoned Mrs Thomas.[37] It appeared quite sure that Mr Thomas, or me, would have to suffer for it. I felt that I could not face the ordeal. Mr Thomas had told me that we should have to attend the inquest. It appeared as if somebody would be charged with murder. I couldn't think of anybody but we two, and sooner than that I felt I would go my own way. I would take my life. I did go to Looe with that intention. I left my coat on the Downs, but later found that I couldn't do what I thought of doing. I have read this statement through. It is made voluntarily and is perfectly true.'[38]

Pill then charged Mrs Hearn with murder. She made no reply, but before leaving the police station, she said:

'I have read the papers and know all about it. I went on the Downs at Looe, took off my coat, but something seemed to prevent me doing what I intended to do. I came back to Looe and bought an attaché case in a shop on the way to the station. Then I booked to Liskeard, and from there to Totnes and on to Torquay. I reached there at about 9 o'clock. With reference to weedkiller, there was a part tin of weedkiller at Trenhorne House when we went there. My sister and I used that and the tin we bought from Shukers on the back ground and at the front of the house'.[39]

Pill said that he wanted to make her make a statement at such a late hour because he wanted to make sure whether she was involved or not and if not Pill could then discharge her.[40] She was taken to the police station at Launceston at 3.30am on 13 January. Later that day she made a brief appearance at the magistrates' court there.[41]

Mrs Hearn explained that she meant to commit suicide, but once on the cliff at Looe found herself unable to do it.[42] It was subsequently ascertained that on the day of her disappearance, John Hedley Pearce, owner of a fancy goods shop in Fore Street, East Looe, sold Mrs Hearn an attaché case for 3s 11d. It would have been before 6pm when his shop shut.[43] She had then taken trains from Looe to Torquay. East Looe station was the terminus of the Liskeard and Looe branch of the Great Western Railway. From there trains could only go eastwards. There was a 6.40pm train from Looe, arriving at Liskeard at 7.08pm (on which she had been sighted). She certainly travelled third class, which would have cost about 8s.[44]

However, Mrs Hearn gave another account of what happened after she left the Looe cliffs:

'I went into a shop and bought a toothbrush. Then I went onto the station still in a dream. I only remember that I thought I would catch the first train no matter in which direction it was going, and on arrival I found that the first train went to Plymouth. So I took a ticket to Plymouth and entered the train.

On the way I found that the train went onto Exeter. So I decided I would stay on the train, and then just as we were nearing Newton Abbott, it flashed across my mind that there were always a number of Launceston people going to Exeter, and I might be recognised. So I got out at Newton Abbott, and got into the train for Torquay... There was no definite plan in my mind as to where I was going'.

She arrived in Torquay at 10.20pm and was one of three people alighting the train there. She drew attention to herself by having to pay an excess fare.[45]

At about 10.30pm Mrs Hearn arrived at St Leonard's private hotel on Newton Road, Torquay, run by John Clarke. She stayed the night and next day signed the guest book as Mrs Ferguson, of Heavitree, Exeter, nationality British. Her idea for this name came from having a friend who had this surname. She paid the bill of 6s 6d and told Clarke that the room she stayed in was comfortable. She then said she was expecting her husband and left to seek a boarding house.[46]

That day Annie went to the library to look at the local press in order to find cheaper accommodation. On the afternoon of 11 November, she met Mrs Beatrice Minnie Marker (1895–1957) of Church Road, Torquay, who let out apartments in her house, in order to take lodgings there. She was carrying a small attaché case and wore spectacles. These lodgings were at 41 Ellacombe Church Road, in a working-class district. Annie also bought a mackintosh for 13s 11d. Mrs Marker let out a room in her house, and she paid her rent in advance on the day of arrival (7s for a week) and said she was Mrs Faithfull (a name 'which I had read in a book') from Exeter. She told Mrs Marker that her husband was in Torquay Hospital. Several people came to see her, but it was Mr Marker who had admitted them. She left on 18 November.[47]

Shortly after arrival Mrs Hearn saw the advert in the newspaper for the post at Powell's house and so her stay with Mrs Marker was short, though she went to the Powells with just three and a half pence to her name.

In 1933 Mrs Hearn made additional comments about her time 'on the run'. Although she had meant to throw herself over the cliffs at Looe, she had thought of Mrs Thomas and that deterred her. She wrote:

'I walked towards some houses and, and then returned again. I was in a dream.

At last I awoke and started walking to the cliffs. I intended to throw myself over. When I got there I couldn't do it...

I took off my coat (underneath which was my rainproof), but I couldn't throw myself over because Mrs Thomas... was there.

It wasn't her ghost, but her image so plainly as if she was in the flesh. I saw her with my mind's eye. She stood in the path. Her arms outstretched. She was very close.

Before getting to the edge I had to pass her. I couldn't do it.

I remember I sobbed out, "Why are you, of all people, trying to stop me? Let me go, let me go".

Then, with a cry, I realised I could not pass her, and I went back. It is not true that I went to Looe to fake a suicide. I went there to end my life. Only the outstretched arms of Mrs Thomas stopped me...

I walked slowly away from the cliff. Darkness had fallen'.

At the railway station she took the first train and so it was chance she ended up in Torquay. She recalled that at Torquay, before taking the job, she was running out of money and was reduced to her last half penny. She was well aware of the search for her from reading the newspapers and she knew that if she was turned out of her lodgings the police would soon find her. After applying for the job, realising that a photograph of her had appeared in the press, she tried to change her appearance by using make up and wearing glasses as a disguise. Her job involved cooking and she was hoping to save enough money to afford a train fare to London and then take a job as a cook in a house in Mayfair or Kensington.[48]

However, Annie was constantly in dread of being recognised. She thought that people recognised her in the street. She regularly read the newspapers in the public library to read about the search for her. She made friends with an old lady who regularly walked her dog and they discussed the Hearn case, agreeing that it took up far too much space in the newspapers. On the day of her arrest she had walked along the coast to Babbacombe and had lunch there. She found being arrested a relief after living in fear of it for so long, or so she claimed.[49]

The discovery of Mrs Hearn marked a new and intensive phase in the investigation. She was not only the major missing witness, but she was also the prime suspect in a murder enquiry and would now be dealt with by the courts. A barrister later wrote, on reading the news of her arrest in his evening newspaper, 'The news was splashed in the paper and clearly the trial would be a sensational one'.[50]

Very shortly after Mrs Hearn's arrest, a journalist for *The Launceston Weekly News* paid an evening visit to Trenhorne Farm. He found the place in darkness, but then saw a light inside and so knocked on the door. Thomas answered and on being told the news of Mrs Hearn's arrest said 'It's the first I have heard of it'.[51]

Stories about Mrs Hearn's time in Torquay were published at the time of her arrest. Powell described how she led a quiet life, attending church every Sunday, and said that she was 'a woman well above the average in education and a person who appeared to inspire confidence'. He explained how his wife had been taken by her. He also noted 'Her manner was frequently preoccupied, and it was noticed she cut references to the missing widow from the newspapers which came into the house. A picture of herself, cut from a newspaper, was found in her bedroom'.[52]

The Markers, whom she had briefly stayed with, were also interviewed by the press. Mrs Marker recalled, 'She appeared quiet and peculiar – a peculiarity that one could not define. She seemed worried, but this I put down to the fact that she said her husband was in a hospital and she was worrying over his illness'. Mrs Marker also recalled that Mrs Hearn had a gold watch on a chain and that she brought in several newspapers each day and asked about any others taken by the household. She did not appear well off and always kept her hat and coat on. Apparently Mrs Hearn had made enquiries for accommodation elsewhere, but the place was full and so the landlady recommended her friend Mrs Marker's to her. Neither of the Markers had any idea that they had been giving room to the wanted woman.[53]

A number of other Torquay residents came forward to report that they had also had dealings with Mrs Hearn. The manageress and waitress at the Lido café thought that in December a woman resembling Mrs Hearn had come in for refreshment. When paying the bill the woman began to discuss the weather and then said, 'I wonder if Mrs Hearn is in Torquay?' Without suspecting anything, the waitress replied, 'She may be for all we know. You never can tell can you?' Mr Scott, manager of the Sun Lounge at the Baths saloon, thought he had seen her there, but she had kept her face hidden. Mrs Joy, owner of a tobacconist and confectioner on Market Street, recalled a woman resembling Mrs Hearn arriving at her shop on three occasions in November. On the first she asked Mrs Joy if she knew of anyone who wanted to employ a cook general, and even asked Mrs Joy for a job, saying, 'I am a good cook but I am unable to keep my jobs as people nowadays expect a cook to do so much more than cooking'. She explained she was a widow living in a single room. She returned the next day to look at newspapers, but was not looking at the situations vacant columns but for the main news. On her third visit the owner's son was present and he later said to his mother, 'Do you know who that woman reminds me of? Mrs Hearn'. Mrs Joy thought 'she seemed very well educated and she was very talkative'. Finally, John Grist of Hesketh garage recalled having talked to Mrs Hearn two days before her arrest when she asked him about trams and he advised taking a bus. He later joked with his wife about having seen Mrs Hearn and thought that she was 'a little vacant, but otherwise seemed to be normal'.[54]

Chapter 7

The magistrates' court hearings

Mrs Hearn now had to be brought before the courts. Her first appearance was on Tuesday 13 January at Launceston Police station. The acting clerk, Vincent Russell Doney (1902–74), asked her if she was Mrs Hearn and in a quiet voice she replied in the affirmative. The charge was then read out:

> 'That you Sarah Annie Hearn of Trenhorne House Lewannick, on October 18 and November 3 1930 in the parish of Lewannick did kill and murder Mrs Alice Maud Thomas'.

Mrs Hearn made no reply to this.[1] The proceedings lasted fifteen minutes and she was then sent to Exeter Prison, arriving at 4pm.[2]

Mrs Hearn later recalled her initial experiences at the prison:

> 'Exeter Prison is a terrible place!
>
> You cannot help feeling a criminal when you enter there.
>
> I was put in the observation cell. There was a bed in it. I lay down on it, shivering in every limb and waiting in dread for the nameless something which I thought was about to happen.
>
> After a while I heard footsteps. The matron came in followed by the nurse and the doctor. They asked me how I was and gave me a sleeping draught. It was no good. I tossed about, a prey to my thoughts.
>
> Some time later the matron came along and talked to me. Another of the officers was also very nice. She was a Devon girl and very superstitious.

One day she told me that twice a spider had crossed her path.

"That's lucky" she said. "I wonder what it will be? It means money".[3]

Mrs Hearn also recalled seeing a baby in prison, who had been born to one of the prisoners a few days earlier. Mrs Hearn was given the baby to hold, but she felt most unconfident, never having had much to do with babies previously, and was happy to pass the little one to a more capable woman.[4] She also did a little light gardening, 'I loved my garden and enjoyed the recreation this gave me'. She also spent time sewing and amending her own dresses and those of the officers. There were letters of sympathy. One was from someone who knew her and the Thomases. Another was from a nurse who once resided in Cornwall and when she became unwell a doctor suggested it was due to the impurities in the Cornish water and on leaving the county she recovered.[5]

O'Donnell offered his newspaper's financial support in exchange for Mrs Hearn's story and her brother found a Grimsby solicitor to represent her, Mr Walter West (1874–1949).[6] Additionally, Powell offered him the £500 reward money he had been given by the *Daily Mail* for finding her as his fee.[7] Powell explained:

'I have thought about it and consulted many of my friends who advised me that I ought to claim the reward.

I feel I have been put to considerable trouble and the matter has affected me so much that I am ill and may have to take a rest.

Since it was known that Mrs Hearn had been at my house, my telephone has scarcely stopped ringing, while people have been continually knocking on the front door. Today has been a pandemonium for me.

Mrs Hearn gave complete satisfaction in her work, and naturally it was a matter of the utmost astonishment to me when I learnt she was Mrs Hearn.

I am a regular reader of the *Daily Mail* and I read in it of the search for the discovery of Mrs Hearn. At that time I had no suspicion that she was working in my own house.

When I began to notice that the maid somewhat resembled the photograph
I pointed it out to the local police'.[8]

O'Donnell was complimentary about West, describing him as 'one of the most
resourceful solicitors it has ever been my lot to meet', adding he 'handled the
case so brilliantly during the police court proceedings'.[9] According to Patrick
Devlin (1905–92) who represented the Director of Public Prosecutions, West was
'a vigorous man and this was a great opportunity'. However, he then thought that
West was unwise in fighting the committal proceedings, 'This was not very wise.
There was not a hope of Mrs Hearn being discharged by the magistrates', and it
would have been better to have reserved the defence for the trial rather than to
reveal his arguments early on. It would also have saved money.[10] However, Edgar
Arthur Bowker, who was clerk to Norman Birkett, claimed 'his brilliant handling
of the witnesses for the prosecution, and the replies he elicited to his searching
questions, contributed greatly to the success of the defence'.[11]

At some point O'Donnell undertook his own amateur detective work. He
talked to Mrs Poskitt and her doubtless sympathetic account of her sister led
O'Donnell to conclude that 'Annie Hearn could never have murdered Minnie
even if she was guilty of poisoning Mrs Thomas – which I did not think she was'.
He took samples of the water at Trenhorne and even collected hair from the floor
of a local barber and concluded that there was a very high ratio of arsenic in these.
He also claimed to have received letters in a similar vein; that there was a disused
tin mine a mile from Lewannick which was contaminated with arsenic and that
there were problems with the local water supply. All this was reported to West.[12]

The reports of the Launceston Medical Officer of Health, which covered
Lewannick, do not support O'Donnell's assertions. The major causes of death
were heart failure and cancer and there do not seem to have been any medical
concerns about deaths due to arsenic in the water as suggested. It should also be
noted that the diary shows strong evidence for the manner of Minnie's death,
which O'Donnell was either ignorant of or overlooked.

Mrs Hearn had another four, purely nominal, but legally necessary,
appearances before the courts in the next few weeks. These were all reported in
the press.[13]

However, the murder charge was not the only one facing Mrs Hearn. She
was also being sued by a Harrogate delivery firm, Lawrence Hall and Company,

for non-payment of money (£20 15s 8d) due to them for delivering furniture from Harrogate to Cornwall six years earlier. Furthermore, Richard Alford, a carpenter of Coad's Green, was pressing for £15 12s 8d owed for funeral costs for the funeral of Miss Everard. A court order was then pinned to the door of Trenhorne House.[14]

For the main business at hand, though, it was on Tuesday 24 February that the first session was held. The next steps prior to a trial were sessions of the magistrates' court, at Launceston, which was held in the Town Hall, and which was presided over by the chairman, Mr Eric Galton Baron Lethbridge (1867–1932).

So Mrs Hearn was brought before the Launceston Magistrates' Court, charged with the murders of Mrs Thomas and her sister. Devlin represented the Director of Public Prosecutions. West appeared for Mrs Hearn. A watching brief in court for Thomas was Mr Anthony Hawke.[15] Apparently:

'Mrs Hearn never lost the composure which has characterised her attitude throughout. She was the most cool and collected person in the building, chatting calmly with her lawyer at the outset, leaning over to pass a few remarks with the matron, and then sitting back in her chair, following with obvious interest, the counsel's opening statement and the legal arguments which ensued'.

There was a great contrast between the two opposing barristers, Devlin being 'confusing in the rapidity of his speech', whereas West 'of mature years, grey haired, who in slow deliberate language sought to controvert the words used by "my friend"'.[16]

This was when the real business of the magistrates' court commenced. Devlin began with the case for the prosecution of Mrs Hearn. He started by stating that Mrs Hearn had ordered a tin of weed-killer. He then declared his intention to use evidence from Minnie's diary during her final months of life. To this West objected. Firstly, because this case was inadmissible as regards the main question at hand, namely the death of Mrs Thomas. Devlin then admitted that the evidence of a deceased person was rarely used in court, but in this case it was relevant because it gave her symptoms preceding her death. West objected to this. He said that it could be used to counter any arguments of the defence but could not be given first. Devlin argued that the prisoner was facing two charges so evidence in both cases was relevant. There was the precedent of the case in which Major Herbert Armstrong of Hay on Wye was accused of killing his wife in 1921; evidence of his attempting to poison another person was used in the case. Armstrong had been found guilty and was hanged.[17]

The magistrates decided that as they were dealing with two charges, evidence from both could be included. Diary entries could be used, but only those which dealt with Miss Everard's symptoms. Devlin read out extracts, some of which have already been cited.[18]

Devlin then described the arsenic in the body and that there was arsenic in the Cornish soil where it had been buried. He described Dr Lynch's tests:

'The total amount of arsenic found in the body was 0.77 of a grain and Dr Roche Lynch is prepared to give conclusively as his opinion that the actual amount of the dose administered must have exceeded two grains, which is a fatal dose'.

Dr Lynch would also state that the poisoning had been going on for seven months. That was the end of the prosecution's case as regards Miss Everard. That for Mrs Thomas was about to begin. Devlin began with some key dates, the first being 1 September when Mrs Hearn ordered the tinned salmon and the second being the third of that month when it arrived. 'I wish you to keep that date in mind and I will take you right away to October 18, on which date Mrs Thomas received what the prosecution will submit was her first dose of arsenic'.[19]

The trip to Bude and the sandwich lunch was then described, with Mrs Thomas eating one or two and the others eating one each, so clearly not all were poisoned to the same extent.

'I think it must follow that only one, or at any rate, certainly not more than two of the sandwiches actually had arsenic in them. We know that Mrs Thomas had a sandwich and suffered severely from the after effects. We know that Mr Thomas ate a sandwich and about half an hour afterwards felt a little queer.

It is therefore probable that Mrs Hearn, after she had administered the poison in the contents of the sandwiches, as the prosecution suggests, only put the poison contents into one or two of the sandwiches. Since there were only three persons present, and apart from Mrs Hearn, Mrs Thomas was the only woman, it is obvious that she would be the first person to be helped to a sandwich, and, since they were arranged in two piles of three each, if you offer one particular pile of sandwiches to a person in 99 cases out of a hundred the person would take the top one'.[20]

Devlin then described the trip home and Mrs Thomas being ill, then being nursed at home by Mrs Hearn and then her mother. He read out Mrs Hearn's letter and described her flight to Torquay. He suggested that this was an attempt at flight. He suggested that there was definitely a case for Mrs Hearn to answer.[21]

During these hearings, Mrs Hearn spent her nights in the police station. Although she slept in the cells, she was not confined to them at other times. Between teatime and bedtime she chatted to others and read the books she had been sent from home. Her favourite reading was thrillers and she looked forward to the arrival of her sister from Doncaster. She learnt that her effects at Trenhorne House were to be sold at auction at Lewannick.[22]

In the meantime, Dr Lynch submitted a report to the Home Secretary in regard to his findings about the bodies of Mary and Minnie Everard. He also submitted it to the Director of Public Prosecutions. It had not yet been seen by the coroner, but the doctor would be seeing him soon. He noted that Mrs Hearn was to be charged with the murder of Minnie Everard but not that of Mary.[23]

Lynch noted that he had examined the contents of several jars. The first three were from Mary Everard and the first contained the contents of her chest and abdomen, the second contained hair and bone and the third some of the earth above the coffin. The other nine jars were from Minnie; firstly the uterus, thigh and arm muscle and bone, the second, heart, liver, kidney and spleen, third, stomach and intestines, fourth, a piece of the shroud, fifth, the brain, sixth, skin, hair and nails, seventh, lungs, eight, earth on top of the coffin and ninth earth under the coffin.[24]

The remains of Mary Everard indicated the presence of arsenious oxide; from jar A this was between 0.45 and 0.33 grains. The second jar revealed 1.7 parts per million of arsenious oxide and the third (the soil sample) 50 parts per million.

Dr Lynch concluded:

'In view of the condition of the coffin described by J.B. Harper and Dr Wordley who in a letter to me states, "Part of the lid had decayed and there was a good deal of earth in the coffin and about the body especially at the front end", and the amount of arsenic found in the soil, it is not possible in my opinion to come to any conclusion as to the cause of the deceased's last illness from the analysis of the viscera.

In view, however, of the statement of Dr Galbraith, it would appear that the deceased's last illness is consistent with arsenical poisoning'.[25]

However, Lynch did not press for Mary to be treated as a murder victim, possibly because he thought the supporting evidence was not conclusive enough.

The doctor then turned to the more numerous jars for Minnie. He weighed the organs and noted that they were all well below the expected weight and thought that this was because 'at the time of her death she was very wasted and also in part due to the loss of fluid after death'. He then went on to list the amount of arsenic in each organ. The total amount was 0.7695 grains of arsenic in the organs (though the doctor's total was an erroneous 0.7765) and 101.6 parts per million. Soil from the bottom of the coffin was initially 62 parts per million and 125 parts per million. Once water was allowed to percolate through the soil, the bottom soil had 0.07 parts in a million and 0.08 in the upper. He concluded that Mrs Thomas died of heart failure following arsenic poisoning. He also referred to the poisoning of Thomas, which had not had much attention hitherto:

'I am of opinion that the illness of the above as described by Dr Hopwood is consistent with a considerable quantity of arsenic having been administered to him, which although making him very ill was not a fatal dose. The illness of Mr Thomas on the 18th October 1930 is consistent with a mild attack of arsenical poisoning. This may receive confirmation when the analysis of a sample of his hair is complete'.

However, Lynch was unable to detect any arsenic in Thomas's hair.[26]

Experiments were also made on Minnie Everard's hair, by cutting a quantity into small pieces and subjecting some to immersion in sodium carbonate. The arsenic content of both was the same. This meant that none was 'deposited on the hair after death'. Another lock of hair was divided into three portions. As to arsenic, the strand nearest the head was found to have 23 parts per million, the middle portion 15 parts per million and the furthest portion 10 parts per million. Lynch concluded that 'the deceased has been taking arsenic for at least 7 months. As the proximal portion contains the greatest amount of arsenic, I am of opinion that towards the end the doses have either increased in frequency or in amount or both'.[27] Taken with the evidence of the diary this is proof sufficient that Minnie was killed by arsenic poisoning.

The second day of the hearings was Wednesday 25 February. The first witness called was John Wilson, the sexton of Lewannick, and he provided some light relief as he was deaf. Mr Paisley, prosecuting solicitor, had to go over to the witness box and bellow in his ear. 'Remember he is very deaf' he told the court. 'He may be deaf but he is not daft. Leave him to answer his own questions,' said West. There was laughter in court, including by Mrs Hearn.[28]

Wilson was questioned about the exhumation and it was established that the bodies were reinterred on 9 December. Photographs and plans were then shown of Trenhorne House and Farm. Ivy Willshire, waitress of Littlejohn's café, stated that she had no clear recollection of the incident on 18 October and so West contended that her evidence not be called at all. The magistrates discussed this and decided to let Devlin use her testimony.[29]

Ivy could not describe the three people, nor tell if there were others present there, and she did not see them eating the sandwiches, but she thought they were in the café for 30 minutes. She did not know the date when they arrived and might have taken on board suggested answers by the police who had later questioned her. There was some laughter at one of her answers about the number of sandwiches.[30]

Dr Saunders was next and he listed the symptoms that Mrs Thomas had been suffering from that he had noticed on his almost daily visits from 18 October to 3 November, and what he had prescribed for her. West asked about her worries. Then there was questioning about what the doctor thought at the time could be the cause of the patient's illness. Devlin tried to clarify matters:

'If I understand the position aright it is this. That up to November 3 you had diagnosed or thought that she was suffering from food poisoning, which you described as ptomaine poisoning, but that on November 3 you perceived certain symptoms and therefore changed your mind?'

'Certainly'.

'To what decision did you come by reason of the change?'

'That she was suffering from arsenical poisoning'.

Dr Fox was then asked about Mrs Thomas's arrival at Plymouth Hospital.[31]

Gilbert Arthur Frank, chief chemist at Messrs Coopers, MacDougalls and Robertson's laboratories in London, was asked about arsenic. He said that the powdered weed-killer sold in 1926 was 70% arsenic, that the Cooper's worm killer tablet pills were 14%, each tablet containing three grains. The powdered sheep dip contained 22% arsenic. Claude Matthews of Shukers confirmed purchases of weed-killer by Mrs Hearn in 1926 and tinned salmon in 1930. The former was debited to Miss Everard's account.[32]

Dr Galbraith was the last witness of the day to be called and was examined by Devlin. He stated that Minnie had 'said she felt as if she was poisoned'.

'Was Mrs Hearn present?'

'Yes'.

'Did Mrs Hearn say anything?'

'Yes. She entered a protest with the remark "How could she say such a thing?"'

'Did you suggest she should go into hospital?'

'Yes, and she refused'.[33]

Thursday 26 February was the third day of the hearing. Dr Galbraith was the first witness. The subject was Miss Everard. The doctor stated that Mrs Hearn had been very attentive to her sister throughout her illness. He could not recall whether the urgent messages came from Mrs Hearn or from someone else; all he knew was that he had been sent them. When he was asked about whether Miss Everard should have gone to hospital, he said that Miss Everard and Mrs Hearn did not want to go there.

Devlin re-examined the witness, who told him that he had gone to the police voluntarily about Miss Everard's illness. This was because, following Mrs Thomas' death, he and his partner thought that it was suspicious, so informed the police immediately about the earlier death.

Thomas was the next witness. All eyes were on him; his arrival in the witness box caused much excitement in the court. He was asked by Devlin to explain the sleeping arrangements after his wife was taken ill on 18 October. Devlin then asked about his taking the sisters out for car trips and he agreed that he had.

Thomas recalled that in 1926 he talked to the sisters about the weed-killer while in their garden, but that Mrs Hearn had never said anything about using it. Thomas was then shown the worm tablets and he confirmed they had lain on a shelf in his house for two years. He also confirmed having Cooper's sheep dip, but this was locked away and was last used in 1929. He then described the trio's trip to Bude on 18 October, of his wife having invited Mrs Hearn and having tea. Devlin then asked what had been eaten and he explained how Mrs Hearn had brought 'fish sandwiches' which she offered to him and his wife. All of them had at least one. He had felt a little unwell and so had Mrs Hearn on the next day.

Thomas then explained that his wife was sick on the way home. They called for a doctor and Mrs Hearn remained in the house for nursing and cooking duties. He said that Mrs Hearn's care was as outlined by Dr Saunders. He recalled that at least eight local people visited the house over the next week; Mrs Parnell did some cleaning and Mrs Pearce brought butter.

Thomas said that he did not think his wife was seriously worried until 29 October. After her mother came to stay with them, she and Mrs Hearn shared the cooking and her mother did the nursing. On 2 November, they had mutton for Sunday lunch, cooked by Mrs Hearn and served by Mrs Parsons, and partially eaten by Mrs Thomas. Thomas had fed his wife on that occasion.

He then talked about his wife becoming worse in the night and crying out. She was then taken to hospital, dying the next day. He was then asked about the talk he had had with Mrs Hearn in the following days, including asking for an acknowledgement about the loan of £38 in 1928.

Thomas recalled once driving either Miss Everard or Mrs Hearn into Launceston about War Savings Certificates (possibly when they sold £30 worth during Miss Everard's worsening health in 1930). Mr West asked about the friendship between the Thomases and Mrs Hearn. Thomas said that his wife had no problem with him being friends with the two sisters.

After further questions, a witness who needed to return to Exeter was interposed. This was Mr Tickle, who detailed his analysis of Mrs Thomas's organs, in which he found 0.85 grains of arsenic. West asked if it was normal to find arsenic in the human body and the doctor told him it was not. West asked:

'Can you give an approximate time when the arsenic was taken?'

'I have heard the date in which the illness took place and that would prejudice my answer?'

'It was very fair of you to say that. Was the arsenic sheep dip arsenic?'

'I could not with certainty exclude sheep dip'.

'Was it weed killer arsenic?'

'The arsenic I found was the arsenic of weedkiller'.

The doctor said that the arsenic found in Mrs Thomas could have been from weed-killer, sheep dip or worm tablets. Thomas was recalled to the witness box, but the magistrates decided to end the proceedings for that day and allow West to carry on cross-examining him the next day. No one was allowed to leave the court until Mrs Hearn had been taken to Launceston police station.[34]

There were moments of emotion and even humour during this day's hearing. When the letter Mrs Hearn wrote to Thomas was read aloud she 'closed her eyes and hung her head, while her fingers twitched the pencil she was holding'. When there was a reference to weeds in Thomas's garden, Thomas replied 'I'm afraid I'm not a very good gardener sir', and there was laughter in court, even by the defendant.[35]

On the next day, Friday 27 February, the questioning of Thomas continued. West asked if it was Mrs Thomas's idea that her husband should invite Mrs Hearn to the picnic on 18 October and he agreed that it was.

'Had she any idea up to then that she was to go to Bude?'

'No'.

'What time elapsed between the time you invited her and the time you called for her?'

'I should say rather more than two hours'.

Thomas was then asked about how the sandwiches were produced and he said that he could not now be sure. The sandwiches were between the two women and in front of him, he then recollected.

'And they were there for all to help themselves?'

'Yes'.

'And each of you in fact did help yourself?'

'Yes sir'.

'I suppose it would have been just as easy for Mrs Hearn to take the sandwich which Mrs Thomas took as it was for Mrs Thomas to take it?'

'As far as I could see'.

'I want to make it quite clear that there was no question of juggling with the sandwiches?'

'No sir'.

'And I want to make it quite clear that Mrs Hearn did not press Mrs Thomas to take one?'

'Not a certain sandwich sir'.

'Was it at your wife's request that Mrs Hearn stayed at the house to look after her?'

'Yes, and I also asked after her'.

'Up to the time she was sick in the car, had your wife made any complaint to you?'

'No'.

'What food was Mrs Thomas eating before Mrs Parsons came into the house?'

'White of egg, milk foods, chicken broth and beef tea'.

'Did she sit up in her bedroom before she came downstairs on November 1st?'

'Yes'.

Thomas then described the trip to Plymouth Hospital, hearing his wife had died and the post-mortem, but he did not know the details of this.

'When did you first know that?'

'I cannot say'.

'Did you ever know that certain organs had been sent away for analysis?'

'I understood there was to be an analysis'.

'Where did you spend the remainder of the night after leaving Plymouth Hospital?'

'Part in the street and part in the garage'.

'When was the next time you went home?'

'The day my wife died'.

'And when you got home, did you speak to anyone about there being an inquest?'

'Yes'.

'With whom did you discuss it?'

'I think with Mrs Horton [nowhere is she mentioned and so it is not clear who she was, presumably a neighbour] and Mrs Hearn'.

'Did you tell Mrs Hearn about your journey to Plymouth and where you spent the remainder of the night?'

'Yes'.

'Outside the fact that you were seeing your wife, was it a shock to see the condition of her?'

'Yes sir, it was'.

Thomas then said that he paid a woman to prepare the body and that he bought white stockings.

'Did you tell Mrs Hearn all about that?'

'I may have done'.

At this point, Mrs Hearn rose from her chair and went over to the table where West was seated and spoke to him. West then addressed Thomas again.

'Did you tell Mrs Hearn that there had been a post-mortem and that there would be an inquest?'

'Yes I did'.

'Did you also say to her, "They are going to send some organs to be analysed"?'

'I cannot say sir'

'Can you say you did not?'

'I would not like to say; I am not sure'.

'Did you also say, "They will find out what it is"?'

I may have'.

'Did you also say "They will blame one of us"?'

'I don't think I did sir'.

'Did you also say "The blame will come heavier on you than on me"?'

'No sir'.

'Will you swear that you didn't'?'

Thomas' reply was inaudible so West repeated the question. He did so again and again but Thomas said he could not be wholly certain. West eventually asked another question.

'Did you also say that a detective may be here at any time?'

'I may have sir'.

'And did you also say, whatever it is, they will find it out?'

'I may have said so'.

'Did you also tell that she would have to attend the inquest?'

'Yes, I said I thought she would have to'.

'Did Mrs Hearn say to you "I had better go home?"'

'Not that I know of'.

'Did you tell her she could do as she liked, but you did not want her to go?'

'I do not remember'.

'About this loan, did Mrs Hearn from time to time offer you an acknowledgement of it?'

'Yes'.

'Until after the death of your wife you did not decide to have an acknowledgement?'

'Yes'.

'When you did ask Mrs Hearn for an acknowledgement she immediately gave it to you?'

'Yes'.

'When you received Mrs Hearn's letter, you knew to whom she was referring when she referred to "I cannot forget that awful man and the things he has said."'

'Yes'.

'You knew what things she was referring?'

'Yes'.

Parsons was then ordered to leave the court, as were all other witnesses then present. West then asked:

'During the whole time you knew Minnie (Miss Everard), was she not often ill?'

'Yes'.

'Mrs Hearn looked after her. Would you say she was devoted to her?'

'Yes, I should say she was'.

'Do you know her death was a great shock to Mrs Hearn?'

'I knew she was worried about it'.

'So you could understand when Mrs Hearn wrote "My life is not a great thing when Minnie has gone"'.

'Yes'.

'You knew she was sorry when Minnie died?'

'Yes, I thought she was'.

'What poison did you have about the house?'

'Cooper's worm tablets, which were kept on a shelf in the kitchen and a tin of Harrison's rat poison, which was kept locked up in my desk'.

'Were you the only person who could get at that?'

'Yes'.

'Is that why the superintendent could not find it on his visit?'

'I think I gave it to him'.

'Are you certain of that?'

'I gave him all the poisons I had got'.

Devlin then asked Thomas a few more questions. He wanted to check whether Mrs Hearn wore glasses and Thomas confirmed that she did. Pill then unwrapped a parcel to show a torn and threadbare black and white patterned coat and passed it to Thomas, who was then asked if he recognised it and he thought he did.

With that Thomas left the witness box. The next witness was Dr William Clayton (b.1891) of Orpington, a consulting chemist and bacteriologist. He had examined 105 tins of salmon, sixty-four of which contained arsenic and forty-one of which did not. In sixty-two of the contaminated tins, only traces of arsenic could be found, there was one two hundred and eightieth part of arsenic and in the other one seven hundredth part.

Clayton had examined seven tins in January and found no arsenic in them. He added that he did not know how arsenic could be introduced or increased if not there immediately. Part of his job was to look into complaints about tinned food. He agreed that food poisoning could be fatal as bacteria could not be isolated.

Mrs Poskitt was next in the witness box. Devlin showed her the red book which was Miss Everard's diary and had been found in Trenhorne House last year, but she could not be sure of the writer's identity. She was then shown a letter signed Annie and Minnie and she was unable to identify the handwriting there. Then there was a letter signed Minnie which was shown to her, which again she could not be sure about.

Devlin then asked her to compare writing from different times that appeared in the diary. Were there differences?

'Perhaps there is a difference, but very little'.

'Can you say which is the handwriting of Mrs Hearn and which is Minnie's?'

'I am sorry I cannot'.

She then described her month's stay in the previous year at her sisters' house during Miss Everard's illness and commented that she had never before stayed so long with them.

'Did these attacks come on suddenly?'

'Sometimes'.

'Do you know the cause of them?'

'They generally followed eating, but Minnie never knew what it was which disagreed with her. The symptoms were severe pain in the body, general uncomfortableness and faintness'.

'For what length of time was she in bed in the month you were there?'

'She was generally in bed two or three days after each attack'.

Dr Wordley, who had carried out a post-mortem on Mrs Thomas and had concluded that arsenic caused her death, was the next witness. Of Miss Everard, he claimed that death was due to a toxic body which caused emaciation and inflammation in the intestines. Devlin examined him first:

'Assuming that subsequent examination showed that there was arsenic in the body, what would be your opinion?'

Arsenic would cause all the conditions which I have found and confirm my opinion of the cause of death. Assuming that arsenic had been found, I should be satisfied that the cause of death was arsenical poisoning'.

West wanted his examination of the doctor to be postponed, but the magistrates would not allow this and so, presumably reluctantly, he began his cross-examination.

'Do you think this death could be due to a dose of arsenic administered on 18 October?'

'I think there must have been a dose subsequently'.

Dr Wordley agreed that it was more difficult to discover arsenic if it was administered in a powdered form rather than a liquid form. The court was then adjourned until 11 March and Mrs Hearn was remanded in custody.[36]

In the interim, the inquest on Minnie and Miss Everard was held at Launceston on 3 March by Dr Thompson, the coroner. Joseph Hopper of Lewannick, carpenter, gave evidence of helping lift the coffins up. He said that of the younger woman was in good condition and was easily raised. That of the older woman was difficult to raise, the lid was broken, and it had burst open at the head. Sergeant Richards of Launceston noted that Dr Wordley took nine sealed jars in the case of the younger woman and three in that of the older one. He took these to London and gave them to Lynch the next day.[37] The inquest was then adjourned indefinitely.

On 11 March the court resumed its hearing. It was expected to last another week as there were twenty-eight witnesses to call.[38] Leslie Albert, the only employee at Trenhorne Farm who also lived there, recalled that Mrs Hearn did the cooking and nursing for Mrs Thomas during her final illness, and was cross-examined by West. He admitted that when he was present his knowledge of such arrangements was nil, but he stated that Mrs Hearn prepared some food for Mrs Thomas. He could not give exact details, however. West continued:

'During the last few says of Mrs Thomas' illness, how many times did you see Mrs Hearn take her food?'

'Four times a day'.

'I do not think you understand. How many times do you think you saw Mrs Hearn take Mrs Thomas food every day?'

'Not any?'

'Then why did you say four times?'

'I was not thinking'.

'Did Mr Thomas do any nursing?'

'Some, not much'.

'So that if he said he did practically all of the nursing to within a few days of Mrs Thomas going into Plymouth, he is saying what is not true?'

'That is right'.

Wilson added that Mrs Parsons did some of the nursing and cooking.[39]

Mrs Wadge was the next witness and she recalled that she visited Trenhorne Farm on 29 October and saw Mrs Hearn and Thomas sitting by the fire. Mrs Hearn was preparing chicken broth or beef tea for Mrs Thomas. Mrs Hearn brought up the tea for Mrs Thomas and when she came down again, she said that Mrs Thomas was too ill to be seen. She did not visit again, but had done so hitherto. Thomas would have seen the food being prepared. West said:

'Mr Thomas told us nothing about it when he was in the box. I suggest to you that Mrs Hearn did not take anything up to Mrs Thomas during the whole time you were there?'

'Oh yes she did'.[40]

Percy Parsons was the next witness. He told of his meeting with Mrs Hearn and what they had discussed, but when pressed by West could not recall having said 'From what I have heard previously, I was not surprised to hear that the sandwiches were part of her tea at Bude'. West asked:

'Is your memory of that sort that remembers only what it suited to remember and does not remember what it does not suit it?'

'No sir'.

The clerk of the court intervened:

'Would it be fair to say that you had heard that they had eaten sandwiches but did not know where they were eaten?'

'Yes sir'.

Mrs Thomas, Thomas's mother, recalled that she had been at Trenhorne from September to 18 October and said that she had not prepared any sandwiches on that last day. She recalled that Parsons had said on 8 November 'This thing must be cleared up' at some stage. Devlin asked her: 'Did Mrs Hearn say anything to you after the funeral about that conversation with Mr Parsons?' Mrs Thomas replied, 'Yes, she said she could not forget that horrid man and what he had said to her'. She testified that she visited her son for about a month per year and that Mrs Hearn and Miss Everard were on good terms with her son and that her daughter-in-law did not object to this friendship.[41]

There were brief appearances in the witness box by Walter Martin, Captain Ollett and the coroner's officer, and the bulk of their evidence has already been related in previous chapters. Pill was the next witness and he explained the arrest and initial questioning of Mrs Hearn. West asked:

'When you first began to talk to Mrs Hearn you wanted to ask her a few questions which you would put to her unofficially?'

'No'.

'Did you put some questions to her?'

'Only of the nature I have given in my evidence in chief?'

'I put it to you that after she had answered certain questions which you put to her, you said to her "Now I want you to make a statement"?'

'No'.

'And you from time to time did question her while she was making her statement?'

'As I have said, leading from one paragraph to another'.

'Such as "What next?" or "After that?"'

'Yes'.

'And you suggested from time to time to her what she should say?'

'No. I repeatedly said to her: "I want to know in your own words"'.

West wanted to know if Pill had said anything unofficially to Mrs Hearn, but he consistently denied this and the magistrates had to conclude with West that nothing more would be gained by continuing to pursue this line of cross-examination.[42]

The statement made by Mrs Hearn, related in Chapter 6, was then read out. Pill said that Mrs Hearn attested her innocence to him. West said that he could not continue to cross-examine Pill until he could have another meeting with Mrs Hearn. The court was then adjourned until the next day.[43]

Pill was once again in the witness box on Thursday 12 March. West continued his questioning and Pill explained that he had entered Mrs Hearn's house in response to the letter given by Thomas.

'Will you tell us the findings of the Coroners' Jury?'

'If that is the question, it was an open verdict. I have not the text before me, but I think it was homicide by person or persons unknown'.

Pill explained that it was only after hearing Mrs Hearn's statement on 13 January that he decided to have her arrested for murder.[44]

Sergeant Trebilcock was the next witness. He recounted his visit to Torquay to identify and apprehend Mrs Hearn. She told him 'Mr Thomas used to come to our house every day but that was only a blind'. This was the only evidence, other than the gossip heard by Parsons that is suggestive of an affair between Mrs Hearn and Thomas and thus indicating a motive for murder by Mrs Hearn. He denied that Pill suggested the answers she gave and the next witness, Superintendent Martin, confirmed this.[45]

West then asked Martin:

'During the whole time the statement was being made, was there anything to show that it was not being made voluntarily?'

'No, she was very anxious to make the statement'.

There was then discussion about whether Miss Everard's diary could be used in evidence. Edward Roberts, a handwriting expert, said it was genuine and Devlin wanted to use it in court. West protested. He said it was not proved to be genuine and even if it were, it would be inadmissible as evidence. Roberts had not actually seen Miss Everard write in the diary so his statement was allegedly invalid. Devlin said that as part of the diary dealt with the deceased's symptoms it should be used. A discussion by the magistrates on this issue ensued and they decided that those parts relating to the symptoms could be used in court.[46]

Percy Rupert Clarke was an accountant employed by Cooper MacDougal and he confirmed that in July 1926 a tin of their weed-killer was sent to Trenhorne House. Shuker and Reed, chemists of Launceston, supplied it.[47]

Mrs Jones of East Looe had found a torn black and white coat in bramble bushes on the cliff at Looe. It could only be found by walking up a steep and ragged path.

Mrs Spear at Trenhorne House produced plans and photographs of the house. It was divided into two halves, one occupied by Mrs Spear and one by Mrs Hearn and earlier her sister. Though Mrs Spear and Mrs Hearn would discuss weed-killer, she was never seen using it. During Mrs Thomas's illness, Mrs Hearn would sometimes return to Trenhorne House and after her death she came to the house and asked for hot water to clean some cups.[48] Devlin asked:

'Did you have any conversation with her at that time?'

'Mrs Hearn said to me that she came over just for a change, I think because she thought the people at the farm thought all tinned food was poisonous'.

Mrs Spear then related how she visited the house when Miss Everard was ill and the latter said that she thought she was being poisoned and that she thought she was going off her head as well as being physically unwell. On this occasion Mrs Spear asked Mrs Hearn about it, and she replied, 'it was an emergency medicine which she had been told to give to her sister when she was in extra pain. She said "I have given her a full dose this time".[49]

Mrs Spear explained that she came in almost every evening in the later stages of Miss Everard's illness and confirmed what Miss Everard had written in her diary about her symptoms of immobility and pain in the legs. Devlin asked:

'During that time was there anyone else in the house except Mrs Hearn?'

'Mrs Poskitt was there in February and Mrs Thomas used to call occasionally'.

'Apart from the time Mrs Poskitt was there, was there anyone else living in the house?'

'No. Mrs Hearn looked after Miss Everard, and after Mrs Poskitt left, she was the only person, so far as I know, who looked after her sister'.

West then asked Mrs Spear about the state of the garden and water supply at Trenhorne House. She replied that the garden had been in an untidy condition when the two sisters had arrived in 1925. She could not recall whether the previous tenants had problems with the weeds.[50]

The hearing was then adjourned until the next morning.

Mrs Spear re-entered the witness box on Friday 13 March. She recalled that Minnie had been unwell since the two sisters took on the tenancy in 1925 and had been seen by Dr Gibson thereafter. West asked:

'Do you know if Miss Everard was often ill?'

'She was always in a delicate state'.

'Do you know what the trouble was?'

'It was some kind of stomach trouble'.

'So far as you know, did Mrs Hearn do all for her sister that she could do when she was ill?'

'Yes sir'.

'From what you saw of her, would you call her a devoted sister?'

'Yes sir'.

'When you visited Minnie in the evenings, did you have evening prayers?'

'Yes sir'.[51]

John Clarke, proprietor of St Leonard's private hotel on Newton Road, Torquay, was the next witness. He attested that a middle-aged woman had arrived after 10pm on 10 November, signing herself in as 'Mrs Ferguson, Heavitree, Exeter, British', the last word being spelt with two 't's. Her only luggage was an attaché case and she left at half past ten the next morning. She said that she was highly satisfied with the place and would recommend it.[52]

Mrs Marker was the next witness. She was asked by Devlin if she had seen Mrs Hearn before, replying 'There is a slight resemblance, but I cannot be certain'. She related how she had let out a room to the woman now known as Mrs Hearn.[53]

Powell then spoke about how he had employed Mrs Hearn in Torquay. Devlin asked:

'Had you any reason to believe that her name was other than Ann Faithful?'

'Not until towards the end of the period when a parcel was delivered addressed to Mrs Dennis'.

Devlin asked Powell if he could recognise the woman known to him as Ann Faithful. He looked around the court and alighted on Mrs Hearn, whom he identified as sitting with a policeman behind West's seat. Powell left the witness box and the magistrates concluded that because of this identification, it was safe to allow Mrs Marker to give evidence. She provided more information about what Mrs Hearn had told her. This was that she had been interviewed by people and she was going to return to Exeter to prepare rooms for them, and that she had been in rooms with them previously in the same city. Dorothy Charlotte Cox, a shop assistant at the Torquay branch of W.H. Smith, said that on 11 November a woman had asked for calling cards to be prepared for her and paid 3s 6d for them. They were never collected.[54]

Mrs Uglow was the next to speak. She had bought a quarter of a pound of arsenic in 1923 at a shop in Launceston for the purpose of killing magpies. Her husband had used some but not all. Devlin asked

'Did Mrs Thomas, to your knowledge, ever have any of that arsenic?'

'No'.

She further said that her farm was 14 miles from the Thomases, but they had not visited since February 1930. Thomas Pearce, a horseman employed by the Thomases, recalled his master having sheep dip but it was used up 18 months ago for washing three dogs. West asked him:

'Have you ever known Mr Thomas using Harris' rat poison?'

'Never'.

'I mean for the purpose of killing rats, of course?'

There was laughter. The court adjourned until the following Tuesday.[55]

On Tuesday 17 March the hearing resumed, with Mrs Parsons being the next witness. She stated that her daughter did not seem too unwell when she arrived at the farm on 29 October and took over nursing and most of the cookery. Devlin asked:

'When your first came was your daughter able to feed herself?'

'Very little'.

The lunch on 2 November was then described and Devlin asked:

'From what you saw would she have been capable of feeding herself?'

'No'.

Mrs Parsons said that her daughter was unable to walk and said 'I believe I am worse'. She described giving her daughter lemon juice which made her sick. She had slept with her daughter that night and the latter was restless, waking in the early hours of 3 November, calling for her husband who took her next door. On the next day she seemed a lot worse and was in a delirious condition. Mrs Parsons agreed that Mrs Hearn did the cooking for Thomas, herself and Mrs Hearn, but the latter made the early morning cups of tea. West asked:

'And Mrs Thomas had tea at the same time?'

'Yes'.

'And you gave it to her?'

'Yes sir… I am not sure about that. I believe I did'.

'Whoever gave Mrs Thomas the tea there was no particular cup for her?'

'Not that I know about. During the time I was in the house, I took all the food up to my daughter. Mrs Hearn may have taken her up a cup of tea once or twice. I do not know'.[56]

Dr Gibson was next called and stated that he had first seen Minnie on 27 November 1922, when she was suffering from long-standing stomach trouble. He diagnosed this as chronic dyspepsia and bowel trouble. He then saw her on a weekly basis until January 1923. Apparently she also said that she had suffered from a gastric ulcer. The sisters were living in North Hill in 1925 and he saw her there for the same problems.[57]

Gibson was then examined on her final illness. Minnie was recovering from the effects of colitis, or so he believed. After visits in January, he next saw her on 12 April when she was suffering from dyspepsia and he diagnosed chronic gastric catarrh:

'My recollection is that Miss Everard constantly complained of inability to digest food. It was rather, according to my recollection, that she was much bothered with vomiting. It was more that she felt that after tasting food, she would be sick rather than that she was bothered with sickness'. He added:

'I saw her the following week, April 18. She said she had been unable to take the medicine. She said it did not suit her and gave her pain'.

'Was the medicine which you describe such as might give her pain?'

'No, it ought not'.

On 26 April Minnie was unable to take the medicine prescribed, so Gibson gave her a fresh prescription of a soothing stomach mixture. On 2 May he found her rather worse. She was sick. On 23 May she said that she could not take any medicine because her digestion and stomach were so bad. It was not just medicine but food that led to this. Devlin asked 'Was the medicine such that she might have difficulty taking it?' and the doctor disagreed.

'In your experience have you known people have difficulty in taking medicine of this type?'

'Yes'.

'Is it common or uncommon?'

'Well, it is uncommon. Giving the most soothing medicine, the easiest medicine for the stomach, is successful in most cases, but there are some patients – do what you like – they cannot take medicine'.

On 26 May Minnie was still ill and on 4 July he found that she had grown thinner. She complained of pain after taking food, of pain in the arms and of difficulty in eating. He could not find any cancer and though she was weak, he did not recognise any paralysis and she was capable of movement. She was far worse at his next visit on 18 July; weak, emaciated and half conscious. She was lying on her left side and had to be helped to move on to her back. He thought she was dying for want of food.[58]

Devlin asked:

'Between July 4 and July 8 her condition got rapidly worse?'

'Yes very much worse than I expected'.

Gibson told Mrs Hearn her sister was dying and on 21 July found her hardly able to speak and in great pain. The doctor wondered if he had missed a gastric ulcer or perforation. Minnie died later that night. He signed a death certificate to the effect that she had died from chronic gastric catarrh and colitis. Inability to take food and digest, allied to a long history of this, had led him to this conclusion.[59]

Devlin asked:

'Did you or Dr Galbraith make up, or was there ever made up in our surgery, a prescription of emergency medicine to be taken in case of extra pain?'

'No. I think she had apparently used the effervescing mixture which I first prescribed, on May 2, somewhat in that way. She took it apparently occasionally not regularly'.

'Did she say that, doctor?'

'No, I am only judging from the fact that she had the medicine on 2 May and May 20'.[60]

Devlin then began to read the portions of Minnie's diary. He read her symptoms and asked the doctor if the medicines prescribed could have caused any of these and he replied emphatically not. There was then discussion about how the doctor had recorded his actions and he said that he did not have a clinical case book for every visit, but had made notes, which he had retained but would be too bulky to bring to court with him. West wanted to see all the documentation, so the doctor left the court to fetch them.[61]

In the meantime, the next witness was called, Mrs Parnell of Trenhorne Cottage. She had worked at Trenhorne Farm when Mrs Thomas was ill and had seen Mrs Hearn doing the cooking. Mr Thomas and Mrs Hearn took it in turns to bring the food to the sick woman. In the second week of her illness, Mrs Thomas told Mrs Parnell that she had stomach pains and tingling in the feet and hands. Mrs Hearn once told Mrs Parnell that she had been home to get something for Mrs Thomas. West asked:

'Did you go the house at all when Mrs Parsons was there?'

'Yes sir'.

'Did you see her preparing food?'

'I only saw her taking up a bit of lunch on Saturday morning'.[62]

Dr Gibson, carrying three large ledgers, then returned to court. West asked him if he was told that the reason why the sisters came down south was that Miss Everard had suffered from a nervous breakdown? The doctor said:

'I do not remember. I understood it was stomach trouble more than anything else'.

'Did she suffer from neuritis whilst at North Hill?'

'Not that I remember'.

'I suggest that she did and you told Mrs Hearn how to treat her?'

'It does not stay in my memory'.

'Were you told that she had been suffering for 20 years?'

'I understood she had been an invalid for some years'.

'Is it a fact that medicine given to a patient often had a reverse effect to what you hoped?'

'It is possible'.

'On April 12 1930, did you tell Miss Everard that you would send some medicine, stomach tonic and a small bottle of stuff which she should take a teaspoonful at the times she felt faint?'

'No'.

'And that might prevent her from getting worse?'

'I don't remember about this bottle of stuff at all'.

Checking his prescription book, he found that he had prescribed a prescription of bismuth, takadiastase and pepsin, but Miss Everard said that would be too strong.

'I suggest to you that is the prescription that you told her to take a teaspoonful of when she felt faint'.

'No'.

'Do you remember telling Miss Everard that Mrs Hearn was a good nurse?'

'I thought Mrs Hearn was a good nurse'.

The effervescing medicine was described as being an emergency medicine and it was frequently used as such by patients. Devlin looked through the ledger and could find no evidence of a small bottle of stuff to be taken in teaspoonfuls. Had it been prescribed it would have been listed there. He asked:

'Would the effervescing mixture have been followed by any pain?'

'No'.

'Did you ever say anything to Mrs Hearn to suggest that this was an emergency medicine to be taken in case of extra pain?'

'No. The mixture was for vomiting, for sickness, not for pain'.[63]

Wednesday 18 March was the next day of the hearing. Dr Lynch was the only witness called that day. Devlin asked what a fatal dose of arsenic would be. Lynch had said that death was caused by two grains of white arsenic in this case. He then said:

'But I would add that this is exceptional. I regard about four grains as a more average fatal dose. It would be fair to add that recovery has taken place after very heavy doses – 100 grains and upwards. It depends on the amount of vomiting'.[64]

Bude. (Paul Lang's collection)

Launceston. (Author's postcard)

Plymouth Hospital. (Author's postcard)

St. Martin's church, Lewannick. (East Cornwall Family History Society, 2022

Gravestone of Mrs Thomas, Lewannick, East Cornwall Family History Society, 2022

Willingham Hall.

De Aston School.

Parish Church Market Rasen.

Middle Rasen. Author's postcard.

CERTIFIED COPY OF AN ENTRY OF DEATH

GIVEN AT THE GENERAL REGISTER OFFICE

Application Number 11298475-1

REGISTRATION DISTRICT BAKEWELL

1915 DEATH in the Sub-district of Tideswell in the County of Derby

Columns:—	1	2	3	4	5	6	7	8	9
No.	When and where died	Name and surname	Sex	Age	Occupation	Cause of death	Signature, description and residence of informant	When registered	Signature of registrar
346	Eighteenth November 1915 Bramwich Wood Wathersage R.D.	Betsy Everard	Female	67 years	Wife of Robert Everard a "Retired" Farmer	Apoplexia pneumonia 21 days. Cardiac failure. Certified by Eliobeth Heam C.R.C.P. +S	Minnie Everard daughter in attendance Bramwich Wood Wathersage	Twenty second November 1915	Clarence Huntlows Registrar

CERTIFIED to be a true copy of an entry in the certified copy of a Register of Deaths in the District above mentioned.

Given at the GENERAL REGISTER OFFICE, under the Seal of the said Office, the 4th day of November 2020

DYE 476554

See note overleaf

7453009 822158 04/18 APSA15P

PMS

Death certificate of Grace Mabel Everard

Magistrates' Court, Weston-Super-Mare. Author's photograph, 2020

North Hill. (Author's postcard)

Looe. (Author's postcard)

Guildhall and Post Office

Plymouth Guildhall. (Author's postcard)

Brooksby, Hesketh Road, Torquay. (Author's photograph, 2021)

41 Ellacombe Church Road, Torquay. (Author's photograph, 2021)

Exeter Prison. (Author's postcard)

MR. NORMAN BIRKETT, K.C.

So many a jury, through its foreman,
Proclaims the conquests of this NORMAN
That " Punch," if yet again he strays
Back to his homicidal ways,
Will do his level best to work it
So that his counsel may be BIRKETT.

MR. PUNCH'S PERSONALITIES.—XCV.

Norman Birkett, KC. (Author's collection)

Assize Courts and Mayoralty, BODMIN.

Above: Bodmin
Assize Court.
(Author's postcard)

Right: Agatha Christie
bust, Torquay.
(Author's photograph,
2021)

every privilege which could be given me under the circumstances, and I appreciated it; endeavoured to make the lot of those connected with me as least irksome as possible.

There was just one aspect which used to make me very sad. I could not see any of my relatives. I only saw my brother once during the whole time I was there. Not because I was not allowed to—do not misunderstand me, but because he lived so far away, and the journey was so expensive that it was impossible for him to come.

The same applied to my sister Bessie. She could not possibly afford to come all that way, although when she was called upon to give evidence, and she was brought to Launceston during the police court proceedings, every facility was given for her to see me, and we spent many happy hours together—as happy as could be under the circumstances—at the little police station at Launceston, both Superintendent Pill, and his wife, Mrs. Pill, the police matron who was in charge of me at the time, being extremely kind in this respect.

Then she was allowed to drive back with me to Exeter after the proceedings were over, and the next morning I was permitted to see her again before she left to go home.

I can never tell you how much those visits meant to me. To be so far away from everyone whom I loved, to be in such a place for ever haunted with the knowledge of the terrible suspicions against me, and to know that I was innocent. It was a fearful ordeal. Yet I tried to bear myself with patience, knowing that some day the truth would prevail.

There has been much sorrow and trouble in my life, but this has been the crowning sorrow of all. Who could help but worry under the circumstances? I frankly admit that there were many nights when I lay awake far into the early hours of the next day wondering what the end would be.

ON TRIAL.

I lived over again all that had happened in the past. The death of my sister Mabel, whom I helped to nurse through a long and trying illness from which she died at an early age. The deaths of my mother and my father. The ups and downs which had come to me during my own life.

All these things passed through my mind as I spent anxious days and nights waiting for my trial. At last the day dawned when I knew that I must face judge and jury. A great peace stole over me.

The day before the trial opened, Mr. Walter West, my solicitor, came to see me. I was greatly comforted, for he had worked so hard during the police court proceedings. And he was confident of my acquittal.

Then the next morning I was taken to the little Assize Court at Bodmin. I could not realise that it was I who was being put on trial for my life. I seemed to look upon that scene with a detached sense of being an on-looker.

The dock is a very narrow one, with scarcely room to stretch your legs. The seat is narrow,

A photograph of Mrs. Hearn taken after her innocence was proved.

but they had kindly provided me with a cushion and tried to make me as comfortable as possible.

I watched the jury being sworn. I looked at them

Annie Hearn. *Peg's Companion,* at the British Library.

Photo: *Graphic Photo. Union.*

Mr. Thomas, of the death of whose wife Mrs. Hearn
was accused.

But all our troubles and all our privations on
tightened the bonds between us, and made us cli
closer together throughout the advancing years.

And I was charged with murdering her. Charg
with killing her deliberately—slowly—in the mc
painful way it is possible to imagine.

For seven months or more I was supposed to ha
given her dose after dose of poison. Supposed
have sat by her bedside whilst she was in the throes
terrible agony, indifferent to her suffering, gloati
over her pain, slowly, yet persistently, sending her
a ghastly death.

My sister and my friend. The friend who h
helped and made things easier for us. The sist
for whom I would have laid down my life.

THE DEAD SHALL SPEAK.

You have heard a lot about the diary which she le
behind, and which was the subject of so much leg
argument both during the police court proceedin
and the trial.

I sat there wondering what it was all about.
knew what was in that diary. Knew that there we
only tender, loving words of thanks for the little
was able to do for her.

It contains Minnie's own story of her long illnes
It contains in detail the grim story of how s
suffered. But it contains many other things besid
and because it throws an entirely new light on how
tended and cared for her night and day during h
illness, I shall in the near future make many quot
tions from it.

The dead shall speak. The mystery which su
rounded this diary must in fairness to myself
raised, so that there can never be any lurking dou
in the minds of those who read the case, and m
have wondered why the diary was not admitted
evidence.

I shall unfold the story of the terrible hours whi
followed the death of Mrs. Thomas, and how t
wagging tongue of scandal, for which there was nev
any foundation, drove me to the point where I almo
took my life.

Thank God that my courage failed me at the la
moment, and I was spared to face my trial, and
acquitted of all guilt.

Why did I run away? Why did I not come forwa
when, after failing in my determination to take n
life, I knew that the police of the whole count
were seeking me? All these things I will tell yc
in due course.

I will tell you of the agony of those months whe
there was a hue and cry throughout the land, and
realised that I was a hunted woman.

But as the days went on, I felt a greater securit
Actually I was within a few miles of the place fro
which I had fled. The hue and cry was dying dow
the tragedy of the death of Mrs. Thomas was grad
ally passing from memory, and I had started a ne
life. But that is a later story.

I want to tell you of my feelings after my arres
When the moment came there was a strange sense
relief. Now at last I should be cleared of all su
picion. Then came the long weeks in Exeter Ga
weeks which lengthened into months.

How kind were all the officials there! I was giv

William Thomas. *Peg's Companion,* at the British Library.

NEW THEORIES IN UNDERGRADUATE MYSTERY

WIRELESS
PROGRAMMES
IN FULL
ON PAGE 16

Daily Mirror
THE DAILY PICTURE PAPER WITH THE LARGEST NET SALE

No. 8,507 Registered at the G.P.O. as a Newspaper. WEDNESDAY, FEBRUARY 25, 1931 One Penny

£1,000
RACING
COUPON
TO-DAY

MRS. HEARN: MURDER CHARGES

Mrs. Sarah Annie Hearn, accused of two murders.

A car taking Mrs. Hearn to Launceston yesterday.

Miss Lydia Everard, sister of Mrs. Sarah Annie Hearn, and (inset) Mrs. Alice Thomas, both dead. When Mrs. Hearn appeared before the magistrates at Launceston, Cornwall, yesterday, remanded on a charge of murdering Mrs. Thomas, the wife of a Lewannick farmer, she was also accused of murdering Miss Everard, by arsenical poisoning. Miss Everard's body was exhumed recently while the police were searching for Mrs. Hearn, who disappeared on November 10, a few days after Mrs. Thomas's funeral and was arrested on January 12 at Torquay. At yesterday's hearing Mr. Patrick Devlin, the barrister appearing for the Director of Public Prosecutions, said that the analyst, Dr. Roche Lynch, was of the opinion that Miss Everard had been slowly poisoned for seven months before her death.

Front page of the Daily Mirror, 25 February 1931, detailing the murder charges against Annie Hearn.

Regarding the poisoning of Mrs Thomas, Lynch said: 'In my opinion a dose of arsenic was administered on that day'. He added, 'My opinion is that that dose ran in to several grains, quite possibly in the region of 10 grains'.

Devlin asked:

'Was the vomiting that you have heard described on that day a severe vomiting?'

'Yes. And it is that fact that I am taking into consideration when I postulate that there were round about 10 grains'.

Vomiting was an important factor, for if Mrs Thomas had tea at 5.15, then felt a sweet taste in her mouth at 6.30, if she vomited at 7.15 and had diarrhoea, these were consistent with having arsenic at teatime. Devlin then asked:

'If the arsenic had been taken in solid form and with food, would that have any bearing on the time of the onset of the symptoms?'

'Certainly. Taken in solid form and with food, particularly if wrapped in a sandwich, it would delay the onset of symptoms'.

He was asked to account for the 'sweety taste' as experienced by Mrs Thomas and replied that it might have been the result of excessive salivation prior to vomiting. He said that the symptoms as described by Dr Saunders, of the vomiting and diarrhoea passing by 26 October and the gastric symptoms passing by 30 October, were all consistent with poisoning on 18 October. Peripheral neuritis could be accounted for by the symptoms described and the mental condition could be consistent with acute arsenic poisoning.[65] Devlin then asked:

'In your view, are the symptoms leading up to the death on November 4 consistent with sub acute poisoning?'

'Yes'.

The significant feature of the post-mortem examination, said Dr Lynch, was the condition of the body's internal organs – the heart, liver, kidneys, gullet, stomach and intestines. Inflammation of the intestines and other damage to these organs suggested toxic poisoning. There was 0.85 of a grain of arsenic in these organs. As he explained:

> 'In my opinion, if Mrs Thomas only received one dose of arsenic on October 18 and she lived until November 4, Mr Tickle would not have found as much as 0.66 in the liver. I am further of the opinion that Mrs Thomas received one or more doses between October 18 and November 4 and that these were not administered within about four or five days of her death'.[66]

Devlin asked if the symptoms were consistent with a single dose of arsenic administered on 18 October? Lynch thought not, saying 'I think the chances would have been recovery, and further, though peripheral neuritis can occur as the result of a single dose its appearance is more commonly associated with repeated doses'.

Lynch then moved onto the topic of Miss Everard, whose organs were rather smaller than normal, due to the emaciated condition of the victim. They revealed, he said, 0.776 grains of white arsenic. He found arsenic in the hair and this showed that poisoning had taken place over a period of six months, and possibly even longer. He concluded: 'So we can take it that arsenic was taken for at least seven months.'

The doctor suggested that the dosage increased near the end of her life. The symptoms described by Dr Gibson in 1922–25 were more consistent with chronic dyspepsia or gastric trouble, which she had also suffered from. The symptoms in her diary and as described by witnesses were consistent with arsenic poisoning. She was not suffering from a gastric ulcer and the diary entry which read 'It seemed as if I was being poisoned' was strongly suggestive that she was suffering from arsenic poisoning. However, no dosage was given in the days before her death. Arsenic in the skin and heart and especially the nails was conclusive.

> 'Having considered all the evidence and the history of the case, in my view death was due to poisoning by arsenic, the arsenic being administered in doses much greater than medicinal doses, but in comparatively small toxic doses over a considerable period of time'.[67]

He was then asked about the death certificate given by Dr Gibson and its accuracy.

> 'I think a medical man, not knowing or suspecting arsenical poisoning, would be quite justified in giving a certificate of that sort on the symptoms which he found. There was no evidence at the post mortem of gastric neuritis or colitis. The condition was found consistent with poisoning by some toxic substance such as arsenic'.[68]

He also argued that the arsenic in the soil around the coffin was insoluble in water and so could not have entered the body that way. He then returned to the case of Mrs Thomas, and reasoned that there were three reasons why her symptoms were not consistent with food poisoning. Firstly, the time elapsed between the eating of the sandwiches and the first symptoms was too short. Secondly, only one person was affected if one discounted Thomas's being slightly unwell. Lastly, there was no evidence of food poisoning.[69]

Devlin asked:

> 'Would it be possible to introduce small doses of the weed-killer into the food Mrs Thomas was having during her illness?'

> 'Quite easy. I think they could be introduced without being detected by the taste'.

> 'Suppose that in that manner, one or more subsequent small doses of arsenic had been put into Mrs Thomas' food, would you necessarily expect to find taking the dose followed by any pronounced symptoms?'

> 'It is quite possible that a dose larger than a medicinal dose but small so far as a toxic dose is concerned, could have been introduced into her food and not have produced an exacerbation of symptoms'.

Devlin concluded his examination of Dr Lynch and with that the day's court hearings came to an end.[70]

The final day of the hearing was on Thursday 19 March. Dr Lynch returned to the witness box and was cross-examined by West about his experiments on the arsenic content of the soil in the churchyard. He said:

'I quite agree that the ideal experiment would have been to percolate water through five feet of soil. I suggest that if you had done that the result would have been more arsenic'.

'Slightly more', conceded the doctor. He then gave figures for the arsenic in the vicinity of the coffin. West pounced on these: 'You found more arsenic in that experiment than you found in the liver of Miss Everard?' Lynch agreed, and then added that he would class her death as due to an acute form of arsenic poisoning. This happened because there were doses given from time to time. The death of Mrs Thomas was due to sub-acute arsenic poisoning; firstly by one dose, but after that he could not be sure how many, if indeed there were any, additional doses had been given. If they had been given, it would have been between 20 and 29 October; there had been none in the last four days of life, in his opinion.[71]

'Then you definitely rule out anything on Sunday 2 November?'

'In my opinion no administration of arsenic took place on that day'.
West then asked:

'Do you say that the final symptoms of delirium, mania and collapse without gastric symptoms and without diarrhoea suggest arsenical poisoning in the case of Mrs Thomas?'

Lynch answered that the symptoms themselves did not suggest arsenic poisoning, but that there was definitely peripheral neuritis. West asked:

'Have you ever known of a case of arsenical poisoning in which a person, fairly well in the afternoon, after taking a fairly heavy meal, suddenly goes into a state of delirium and mania?'

'No. Generally, there is a period of excitement prior to the actual mania'.

Lynch went on to say that he thought that on 18 October, 10 grains of arsenic had been administered, because only two hours later there was considerable vomiting and this would result in much of the arsenic being removed from the body.[72]

Mrs Hearn was asked to stand whilst the two charges were read out to her. 'Have you anything to say in answer to these charges?' the chairman asked. 'Only that I am not guilty,' came Mrs Hearn's reply.

West then said:

'I submit that it is your duty to discharge her. I have been here 10 days patiently listening to the evidence, but simply in vain, for one jot or tittle of evidence which suggests definitely or in any other way that my client was responsible for the deaths of these two women.

The prosecution have called nearly 50 witnesses in order to get you to commit this woman for trial, but what is the net result? Only the opportunity to do what is suggested by the prosecution Mrs Hearn did so. If you commit Mrs Hearn on opportunity only, then I say it will be a great injustice, to put this woman in peril on such grounds'.[73]

West then dismissed the evidence presented by the prosecution and added, about Mrs Hearn's disappearance:

'Remember she was a lone woman who had lost her sister a few months before. People were accusing her of being responsible for Mrs Thomas' death. She did a thing which perhaps in similar circumstances many others would have done. She left the village. Just imagine the scandal that was going on and the lies that were being told. She had no one to confer with, no one to talk to; she decided that she would end her life and went off to Looe...'[74]

He finally noted that the jury at the inquest had not named Mrs Hearn as the killer and so asked the rhetorical question 'Are you gentlemen going to say that the jury were wrong?'[75]

However, the magistrates felt that there was enough evidence to commit Mrs Hearn for trial at the Cornwall Assizes to be held in two months' time. For the present Mrs Hearn's appearances in public were over, but her biggest ordeal was about to begin. She was returned to Exeter Prison by car.

Devlin recalled that Mrs Hearn sat:

'directly behind [me] with a wardress on either side of her. She was reported as being completely at ease and chatting happily to the wardresses; occasionally she would write a little note to Mr West'.[76]

As an aside, on 18 February at Launceston County Court Mrs Hearn was sued in absentia.[77] A notice of this was pinned to the house door. Mrs Hearn's possessions were auctioned by order of the high bailiff of the county. These included a grandfather clock, a violin, a pianoforte, a Singer Treadwell sewing machine, a dinner wagon and dining and bedroom suites.[78] There were also many books, including one or two works by Dickens (presumably those read by her late sister), devotional literature, including the Old Testament, commentaries, books of miracles, biblical texts hanging from the wall and some books of modern fiction such as *The Sheik* and *The Apple of Eden*. Both suggest that Mrs Hearn enjoyed the escapist romantic fantasy that many women devoured at this time. There was homemade loganberry jam and marmalade. Many people flocked to the house on 28 February to see the items. The goods were sold in 300 lots and made £100 in total.[79]

To return to the main issue, Mrs Hearn and Mrs Poskitt met together in the police station, and 'we spent many happy hours together – as happy as could be in the circumstances'. Then the sisters were driven back to Exeter and Mrs Poskitt visited her sister in prison the next day before travelling northwards. According to Mrs Hearn, 'I can never tell you how much these visits meant to me... It was a fearful ordeal. Yet I tried to bear myself with patience, knowing that someday the truth would prevail'.[80]

The date for the trial was announced as 15 June and the names of the prosecuting counsel were given as Mr Herbert du Parcq (1880–1949), a KC since 1926 and since 1929 Recorder for Bristol, and a member of the Western Circuit.[81] He was aided by Devlin, continuing his role from the lower courts.[82] For the defence was William Norman Birkett, KC (1883–1962). He was a well-known criminal lawyer and had successfully defended two women on the charge of poisoning their husbands; Harriet Crouch in 1926 and Beatrice Pace in 1928.[83]

According to an admirer, 'Norman Birkett seemed to me then to be everything the model advocate should be; alert, courteous, of impressive bearing and possessed of a most melodious speaking voice'.[84] Bowker wrote that his boss needed to remove the 'sinister aspect of guilt' surrounding Mrs Hearn.[85]

Meanwhile, Mrs Hearn appeared to be in good spirits, according to her sister Mrs Poskitt, who told journalists, 'All I can say is that Mrs Hearn, who is my only sister, is very cheerful. She asks us to cheer up in this trying time. She speaks well of her treatment at the prison'. She was also writing to her brother in Grimsby.[86] A few of Annie's letters to Bessie from prison survive. She wrote:

'Many thanks for both your dear letters. I always think of you, especially on Sunday evening, because I have a good idea of what you are doing then. I wish I could come over in person as well as in thoughts. I suppose you never get a glimpse of me sitting there? Sitting in your old "easy"? Just turn around quickly next time, and see when you are playing "What are these?" [referring to the well-known anthem].

I don't seem to have much to say in reply to your nice letters. The time is going. Five weeks only now, 4 weeks next Monday. It will be a long drive to Bodmin which is about 20 miles from Launceston'.

Another letter ran as follows:

'Thank you so much for your dear letter. I expect you wrote it on Sunday. It was a lovely sunny day here. I was outside a nice long time. These long evenings I am generally out an hour or more, as well as the ordinary daytime exercise.

I wonder if you have your hammock fixed to use. I am glad we sent that. Yes – the long wait is nearly over. Three weeks next Monday. I wonder if you will be in Grimsby at all before you come. If so, I wish you would bring the little fawny coloured felt hat out of my parcel.

It would be so comfortable for your journey home. And also a change of wear just after things are over – more unnoticeable than the same all the time.

I am managing all right for clothes. I wear the old tweed frock all the time.
I have not found it too hot, as of course it is different in a place like this.

I also have the woollen coat for outside or anytime I want it. I also have the
little old black frock you saw me wearing at Launceston. I have taken out
the black front and the collar off and made a white silk collar and front. So
I think it will be all right under a coat to wear.

I shall have such lots to tell you when all this is over and we are together
properly. Mind you keep yourself up Bessie dear, for my sake. Love to
all–Your own Anne.'

The last letter before the trial was brief:

'Dearest Bessie, Many thanks for your letter. I can now say one week next
Monday. It would be nice to go back together… We will have the 2nd of
June next month, won't we?'[87]

Meanwhile, the prison's medical officer, Dr Charles Newton Lovely (1863–1947)
had to examine Mrs Hearn's mental state, as was necessary for any defendant in
a murder trial, and on 5 June concluded 'This woman has exhibited no evidence
of insanity whole under observation here. I consider her fit to plead'.[88]

Dr Lynch made a report on 10 June to the effect that weed-killer could be
added to Ovaltine and Benger's food without causing these to be discoloured;
clearly he knew that Minnie's diary referred to her being given these substances
by her sister. Two to four grams of arsenic could be added to the Benger's food
and two to ten to Ovaltine without any discolouration, thus showing that Minnie
could have been poisoned by her sister without the former's knowledge.[89]

Chapter 8

Case for the prosecution

The defence was greatly helped by Dr Sydney Smith (1882–1969), who was a pathologist who, after qualifying at Edinburgh University, worked in Egypt in the 1920s, before taking up a teaching post in pathology. Fellow pathologist Dr Keith Simpson later wrote of him, 'a remarkable man... He had flair and ability, an enthusiasm for police problems, tolerance of the human nature and pathos of crime and killing, and a real interest in his pupils'.[1] Having been shown the relevant documents by West, Smith wrote a report outlining his concerns about the medical evidence of the prosecution and sent it to Birkett. Smith did not doubt that Mrs Thomas died of arsenic poisoning, but thought it most unlikely the poison was in the sandwiches. As to Miss Everard, 'the evidence was even less conclusive' and as to the death certificate, 'I thought – and I still think – that he was right'. One wonders how he thought the arsenic was administered, when and by whom. He told Birkett he could not attend the trial because his university work was too demanding. However, on 11 June he received a telegram from West which read:

'BIRKETT THINKS IT VITAL YOU SHOULD BE IN BODMIN THIS SUNDAY FOR CONSULTATION ABOUT SIX EVENING. I THINK SO TOO AND MOST EARNESTLY BESEECH YOU TO COME. WIRE REPLY AT ONCE. WEST.'

The pathologist's reaction was as follows:

'My impulse was to refuse on the grounds that my first duty was to my students. Then I thought it would be a negation of all my teachings if it meant that an innocent woman might be convicted and hanged. So I went'.

He met Birkett for the first time and was impressed.

'I had never known anyone quite like him. He grasped the technicalities
of the evidence with extraordinary speed and saw the implications of my
points at once'.

They had a conference on the Sunday evening, 14 June, and then Birkett asked,
'Will you be here to give evidence if it is needed?' and Smith agreed. Birkett
continued, 'I don't know if I shall call you. I hope it won't be necessary, but
I would like to have you beside me in court'.

The advantage of only calling the defendant as a defence witness meant that
the defending counsel could have the last summing-up speech before the judge's
final address. Thus he would need to obtain all the evidence he needed against
the Crown's case by the successful cross-examination of their witnesses.[2]

Just before this trial, which was part of the wider assize, where several cases
were dealt with, the judge gave a lecture to both the public and the press who
would be dealing with the case. Noting that there was great public interest in the
case, he warned that this must not interfere with the principal aim of the trial,
namely to establish the truth of the matter. Press reporting must be most careful.
Headlines and reporting must not seek to influence opinion. The Hearn case was
expected to last for a week.[3]

Understandably, Mrs Hearn was not feeling too well and she later wrote:

'Long before my trial I was in a poor state of health and worn down by
worry and anxiety. I had lost strength and energy. I never slept properly
the whole time'.[4]

On the evening of Sunday 14 June Mrs Hearn was taken from Exeter Prison to
Bodmin Police Station. She recalled:

'There a bed had been put into a cell and blankets sent on from Exeter
prison, so I would be comfortable.

Everyone was very kind. They offered me something to make me sleep
soundly.

"No" I said "It is very nice of you, but I will face it all without drugs. I don't want anything that will make my head less clear than it is now".[5]

West reassured her that all would be well. Mrs Hearn later wrote, 'I was greatly comforted, for he had worked so hard during the police court proceedings. And he was confident of my acquittal'.[6]

On the next morning the judge in full robes and heralded by trumpeters arrived in court, along with the Mayor Alderman John Albert Jago (1867–1949) and the High Sheriff, Lieutenant Colonel Edward Hoblyn Warren Bolitho (1882–1969), after having attended a service at the parish church.[7] There were crowds outside waiting to see any of the principals. They saw Thomas arrive in a car with his mother and Dr Lynch.[8]

Arthur Smith, clerk to Lord Goddard, was present and he recalled the scene:

'I remember the excitement of our arrival in Bodmin for the case had aroused intense local interest… for in that remote and gentle county, violent crime is a rarity. Almost before it was light crowds had gathered in the small grey square and people were queuing for places in the public gallery. I recalled how they booed and hissed the prisoner… how frail and ill Du Parcq looked that morning and how anxious I felt for him. He had not told me that he had a weak heart. It was to play him a cruel trick at a later stage'.

Smith seems to have been convinced of Mrs Hearn's guilt, as he stated as fact that she was in love with Thomas and killed his wife in order to marry him.[9]

The trial took place at Bodmin Guildhall on Fore Street.

Once 'Mrs Sarah Annie Hearn' had been called, she slipped into a seat behind Birkett. She rested easily against the railing there, glanced around the court and then listened attentively to the proceedings. She wore a different outfit from the earlier proceedings; a brown hat trimmed with yellow and brown flowers and a lighter brown coat. She wore spectacles and was accompanied by three wardresses and a nurse. At one point she asked for a pencil and paper to make notes.[10] She later recalled how she felt at this time:

'I could also see Mr Norman Birkett. So far I had never seen nor spoken to the man who had my life in his hands. He was tall and his strong face gave me confidence. When he looked up at me, his kindly eyes sent a message of hope to my heart. I liked his eyes.

The Jury was called into the box one by one. I realised that my hopes largely rested on them. When I looked in the direction of the box I felt comforted. They looked like people of my own class. I felt somehow they would understand. But for this and my confidence in Mr Birkett, about whom I had already heard so much, I should have no hope at all'.[11]

She added that she:

'felt sorry because I had heard that all during the trial they would have to be away from their homes. I tried to visualise their feelings knowing that they had a fellow creature's life in their hands, and wondered how I would feel in similar circumstances.

I looked towards the judge and speculated what his feelings must be. It is a terrible responsibility this responsibility of life and death. Yet it is one that must not be shirked'.[12]

The judge was Sir Alexander Adair Roche KC (1871–1956), a barrister of the Inner Temple, KC since 1912 and a Judge of the King's Bench Division of the High Court since 1917.[13] Defence costs added up to £1,000; in part at least paid for by O'Donnell's newspaper for Mrs Hearn's exclusive story after the trial. Birkett was assisted by Mr Dingle Mackintosh Foot (1905–78), who had been admitted to Gray's Inn in 1925 and was admitted as a barrister in July 1930.[14] Anthony Hawke (1895–1964), another barrister, was also present, as he had been at previous hearings.

There was discussion about whether the diary of Minnie Everard was admissible in court. Du Parcq argued with the judge that it was admissible. Birkett argued against it, stating that it could only be used if it would provide evidence of a system. Such had been the case with trials of multiple killers. The judge agreed with Birkett and cited a precedent case. The defence had thus won an initial victory.[15]

The clerk of the court formally asked Mrs Hearn how she would plead to both charges and in a loud voice she declared after each, 'I am not guilty'.

The bulk of the day's session was made up of Du Parcq's opening address to the jury, in which he laid out his case against the defendant; this took an hour and forty minutes. He first impressed on them the responsibility that was theirs and the seriousness of the task which lay before them. He told them to forget anything that they had previously read about the case and to only rely on the evidence that would be brought before them in court. He then launched into the Crown's case. This was that Mrs Thomas had been poisoned by arsenic on 18 October and at a later date and died on 4 November.

Du Parcq told briefly of Miss Everard's death and the friendship between the Thomases and Mrs Hearn since 1925. He then talked of the trip to Bude and the eating of the sandwiches prepared by Mrs Hearn and the subsequent death of Mrs Thomas. Du Parcq then interjected to tell the jury about arsenic and how it could easily be purchased in the form of weed-killer, and how its symptoms resembled those of food poisoning, with which it was often confused. It acted more slowly if indigested with food, such as sandwiches, as in this case. Small amounts of arsenic could be found naturally and in medicines and foods.

He then described Mrs Thomas's death, paying particular attention to the fact that the symptoms she endured were those of arsenic poisoning. He described the findings of the post-mortem and those of the analyst, which all went to show that Mrs Thomas had died of arsenic poisoning. He then turned to Mrs Hearn:

'I submit that the fact was first, that Mrs Thomas died of arsenical poisoning, that she had a dose of arsenic in these sandwiches, that they had been prepared by Mrs Hearn and no one else, that no one else had the opportunity of preparing them, that Mrs Hearn had the opportunity of giving another dose, or doses afterwards, and no one else had such opportunities'.

Du Parcq noted that in 1926 Mrs Hearn bought weed-killer, but added that there was no evidence she ever used it in the garden and even if she did, only a few grains were required to kill. In fairness he added that Mrs Uglow and Thomas also had products containing arsenic. He then described the letter sent to Thomas on 10 November, Mrs Hearn's journey by car to Looe, buying an attaché case, planting her coat on the cliffs and taking a train to Torquay and arriving that evening. On 18 November Mrs Hearn had left Mrs Marker and told her she was going to Exeter, to prepare rooms for the people who had seen her. He then told of her recognition by Powell, her arrest and read out her statement to the police made on 12 January.

When the jury was out, Du Parcq stated he would discuss the death of Miss Everard as the symptoms were so similar that it was relevant here. Birkett argued that he should not use Miss Everard's diary as it was inadmissible. As with the lower court, the judge agreed that it was as regards Mrs Thomas's death, but not as regards the diarist herself. When the jury returned, Du Parcq stated the details of Miss Everard's death and then said that he was not going to discuss motive, as none could justify murder. What he relied on was the evidence of murder having been committed. He finished his speech at 4.30pm. Very little evidence was actually given; only the showing of plans and photographs of the farm, evidence of an order for weed-killer and a chemist who spoke of the properties of arsenic.[16]

Smith thought that the prosecution had blundered already, later writing 'In a sense the Crown played into our hands'. This was because they had insisted that Mrs Hearn had killed her sister as well as Mrs Thomas. He wrote 'The medical evidence was definitely weaker in the case of Miss Everard; if this charge could be destroyed, then the case in respect of Mrs Thomas would be badly shaken'.[17] Yet in this he was surely wrong; the evidence of the diary and Dr Lynch's post-mortem findings give firm proof of death by arsenic poisoning.

On Tuesday 16 June, the second day of the trial, the focus was on the death of Mrs Thomas and so Thomas was the principal witness, along with his mother, mother-in-law and Dr Saunders. The first, however, was Gilbert Arthur Freak, chief chemist of Messrs Cooper, London, who was asked questions about the physical properties and appearance of arsenic. One significant exchange was as follows, with Birkett asking:

'And then you would have it completely dissolved?'

'Everything would be in solution except the blue pigment which is insoluble'.

'And when you have the solution it is a blue solution?'

'Yes'.

Mrs Uglow was next, and the sister of the late Mrs Thomas whose farm was fourteen miles from Trenhorne, who admitted that they had bought weed-killer to kill magpies in 1923 and had not used it all. Thomas Pearce, a farm worker at Trenhorne, recalled buying sheep dip containing arsenic to wash some dogs, but it had all been used up two years ago.[18]

Thomas gave a brief account of his life at Trenhorne Farm and relations between him, his wife, and the sisters. The judge then asked:

'When did you first know there were any sandwiches?'

'There was no arrangement about taking any, I did not know there were any before we were asked to take some at the table'.

'How did you do it?'

'I did not see the sandwiches put on the table. I cannot say who took the first. They were placed there between the two ladies'.[19]

Du Parcq then took over the examination.

'Who asked you to have some?'

'Mrs Hearn. She asked me if we would like a sandwich. I cannot say who took the first. I cannot say whether I took the first one. I did take one and my wife and Mrs Hearn took one each'.

'How many did you have?'

'I only had one. I could not say whether they had more than one or two'.

Thomas could not remember how many sandwiches there were – perhaps six – or what happened to any that were uneaten. He recalled having two whiskies and his sick feeling ceased. He said that he rejoined the ladies at 6.30pm, and his wife said, 'Are there any fruit shops? I have a sweety taste in my mouth', and he bought her some bananas but was not sure if she ate any. Du Parcq resumed his examination.

'At the time or at any other time in the day did Mrs Hearn make any complaint about feeling anything wrong with herself?'

'No, I never heard her say anything'.

'Did Mrs Hearn say anything to you about her own condition?'

'A day or two after we had been to Bude I asked Mrs Hearn what type of fish was in the sandwiches. She said it was tinned salmon and she herself felt funny'.

Birkett then asked:

'Whoever took the first sandwich, they were all taken about the same time?'

'Yes, but I could not say who took the first sandwich?'

'But as to taking of the first sandwich, there was no pushing of the plate or juggling with them?'

'No, there was no juggling'.

'Did your wife take the second sandwich?'

Thomas was uncertain about this. He then said:

'I was asking Mrs Hearn what was in the sandwiches?'

'But you knew what was in the sandwiches – you had eaten one?'

'Yes, but I did not know what kind of fish it was'.

'Did you tell the doctor what your wife had had for her midday dinner?'

'I cannot remember'.

'Do you remember what you had?'

'No'.

'I suggest to you that from the 18th to the 29th October your wife steadily improved?'

'She did not improve all the time but on some days'.

'Is it true to say that apart from one setback, your wife's condition improved until the 29th?'

'Yes, but very little'.

'Your wife's serious relapse was on November 2?'

'She had a relapse before that, on the Wednesday the doctor did not come'.

'You probably mean the Tuesday, but there is no doubt that the serious relapse was on November 2?'

'Yes'.

Thomas spoke about how Mrs Hearn and Mrs Parsons shared the cooking on 2 November and he fed his wife. It was suggested by a doctor she could go to a hospital on 28 October but she refused. Thomas then denied the words attributed to him by Mrs Hearn after his wife's death.

'Did you say "The blame will come heavier on you than me. People are saying so"?'

'No, I did not'.

'Did you say anything to her about what you knew people were saying?'

'I did not'.

'If, after the death of your wife, you had said to a woman "The blame will come heavier on you than me", is that a thing you would be likely to forget?'

'There was no blame to come on me'.

'In a letter to you, Mrs Hearn wrote "I am going out if I can". I suggest you said that she was that woman that people were talking about?'

'I may have said so'.

'Did you tell her that people were talking about you both?'

'I might have said people were talking about the sandwiches and that my wife had died from eating poisoned sandwiches'.

'Had the doctor said that to you?'

'Yes'.

'Might you have said "The blame will come heavier on you than me"?'

'I may have. I cannot remember. It was Mrs Hearn's sandwiches my wife took'.

'Did you say "A detective might be here at any time"?'

'I said someone might come to make enquiries. I may have said detective, I cannot remember'.

'Did you say "Whatever there is they will find out?"'

'Yes'.

'Were you referring to food poisoning?'

'Yes'.

Did Mrs Hearn say "If people think like that I had better go to my own house"?'

'Yes'.

'It is true, then, that she said people were blaming her?'

'I might have said that people were talking about the poison in the sandwiches'.

'Poison, sir. Did you use the word "poison" to her?'

'No'.

He then asked, did Thomas think that Mrs Hearn's letter to him meant 'she was meaning to take her own life if she could screw her courage to the sticking point, is that how you read it?'

'Yes'.

'Then when Mrs Hearn wrote "I cannot forget that awful man and the things that he said" did you know she meant Parsons?"'

'Yes'.

'Did he say "Is it that woman, Mrs Hearn"? Did you know that had been said about her?'

'I knew Mr Parsons had said things. I did not know exactly what he had said'.

Birkett then asked about the words 'I am innocent – innocent' in Mrs Hearn's letter and whether these were underlined. Thomas agreed that this was the case and Birkett asked again if Thomas knew that people were talking about the sandwiches and he agreed this was so. He then asked:

'Do you think that letter was of a distraught woman, of a woman very upset and very grieved?'

'I took it that she was upset'.

Birkett cited the letter again:

'"My conscience is clear and I am not worried about the afterwards". You knew she was referring to the great hereafter?'

'Yes'.

'That money she owed you was lent in 1928?'

'Yes'.

'How came it that after the funeral you asked for an acknowledgement of that money and never before?'

'Mrs Hearn had offered to give me an acknowledgement before'.

'Why did you not take it?'

'I did not worry about it'.

'Why did you mention it immediately after the funeral?'

'I did not know what my arrangements would be. Everything was upside down, and I thought I should have an acknowledgement'.[20]

Birkett was, a journalist noted:

> 'tall and gaunt, and covers his most piercing questions with a disarming smile. For the most part his style is almost conversational, but occasionally there was eloquence in his tone and words… also there is suggestion of steel in his tongue. Now and then he thrust aside his grey wig, revealing the burnished auburn of his hair and always he used his hands and fingers expressively. He has a habit of repeating the last few words of his witness' reply'.[21]

Birkett ascertained that Mrs Hearn had agreed to repay Thomas the £38 once she opened her house to lodgers, but she had been unable to do this as her sister had been so ill. Birkett then asked:

> 'How came it that it was at this moment after your wife's funeral that you suggested she should give you an acknowledgement of the money when she had offered it before and you had not bothered about it?'

> 'I think I went on very well going on nearly two years without any acknowledgement'.

The judge intervened to tell Thomas that Birkett was not blaming him for this, but just wanted to know why he had chosen that moment. He replied:

> 'No particular reason, except the loss of my wife has made a lot of difference to me. I did not know if I could keep on the farm. It is only reasonable if a man lends money for him to have an acknowledgement'.

> 'What advantage would it be to you to have an acknowledgement which had never been refused before and which had been offered before? Is that the best explanation you can give?'

> 'I think I have given a good explanation'.

'Between October 18, the day of your visit to Bude, and the 29th, when your mother-in-law came, you took up a morning cup of tea which you had made yourself, to your wife?'

'Yes'.

'Did you give medicine to your wife in that period?'

'I don't remember giving her any medicine. I gave her brandy and tea'.

'Between the 18th and 29th were you really your wife's nurse?'

'I did everything I could for my wife'.

'What did you do with the letter from Mrs Hearn?'

'I gave it to the police the same day that I received it'.

'You have been asked if Mrs Hearn wears glasses many times'.

'Yes I have'.

Du Parcq re-examined the witness.

'You say you do not remember giving any medicine to your wife, but you may have done?'

'Yes'.

'Who else took medicine to your wife?'

'Mrs Hearn'.

'When were you first told that arsenic was administered to your wife?'

'When Superintendent Pill came to my place about November 14'.

'Did you know anything about poison having been administered?'

'I thought that my wife had been suffering from ptomaine poisoning'.
The judge then asked a very definite question to Thomas:

'Did you, from first to last, ever yourself, give your wife any arsenic?'

'No sir, never in my whole life'.

'Are you sure?'

'I have never had arsenic in my possession except sheep dip and tablets
which are things any farmer might have'.

Thomas then stood down. The examination had lasted three hours; the cross-
examination another hour and a half. A journalist wrote:

'He was a good witness. Wearing a navy blue suit and a black tie, his face
still bearing traces of his bereavement and anxieties, he stood quietly in the
witness box, answering questions briefly but clearly in a strong firm voice,
which was seldom raised above conversational level. The rich Cornish
accent which he speaks contrasts sharply with the perfect English of Mr
Norman Birkett'.[22]

Mrs Parsons was the next witness and described her time at Trenhorne Farm,
nursing and cooking for her daughter, and of her being taken to hospital. She
agreed she took tea to her daughter in the morning. Birkett asked another question.

'On November 2 did you not put in the milk and sugar in the kitchen while
Mrs Hearn poured out the tea?'

'No, I never helped Mrs Hearn that day?'

Mrs Parsons said lunch on that day was eaten in the kitchen and that she brought up her daughter's herself into the dining room; Mrs Thomas ate half and the rest was put in the oven. Birkett then asked:

'Mr Thomas a little later took that food into the dining room, saying that he would try to persuade his wife to eat?'

'Yes, and when he came back the plate was empty and he said "I have made her eat".'

After dinner, Mrs Thomas had a sweet taste in her mouth and was given a lemon drink which Mrs Parsons had prepared. She was then sick for the first time since Mrs Parsons had been there.[23]

Mrs Elizabeth Hick Thomas was the next witness. She recalled staying with her son for the month up to 18 October. Then Mrs Thomas junior was quite well. She then spoke of a conversation she had heard with Mr Parsons, who had said 'Tis that woman'. On 10 November she talked with Mrs Hearn who had referred to Mr Parsons as 'that horrid man'. Mrs Hearn asked if she could go to Trenhorne House and have a look around and she agreed and then waited for Mrs Hearn to reappear, but she never did.[24] Birkett asked:

'Was Mrs Hearn very upset by Mr Parsons's words "Tis that woman"?'

'Yes, I was talking to her in the kitchen and I spoke of life's troubles and worries. Mrs Hearn said "I do not think life is worth living". She seemed very quiet.'

Next to speak was Ivy Willshire who spoke of serving the Thomases at Bude on 18 October, saying she could not recall chocolate cake being eaten and that the sandwiches were served on paper and it was all taken away when they left. Leslie Wilson, the farm worker at Trenhorne Farm, recalled Mrs Hearn taking food up to Mrs Thomas when she was ill.[25]

Mrs Wadge recalled her visit on 29 October and that when she was there Mrs Thomas was unwell and was upstairs. She did not see Mrs Thomas, but had found Thomas and Mrs Hearn in the kitchen. She did not remember saying to Mrs Hearn that she would like to see Mrs Thomas very much. Birkett asked: 'You may have done so?' Mrs Wadge remained quiet and had to be prompted by the judge for an answer and eventually she said, 'I don't think so'.

Dr Saunders talked of attending Mrs Thomas's illness and on 29 October trying to persuade her to go to hospital. He thought it was a food poisoning case and Mrs Thomas was mentally agitated, was weak and tingling in her limbs. On 3 November, when he saw her again, she was far worse; delirious, lacking in reflexes and could hardly move her legs. Du Parcq asked:

'Did you then form any different view of her illness?'

'It was then that I thought she was suffering from arsenical poisoning and decided to send for another doctor'.
Birkett then cross-examined Saunders:

'From October 18 to November 3 you were satisfied that this was a case of ptomaine poisoning?'

'Yes, in my own opinion'.

Dr Saunders agreed that there was an improvement in some of Mrs Thomas's symptoms. She was much better on 29 October and on the next day the gastric symptoms had entirely cleared up. This improvement was maintained on the next two days, but on 3 November she was mentally agitated and her limbs were weak, perhaps due to confinement in bed. The court then adjourned until the next day.[26]

Mrs Hearn, with her accompanying women, to whom she chatted, slipped in and out of court almost unnoticed. She sat quietly and motionless, her eyes flitting between lawyer and witness. Again, she made pencil notes throughout.[27] She later wrote:

'I listened to every word of the evidence. I tried to place myself in the position of the jurors. What would I be feeling if – without my own knowledge of all the circumstances, and the knowledge of my innocence, I was called upon to sit in judgement?'[28]

On Wednesday 17 June the case resumed, with Birkett cross-examining Dr Saunders, who had attended Mrs Thomas up to her removal to Plymouth Hospital on 3 November. Birkett 'revealed a remarkable knowledge of arsenical and ptomaine poisoning, their symptoms and their effects'. The barrister had a treatise which he cited from but mostly he did not use it. Saunders thought Mrs Thomas's physical and mental states were entirely disconnected. She was a mix of cheerfulness and apprehensiveness. The judge then addressed him

'You first became suspicious it might be arsenical poisoning on October 27 or 29?'

'That was a very fleeting suspicion – so fleeting as to be fantastic'.

'You had never seen a case of acute arsenical poisoning before?'

'That is so'.

'On November 3 neuritis suggested arsenical poisoning?'

'Yes'.

'About her mental condition. What sort of things did she say to you? What made that condition manifest?'

'She did not say very much, and I could never get very much from her. She was not sleeping well. She told me that at the beginning'.

'I wish I could get you to help us to envisage her condition'.

'She appeared to be very agitated and worried. I asked her practically every day if there was anything that worried her and she said there was not'.

'But in a way that did not convince you?'

'Yes, I still thought she was worried'.

'That continued the same?'

'Yes, except on 29th, when her mother arrived. Then she was better'.

Dr Lister was called. He recalled seeing Mrs Thomas at 1 am on 4 November, the day of her death. Birkett then asked a question, as he had with Dr Saunders, to underline their lack of experience and thus to undermine the value of their evidence.

'You had not much experience of arsenical poisoning?'

'Not acute arsenic poisoning, but I have seen chronic cases'.

'You said before the magistrates at Launceston did you not, that you had little experience of arsenical poisoning?'

'Yes'.

'If you had not had the conclusions of Dr Wordley and the analyst, might you have come to a different conclusion yourself?'

'I came to my conclusion before then'.

'And their conclusions confirmed your view?'

'Yes'.

Dr Lister agreed that anything affecting the nervous system would also affect the muscles, and was asked if food poisoning also affected the nerves; he replied:

'Botulism affects some part of the nervous system'.

'But food poisoning generally does affect the nervous system?'

'I have never heard of neuritis following every case of food poisoning'.

One of the most common forms of peripheral neuritis was caused by alcoholism. The nervous system becomes disorganised due to alcoholism. There were several types of peripheral neuritis; bacterial, metallic, organic and metabolic. Arsenic poisoning was the latter. Birkett asked:

'There is the bacterial form. That is the important one for me in this case. There are many medical schools of thought which recognise that form equally with the other three?'

'There are definitely bacterial causes. Diphtheria is the commonest. Then you get a certain number of cases in which there is no obvious cause'.

'Suppose a person is suffering from food poisoning and cannot sleep from day to day and week to week, you would get a condition of reduced vitality which might produce peripheral neuritis?'

'I have never heard of such a thing'.

'I am speaking hypothetically. Are you agreed that you can find peripheral neuritis arising from a reduced condition caused by the reasons I have indicated?'

'Not in a week or two'.

The judge intervened to ask whether the peripheral neuritis in this case was medium or grave and the doctor said that it was very severe. Answering a question from Birkett, the witness said that arsenic had been taken at the onset of her illness. Birkett then asked:

'The question is whether she had any subsequently. What do you say to that?'

'At first I thought she must have had, or she would not have got worse after improving for a time'.

'The change after the history of the case had been indicated to you suggested that the only explanation in your mind was that arsenic had been taken shortly before death?'

'I do not think I had better give an opinion on that'.

'You had the view that it needs some explanation to account for the relapse when you were called in as compared with the history of the case?'

'I thought she must have had some more'.

'It was that you need some explanation to account for the change from the progress to the relapse that you thought arsenic must have been taken to account for it?'

'A second dose, yes'.

'You say a second dose; I put it this way: Arsenic according to your evidence, must have been taken to account for the fact of the relapse, whatever the original cause?'

'I thought arsenic was the cause of the original illness, and some more had been taken to account for the relapse'.
The judge then asked for clarification:

'If there were no original dose, you must take it that something else must have caused the relapse. Your evidence is based on the fact that there must have been an original dose?'

'Yes my Lord'.

Birkett returned to the questioning.

'Dr Saunders had been treating the patient for food poisoning. That is certainly a possibility, is it not, that there had been an original illness of food poisoning, which was progressing and that there was arsenic to account for the relapse?'

'No. I would put it this way: There had been at the onset vomiting and diarrhoea, which are by far the most commonly caused by food poisoning. But that common diagnosis had to be revised as the illness progressed'.

Lister said he diagnosed arsenic before Mrs Thomas was dead and the judge asked if he still believed that there had been a second dose of arsenic. He said that he had thought so at first but on hearing other evidence he was now convinced that there must have been. The judge then asked:

'What it comes to is this: I gather you to say you are not sure about the matter now having regard to other circumstances which would account for everything without a second dose?'

'My present view is that it is more likely she had a second dose'.

Wordley was the next witness and he said that there was no evidence by testing of food poisoning. Birkett then asked:

'You would not exclude the possibility that you might have food poisoning, though the tests were negative?'

'Yes, by one test, but when one bears in mind the combination of tests – there were 13 in all and they were all negative – it is another matter'.

'Assuming food poisoning on October 18 and a post mortem on November 4 the process of time is material, is it not?'

Yes, it is important'.

'You have given your view that death was due to arsenical poisoning. At this stage is it your view that arsenic was taken into the body at a late date before the post mortem examination?'

'Whatever arsenic was given, some arsenic was given, in my opinion, within a relatively short period of death'.

The judge then asked:

'What do you mean by over a short time?'

'I should say about four or five days before death'.

Birkett returned to his questions:

'You gave evidence at the inquest. Did you not say that the symptoms of food poisoning would be exactly the same till paralysis of the limbs set in, and it is just a possibility that after the ordinary food poisoning arsenical poisoning occurred on the Sunday previous to death?'

'Yes, I said that before any full analysis was known. I knew only the contents of the liver'.

Wordley added that at the early stages of the inquest there was no evidence of arsenic, but at the post mortem it was found. Arsenic might have been taken on the Sunday.

'I am not seeking to make you say that there was no arsenic on October 18. What I suggest is this: that when you made that answer you made it on this fact: the symptoms of food poisoning and arsenical poisoning are up to a point the same?'

'Yes'.

'When there was a violent change on November 3 – it may be – I do not say it was a fact, but we cannot exclude the possibility that it was food poisoning up to that point and after then arsenical poisoning?'

'No. There may have been an acute condition of arsenical poisoning on the Sunday, but you have left out the statement I have made about the arsenical poisoning setting in when the paralysis of the limbs began'.

Wordley said that he did not think that death came only from the poisoning on 18 October, because there was too much arsenic in the liver to account for just one dose. Du Parcq then asked:

'Have you ever thought it consistent with the facts of the case that no arsenic was administered at all until the Sunday before death?'

'No, that would not be consistent with the facts'.

Tickle then stated that there were 0.85 grains of arsenic in Mrs Thomas's organs. It could have been there long before death and was consistent with the arsenic found in Cooper's worm tablets. Dr Clayton discussed the tins of salmon and pointed out that the legal maximum amount of arsenic was a hundredth of a grain per pound. Birkett recalled the Lochmaree botulism case which had resulted from a tin of salmon (in 1922 eight people had died from this at the Scottish hotel in question) and asked if Clayton recalled this. He did.

'That was a very serious case of food poisoning?'

'Yes'.

The judge stated:

'It was so serious that all the persons who ate the paste were affected to the extent that they died?'

'Yes'.

Du Parcq intervened to ask:

'With the advance of science is it now usually possible to isolate bacillus?'

'Yes, except in very rare cases'.

Percy Parsons was the next witness and spoke of his conversation with Mrs Hearn just after the funeral. He concluded by stating that an investigation would then be needed. Du Parcq began his examination:

'Did Mrs Hearn say anything?'

'No. She did not make any reply that I know of'.

Birkett then intervened.

'Were you invited to the funeral?'

'No'.

'Had you ever been in the house before or since?'

'No'.

'Or speaking terms?'

'With my sister, yes'.

'Were you on speaking terms with Mr Thomas?'

'I suppose we were not. There was a disturbance years ago and we never spoke'.

'Have you been harbouring resentment all these years?'

'No'.

'Is it a fact that you have not spoken to him for years?'

'I have given him the time of day'.

'You did not speak on the day of the funeral?'

'Yes, we shook hands then'.

'Do you know when you first heard about the sandwiches?'

'No'.

'Did you ask Mrs Hearn who made the sandwiches?'

'I asked Mrs Thomas'.

'When you asked whether the sandwiches were made at the farm, did Mrs Hearn say "I made them"?'

'No. I asked Mrs Thomas if she helped my sister and Mrs Thomas said "Certainly not. Mrs Hearn made the sandwiches and brought them with her"'.

'You are answering now a little emphatically. Did you raise your voice and talk like that on the day of the funeral?'

'I may have'.

'When you said "this is important, looks serious, and has to be seen to" did you raise your voice and use a threatening manner?'

'I cannot say. I may have'.

'Did you say "It is that woman" or anything like that?'

'No'.

'If Mrs Thomas says you did, is she mistaken?'

'Yes'.

'Have you seen the letter in which Mrs Hearn wrote "I cannot forget that horrid man and the things he said"? You know the horrid man was you?'

'Yes.'

'You had spoken to her bitterly that day, had you not?'

'No'.

'Did you say "This is serious and has to be seen to"?'

'That I did say'.

'Do you think you were horrid that day?'

'No'.

'Did you say at the inquest "I knew my sister and her husband did not get on together from the first"?'

'Yes'.

'Did you also say "I put down the fact that they were not happy because on one occasion I saw them not getting on well together"?'

'I did say that'.

'Did you say also "A relation of mine died some years ago and there was some money to be shared by my branch of the family?"'

'Yes'.

'Did you say "There was some friction between members of my family about this including a member living in the same district as Mr and Mrs Thomas"?'

'Yes'.

'How many years was it before you had spoken to Mr Thomas?'

'I could not say'.

'About 10 years?'

'It might have been'.

Du Parcq then re-examined Parsons.

'Had you seen some incident between Mr Thomas and his wife 10 years ago?'

'Yes'.

'Was it a quarrel?'

'Yes'.

Thomas was then recalled to state that his wife's life was not insured and he gained just over £100 from her death.

Pill gave evidence of the arrest of Mrs Hearn and the statement she gave him. Birkett cross-examined him, ascertaining that a tin of weed-killer bought in 1926 was found and that Mrs Hearn had been eager to help the investigation and was cool when making her statement. He then asked:

'You thought it right to ask her a special question about the food prepared at the farm on the Sunday before Mrs Thomas died?'

'Yes'.

'That is the explanation of the fact that she said in her statement that she cooked some mutton, but did not carve it or have anything to do with the gravy?'

'Yes'.

Trebilcock was next to speak and he recalled that initially Mrs Hearn called herself Mrs Dennis and said to him in a low voice, 'Mr Thomas used to come to our house every day with a paper. Of course that was only a blind'. Birkett cross-examined him.

'Have you ever found a sentence of yours not properly caught by the hearer?'

'Yes, at times'.

'Your voice is not too clear. It is possible to make a mistake about what you said?'

'I thought I had spoke very plainly'.

'But this statement of Mrs Hearn's. Do you not think it was a misunderstanding of what she said?'

'I made no mistake about that.'

'Well, listen to this "Mr Thomas used to bring a paper. He was very kind". "Mr Thomas used to bring a paper. It was only a blind". Don't you think you could have made a mistake?'

'No'.

'Do you suggest in this serious case that while your superintendent was taking the statement down, Mrs Hearn turned and whispered confidentially to you the statement you have told us?'

'That is what I am telling you.'

'Was that the only thing she uttered in a low voice?'

'I don't remember anything more'.

'I suggest Mrs Hearn never said anything of the kind about it being a blind?'

'I say she did'.

Given the numerous visits of Thomas to Trenhorne Farm, as previously noted, it is possible that he used the giving of gifts as excuses to visit so often, though he did not do so the majority of times he went there. If Mrs Hearn made the comment that she did it is not contrary to the known facts.

The judge announced that he did not think the case would finish that week and that the effect of the weekend on the jury might be a problem. The jury then adjourned until the next day.[29]

Mrs Hearn, who had arrived just before the judge, followed the evidence attentively. Just after lunch she had an animated talk with Mr Foot. When Parsons spoke, she 'leaned forward and turned slightly to the right, keeping her gaze fixed unwaveringly on the witness throughout the whole time he was testifying'.[30]

The trial resumed the next day, Thursday 18 June. Mrs Hearn followed the examinations closely and when she saw her sister she nodded and smiled. She was also seen passing a note to Birkett. Sometimes she leaned forward to whisper to him.[31]

Claud Matthews, director of Shuker and Reed, said that they had sold Mrs Hearn a half pound tin of salmon on 3 September, but she was not a regular purchaser of such tins. Edward Roberts, bank cashier at Launceston, experienced in handwriting, was called upon to say whether Mrs Hearn's signature on the statement she gave to the police was genuine. To do so he was shown other known samples of her handwriting and in light of them he thought that it was genuine. 'I believe it is my lord' was his final comment when questioned by the judge. Birkett did not cross-examine either witness.[32]

Mrs Spear was the next witness and she explained about the living arrangements and that the sisters once left the house for 12 months. She was asked about the garden in particular. Du Parcq asked:

'Let me ask you this. At any time when Mrs Hearn was living in the house, do you remember any conversation with her about weeds in the garden?'

'No sir, not particularly'.

'Did she ever say anything to you about weed-killer in the garden at any time?'

'No'.

'Did you ever see her using weed-killer?'

No'.

'Did you ever see any sign of weed-killer being used?'

'No sir, but I didn't go out into the back garden very often.'

Du Parcq then moved on to Miss Everard's illness.

'When did you first hear from Mrs Hearn that her sister was ill?'

'She was always in a delicate state of health'.

'When did she get worse, do you know?'

'12 months last January'.

'Used to visit often?'

'Not very often'.

'Do you remember being asked to go in?'

'Yes sir'.

'When was that?'

'I can't remember the date, but I should say it was April or May 1930'.

'Did you have a conversation with her about the state of her health?'

'She didn't say much about the state of her health'.

'Was Mrs Hearn in the room?'

'Yes'.

'What did Miss Everard say to you?'

'I don't remember anything in particular. I read a chapter of the Bible and said a prayer'.

'Was there any occasion, or were there any occasions, when Miss Everard said anything to you in Mrs Hearn's presence about her condition?'

'Mrs Hearn came one day to me in May between five and six o'clock'.

'Tell me what she said'.

'Mrs Hearn said that her sister was worse and she asked me to come in and I went in and Miss Everard seemed very much worse. Miss Everard said she thought she had too strong a dose of medicine, which was going into her hands and legs and numbing them'.

'Did Mrs Hearn say what the medicine was?'

'She said it was an emergency medicine to be given to Miss Everard when she was in pain and "I gave her a full dose".'

'You didn't see the medicine, I suppose?'

'No'.

There was some discussion between Birkett and Du Parcq as to whether the witness's testimony in June to Miss Everard's symptoms should be allowed, but it was decided it was relevant, so Du Parcq asked:

'What did you hear her complaining of at the time you were there?'

'She complained of sickness'.

'What kind of sickness?'

'Vomiting'.

'And was that a frequent complaint she made?'

'Yes, but sometimes she said she felt better'.

'Apart from vomiting, did she complain of anything else?'

'She seemed to suffer a good deal of pain in her legs and shoulders'.

'Besides the pain in her legs, had she any other complaint about her legs?'

'She said she could not move them except when her sister moved them'.

'Towards the end, towards her death, did you notice a change yourself in her condition?'

'Yes, the last two or three days'.

'How did that occur?'

'In weakness. She could not move'.

'Was she in pain the last few days?'

'Yes'.

'What sort of pain?'

'Pain all over the body, and weakness'.

There was then discussion as to visitors in the house; one Mr Roberts, a lodger in January (not mentioned in the diary), then Mrs Poskitt for a month soon afterwards. Thomas was said (erroneously) to have occasionally visited as did a few enquirers. Mrs Hearn did all the cooking and nursing. Du Parcq then turned to Mrs Thomas's illness later in the year. Mrs Spear asked after her three times but only saw her once, on the last Sunday.

'Did she tell you anything about how she was feeling?'

'She was feeling better'.

'Did she make any complaints?'

'She said she was having sickness, once a day in the morning'.

'Did you hear anything about any other symptoms?'

'She had no strength in her legs, they were numb'.

When asked if she had spoken to Mrs Hearn in these weeks, she answered: 'She came in and said she did not want any milk, but said Mrs Thomas was ill, suffering from food poisoning'. After Mrs Thomas's death, Mrs Spear said 'She said she couldn't stay down any longer. Everyone seemed to think that all tinned food was poison'.

Birkett cross-examined Mrs Spear about the fact that Miss Everard's health was poor before she arrived at Lewannick and the witness accepted that this was correct. He then asked about the prayers that were said.

'When you say the three of you joined in you mean that they said the response "Amen"?'

'Yes'.

'And as far as you know they both welcomed your coming?'

'Yes'.

'So far as you can judge from start to finish in all that she did Mrs Hearn gave you the impression of being very devoted to her sister?'

'Yes'.

'In her solicitation, her sympathy for her sister, did she seem genuinely aggrieved at the illness of Minnie?'

'Yes'.

'The garden was not always so wild?'

'Not so bad'.

'It was always a weedy place?'

'Yes'.

'You have seen Mrs Hearn weeding the garden and keeping it in order?'

'Yes, working in the garden'.

'After Minnie became ill, Mrs Hearn didn't have much time for gardening, lodgers or anything else, had she?'

'No'.

'And, of course, it was quite possible, was it not, that she may have used weed-killer in the garden at that time or shortly afterwards, and you did not know about it?'

'That is quite possible, yes'.

He then turned to the question of Miss Everard's illness.

'But it was Mrs Hearn who wanted the doctor to come, and he came quickly?'

'Yes'.

There were then a number of questions aimed at showing that Miss Everard was unwell, suffering from anaemia and hysteria.

'There were times when she was hysterical, were there not?'

'I do not know'.

'Perhaps I will use the words "a bit excited"?'

'She was on occasions, as on the night she thought the medicine was too strong'.

'Would it be right to say "rather hysterical that night"?'

'Well I would not say hysterical, but she was frightened by the medicine'.

'Now about these complaints you gave evidence about. You never saw her vomiting?'

'No'.

'And of course, the complaints that you told us about, the pains in the legs and shoulders. Do you know whether she had a touch of rheumatism at all?'

'She considered it neuritis, I think'.

'She had been suffering from that for a very long time, had she not?'

'Yes'.

'If Mr Thomas came every day with papers, you would not know? And Mr Roberts, did you know how long he had been there?'

'Since about November 1929 I should think'.

There were then questions about Mrs Thomas' sickness and Mrs Hearn's exchanges with Thomas after his wife's death. Du Parcq intervened:

'Have you told us everything that was said on that day when Mrs Hearn was there? Did she say anything about being put out by the medicine?'

'Yes'.

'In the presence of Mrs Hearn?'

'Yes, she was in the room all the time'.

The judge intervened.

'What did she say?'

'She said she would not take any more of the medicine. It seemed to do more harm than good. The medicine seemed to be going into her hands and legs. She seemed to be losing the use of her hands and legs'.

'When you said she was frightened of being poisoned by the medicine, were they the words she used or is that what you thought as a result of what she said?'

'I do not think she used those words, but she seemed frightened, to me'.

The evidence of the diary would have been useful here, to show that Minnie did indeed think she was being poisoned on one occasion, as well as showing the symptoms of being killed by arsenic. Yet this evidence was not available and so the defence enjoyed an easier ride.

The next witness was Mrs Poskitt. It was established that she had not seen her sisters for some years but was with them from 17 February–17 March 1930. Mrs Hearn recalled that Mrs Poskitt was her only living sister and that 'she was an unwilling witness for the prosecution'. Although they lived miles apart they had a close bond.[33] Mrs Hearn later wrote:

'Only once [during the trial] did I feel unhappy. That was when my sister Bessie was called to give evidence for the prosecution. Like myself she has had a hard and difficult struggle in life, and we have always been devoted to each other. It was a terrible moment, therefore, when her name was called, and she entered the court.

She passed behind me so close that I could have touched her. I could see her trembling fingers as she lifted the Bible to take the oath. It was for her that I felt unhappy, knowing full well that she would rather have died before being called upon to give evidence.

And I would rather have died than have her called. That much at least I would have spared her had it been possible, but the law is cruel as well as just, and I know it could not be helped.

But what was worse was the fact that until she had given evidence she was not permitted to see me at all.

I am not complaining, for I quite realise that these things have to be, but it was a great hardship, knowing that she was simply longing to see me as I was longing to see her, that the days of the trial would drag on without our being able to so much to say "How are you?" to each other.'[34]

Mrs Poskitt was asked:

'When you went to stay, was your sister Everard in good health?'

'Sometimes better and sometimes much worse'.

'She was suffering from gastric stomach trouble, which had plagued her for 30 years'.

'At the time you were staying with them, was she able to be up and about?'

'Some of the times, other times she was in bed'.

'During the time you were there, who was doing the cooking in the house?'

'My sister and Mrs Hearn'.

'When your sister, Miss Everard, was in bed, who nursed her?'

'We both did'.

'And Mrs Hearn, did she give her any food?'

'Yes'.

'What sort of food was she taking in bed?'

'Very little'.

'During the time you were there, how much time did she spend in bed?'

'There were two or three times, perhaps a few days each time'.

He then discussed the letters that were reproduced in Chapter 3. Part of one letter, written after her visit to Trenhorne, had been cut off.

'You don't remember cutting off any part of this?'

'No sir, I don't'.

'This is the condition in which it was when you passed it to the police authorities?'

'Yes'.

'Did you cut the rest of the letter off?'

'No, sir'.

'When you received this letter, it was complete, was it?'

'As far as I know it was'.

A journalist noted:

'she gave her evidence with a voice strongly marked by a north country accent, the broad vowels contrasting with the burred Cornish consonants in which much of the evidence has been given. Once she had to be asked, as with other witnesses, to raise her voice. Mr Birkett suggested to her that her evidence was very important and immediately her voice became audible throughout the court'.[35]

After Mrs Poskitt had given her evidence, there was questioning of those present at the exhumation. Birkett wished to establish whether, on that windy, snowy day, any foreign bodies had contaminated the corpse. Neither the carpenter, the policeman nor the analyst who had been present thought that this was the case, and when Birkett asked the latter 'Was there any foreign matter in it, soil, earth or wet?', Dr Wordley answered with an emphatic 'No'.[36]

Birkett then asked: 'Am I right in saying that a piece of soil, so small that you could hold it between your fingers, dropped on to the body would make every single calculation wrong?'

'Yes,' came the answer, which was a pretty damning reply, apparently destroying the case for Miss Everard being a murder victim. However, according to a late twentieth-century pathologist, Dr Patrick Toseland, Birkett's statement 'is quite untenable'. He added, though, that for Birkett to get away with this was an indication of how the prosecution and its experts had failed to prepare.[37]

Friday 19 June was day five of the trial. Dr Clayton was cross-examined by Birkett throughout the day. The latter wanted to show that Mrs Thomas might have died of food poisoning, not arsenic, and if that were the case, his client should be acquitted.

'You have heard that food poisoning might be caused by the bacteria being present in a living state?'

'Yes, that is food poisoning by infection'.

'It might be caused by the toxins in this bacteria?'

'Yes'.

'Sterilisation of food by heat might kill the bacteria but not the toxins?'

'Yes'.

'So that a tin of salmon which had been infected and subsequently sterilised were examined bacteriologically, you might find no bacteria, but food poisoning from the toxin might occur?'

'Yes, on the examination of the salmon itself'.

'Do you know the salmonella group?'

'Yes'.

'And the toxins of that group are very numerous?'

'Yes'.

'And are invariably associated with tinned foods?'

'Yes, and other foods'.

Du Parcq intervened to ask:

'And in such cases are you able to say whether the experience has been that where there are toxins some people suffer and others do not?'

'In my reading of it there are several such cases'.

Dr Wordley was recalled and there was discussion as to whether Miss Everard died of a gastric ulcer. He stated that she may have had one shortly before her death.[38]

Dr Lynch was the next witness called. Bowker wrote of him, 'The name of Dr Roche Lynch is one to conjure with in the realms of analysis. Like that of Sir Bernard Spilsbury in pathological matters'.[39] Lynch explained that after a large dose of arsenic was administered, the victim would suffer vomiting and diarrhoea, dying 30 hours later. However, recovery sometimes happened and sometimes poisoning resulted in the victim going into a coma and dying 12 hours later. This was rare, however.[40] Dr Lynch then said:

'Then we have the possibility of a person after an acute attack getting better, and receiving a second dose, as a result of which death is delayed by a period of days and possibly weeks. It is an acute attack followed by sub-acute attacks.

Peripheral neuritis follows an arsenic ingestion. First symptoms follow within a week and it is often fully established in four to five days. Or it might not appear for weeks after the first dose. Feet tingling and disordered sensations in the feet are the first symptoms. These are followed by paralytic symptoms and the loss of the ability to walk. Inflammations of the facial organs may also be felt. There might also be rashes. Small doses might not lead to these symptoms, however'.[41]

Du Parcq then began to re-examine his witness on specifics:

'Will you now tell us what is the general medicinal dose?'

'One thirtieth of a grain is the general medicinal dose'.

Roche intervened:

'What is the maximum medicinal dose?'

'Eight hundredths of a grain or roughly one tenth of a grain'.

Du Parcq returned to his role:

'What is a fatal dose?'

'The recognised possible fatal dose is two grains. Up to four grains may be required to kill. A recovery has taken place with much larger doses'.

'With the absence of acute symptoms, what would be the dose?'

'I think it would be up to half a grain or less. After that you should get acute symptoms'.[42]

Du Parcq then said that there was another form of arsenic poisoning when the acute symptoms wore off and others took their place: sleeplessness, restlessness and worry. Skin rashes and peripheral neuritis appeared and the patient died in a coma. He then asked the doctor for his opinion on the death of Mrs Thomas and Lynch replied:

'On the data in the case I have formed the opinion that she died from heart failure resulting from arsenical poisoning'.

'Do you wish to qualify that in any way?'

'No. I am satisfied that she died from arsenical poisoning'.[43]

Could the doctor say when the main doses of arsenic were administered? According to him it was quite consistent to have taken it in sandwiches eaten at Bude on 18 October.

'Do you think that was the only dose?'

'No, I think there was another dose or doses'.

Du Parcq asked how much arsenic would have been in the sandwiches.

'I am making a very rough guess, but I think she received about 10 grains of arsenic. That would mean 14.3 grains of weed-killer'.

'Is it possible to administer that quantity in a sandwich?'

'Yes'.

'What about the taste of it? Would it be perceptible?'

'White arsenic is practically tasteless'.[44]

Du Parcq then moved onto Mr Tickle's analysis, in which less than a grain had been found in the body. This overlooked the fact that muscle tissue had not been analysed. Du Parcq tasked Lynch with this:

'The finding of the quantity of arsenic in the body amounting to 0.85 grain, compared to the fact that the muscle tissue was not analysed, suggests. Does it not suggest a conclusion to your mind?'

'If the muscle tissue had been analysed, one would have said with certainty the quantity of arsenic would have been well over a grain. These facts, of course, confirm that death was due to arsenical poisoning'.

'Now can you have any conclusions on the whole of the facts as to what other dose or doses may have been administered?'

'First of all, if Mrs Thomas had only received one dose on 18 October, I should not have expected to find that comparatively large quantity of arsenic in the liver. There was nearly seven tenths of a grain. I should have expected to have found approximately one tenth of a grain. The liver in a sense acts as the first line of defence and absorbs as much of the arsenic from the blood as it can to prevent other tissues like the brain being affected'.

The judge asked if the liver in turn gets rid of the arsenic and Lynch agreed.[45] Du Parcq continued his examination.

'If you find as much as two thirds of a grain in the liver, you expect that the dose has been more recently taken?'

'Yes. From October 18 to November 3 is about 17 days, and I would expect to find only a very small amount – a tenth of a grain – if there was only one dose on the 18th'.

'Can you say whether a dose was given in the last few days?'

'In my opinion a dose was not given in the last few days'.

'Can you be more accurate than that?'

'I should say within the last three or four days. That, of course, is a very general estimate. I say so because in the last stage of Mrs Thomas' life I understand there was no diarrhoea, and therefore her bowels were moving naturally and food and other substances were passing through in the ordinary natural way. If a dose had been taken by mouth in that period, one would expect to have found a larger quantity in the intestines'.

'When you formed that opinion, did you know any of the circumstances of the household? Did you know Mrs Parsons had taken charge of the household?'

'No. The only fact I knew was that Mrs Thomas had vomited on the Sunday afternoon'.

The judge then intervened:

'You know it has been said that Dr Wordley found a good deal of liquid in the stomach and if that, like the muscle tissue, had been sent for analysis, it might have contained some signs of arsenic, was administered within a few days of death?'

'The first thing I have noticed is that the contents of the stomach was a black offensive liquid. Therefore it is not stomach contents in the true sense of the word, which is usually taken to mean food'.

Birkett then wanted to put his oar in, saying: 'In view of the matter in hand, is it not dangerous that he should speculate on the subject?' The judge replied: 'He will speculate on matters fast enough when you are cross-examining him'. Birkett then said: 'If your lordship is anxious to assist me, I will sit down at once'. The judge said 'I think it will help everybody, not only your side, but perhaps we had better leave it alone. Mr Birkett can ask about it if he likes'.

Lynch declared that giving a dose of arsenic between two and four days before death and if that was the only dose of arsenic, then it would not be detected in the hair or if it was, only in the smallest of traces.

Du Parcq then asked if the symptoms were consistent with ptomaine or food poisoning and Lynch replied:

'They are not'.

'Will you state your reasons?'

'The whole history of the case, the evidence of various witnesses, but above all, the evidence of the analysis'.

'You heard Mr Thomas say that he felt a little funny inside after his tea. Do you attach any importance to that?'

'I do not attach any importance to it. I think if this were a case of ptomaine poisoning that the symptoms in the case of Mrs Thomas were very severe, but there should have been at least some symptoms if he had eaten an infected sandwich'.

'Would it be possible for the symptoms of Mrs Thomas to be produced by quite a small dose of arsenic?'

'That is a very a hard question to answer, but on the whole, I should say not'.

'Does peripheral neuritis ever follow ptomaine poisoning?'

'I have never known it in my experience, and I have never heard of it in my studies'.[46]

Lynch then described the results of his analysis of Mrs Thomas's organs. There was arsenic in each one. The total was 0.776 grams, he said, and the judge asked him to confirm that that was about three quarters of a grain, which he did. He had examined the organs for other poisons but all he had found was a trace of copper in the liver and that was always to be expected there.

Du Parcq asked him to explain about the level of arsenic:

'Small though your figures may be, are they larger than one would expect to find in a case of person who has not died of arsenical poisoning?'

'Oh yes'.

Justice Roche asked if they were much larger and Lynch replied:

'I regard arsenic as practically always being found in the body and the figure you get is something like 0.01 per 1,000,000'.

'Can you give any idea as to the arsenical content of the normal human body?'

'I have never worked it out, but it is probably a 100 million times less'.[47]

Lynch then went on to explain the analysis he had made of Miss Everard's hair. He had found arsenic there to be 10 parts per million and that was a large quantity indeed. A normal person would expect to have 1.6 parts per million. Judging from a lock of the deceased's hair, arsenic had been administered for the last seven months of her life. Frequency and amount increased towards the end, he suggested. Her nails had 40 parts per million in them and this was exceptionally high. Soil from the top and bottom of the coffin had been tested for arsenic and proved positive, but it was insoluble and so would not have entered the coffin in water except for a very small amount.[48] He stated:

'I am, therefore, in a position to say that arsenic was being administered during the last seven months of Miss Everard's life and further I suggest that towards the end the doses of arsenic increased in frequency, or amount or both'.

A journalist noted:

'Dr Roche Lynch is able to explain the most difficult technical experiment in simple everyday terms, and make his remarks interesting. Under cross-examination, he is clear and deliberate, occasionally fingering his horn-rimmed glasses while pondering a reply'.[49]

The court adjourned for lunch and afterwards Lynch stated that the medicines prescribed by doctors Galbraith and Gibson would only have contained minute portions of arsenic. Birkett, with Smith by his side, then began his cross-examination with a question he had asked of earlier medical witnesses in order to undermine their evidence. 'Throughout the afternoon, the duel of words continued, the attention of everyone in court being held despite the technical language'. He began:

'Have you ever examined a living person suffering from arsenical poisoning?'

'No'.

Smith later noted: 'In fact, of course, this did not make it any less valid; but Lynch's admission made an unfavourable impression on the jury, who were mostly practical men'.[50] Lynch continued to add that he had never examined a corpse which was in a coffin in ground that was impregnated with arsenic at such a high level as in that churchyard, which was far higher in proportion to that found in the body samples analysed. Birkett was keen to press home his apparent advantage:

'With soil so heavily impregnated as the soil of Lewannick churchyard, if that impregnation is at all widespread in Cornwall is there some chance of arsenic being found in drinking water?'

'Traces, I have no doubt'.

'In people who have been drinking the water in Cornwall for a long time, you would expect to find some arsenic?'

'Minute quantities of the amount of which I have been speaking'.

'Do you know the precise chemical form in which arsenic is present in the soil of Cornwall?'

'No'.

'Is it not a most remarkable feature of the case that in the soil above the coffin you should have twice the arsenical content that you have in the soil below it?'

Dr Lynch said that it could have been because the stones which were insoluble to acid had been removed and this accounted for the difference. Birkett continued:

'How do you account for the marked change in the condition of Mrs Thomas on November 3?'

'The symptoms had been slowly getting worse and had come to a climax on that date'.

'I put it to you that in November 3 there was a sudden change for the worse, something totally different to what the doctor had seen before?'

'That is not how I read the evidence'.

'When do you think the last dose of arsenic was taken?'

'I think arsenic was taken into the body somewhere about October 30. I do not think it would be later than that'.

'Do you not think the symptoms in the case point to an administration on November 2?'

'No the symptoms point to a much earlier date'.

'I mean, excluding October 28, after that date there was the taking of one or two doses in the last three or four days before death. On that point I suggest that the symptoms point to November 2, and not an earlier date, because of the progressive improvement?'

'I do not agree that the symptoms would help you at all'.

Dr Lynch agreed that there were some similarities between food poisoning and arsenic poisoning, but said that there were important differences and these were noticeable in this case.

'Excluding arsenical poisoning for a moment, from your mind, the symptoms exhibited might for the most part have been due to food poisoning?'

'Yes'

'If you had had no post-mortem, the symptoms could have been attributed to food poisoning?'

'Not peripheral neuritis, or in my opinion, the mental agitation'.[51]

Birkett also attempted to show that arsenic could not have been in the sandwiches.

'And placed upon the sandwich it depends very much on how the sandwich was made and I suggest that it was a moist sandwich carried for hours and it is inevitable that that sandwich is discoloured and blue?'

'I have not tried it and my expressed opinion for what it is worth is that it would not'.

Smith later commented:

'The celebrated analyst little knew how easily Birkett could have proved his opinion worthless. His rather pompous opinion escaped deflation only because Birkett wanted to having to avoid calling me as a witness if he could'.[52]

Birkett continued:

'Upon the theory that is put here by the Prosecution, that such a sandwich had been prepared, according to your evidence in solid form, it would be a terrible risk to run that the sandwich would have been stained?'

'Personally, I do not think so'.[53]

Birkett also cross-examined Dr Lynch on the subject of Miss Everard. He suggested that since she had been prescribed laxatives this was not consistent with her being poisoned, but Dr Lynch disagreed and then Birkett suggested that the corpse's hair, which contained arsenic, might have been contaminated from another source. He then focussed on the nature of the exhumation and how that could well have led to a faulty conclusion on Dr Lynch's part:

'You agree the conditions under which the post-mortem examination was conducted were not as satisfactory as a laboratory?'

'Yes'.

'Was there no one to assist Dr Wordley except inexpert people?'

'Yes, there was the police sergeant'.

'You cannot exclude the possibility of contamination?'

'Some little matter might have got into some of the jars, but that could not have account for the arsenic I found'.

'I make the plain suggestion to you that the possibility cannot be excluded of contamination of the hair and of the organs by diffusion from the surface of Lewannick churchyard?'

'I agree it cannot be absolutely excluded, but it is extremely unlikely'.[54]

Bowker wrote, in regard to the microscopic pieces of dust, 'to the lay mind these questions about specks of dust may seem rather futile and immaterial. But I would remind you that... they are very much to the point'.[55]

Mrs Hearn listened closely to the evidence but leant forward less frequently than previously. Most of the time she sat still, looking ahead. After lunch she had a few words with Foot.[56] She had been impressed with Birkett's cross-examinations and later wrote:

'Only the clever cross examination of Mr Birkett kept me from giving up all hope that the jury would find a single point in my favour.

Death seemed to be sitting by my side I could almost feel his cold breath on my face.

Very soon, however, I began to feel better when Mr Birkett began to bring out some very remarkable points.

Of course, I had not the least idea what these clever lawyers were acting on my behalf and had been doing behind the scenes. They did not tell me a great deal and it came as a big surprise when Dr Lynch said that there was actually arsenic present in the soil at Lewannick churchyard.'[57]

Saturday 22 June was the sixth day of the trial and the case for the prosecution was nearing its end. Dr Lynch showed the judge and jury a Cooper's tablet containing arsenic, one of which the judge managed to drop, but the doctor had others, which he then passed around in an envelope. Du Parcq asked if such worm tablets had been taken in the sandwiches at Bude, what would the result have been, given that they contained copper?

'Copper sulphate is a recognised emetic and begins to produce immediate vomiting... I mean within the first half hour or so'.

'Coming to November 2, would vomiting follow very quickly if given in tablet form?'

'Half an hour'.

Du Parcq reminded him that Mrs Thomas had vomited after eating her Sunday lunch on that day.

'You would expect sickness?'

'Yes'.

'Will you make it quite clear once more, why it is, taking the analysis of the liver and the result of the analysis of the intestines, together you draw the inferences you do as to when the doses of arsenic were given?'

'When a dose of arsenic is taken by the mouth it passes to the stomach and through the intestines. During that time a portion, or all of the arsenic, depending on the dose, is absorbed and goes to the liver. If one finds an appreciable quantity in the liver, and in the intestines, one is able to say that the dose was given a short time before death. If one finds an appreciable quantity in the liver and none in the intestines, one has to antedate the taking of the arsenic, and in this case I put it at three or four days'.

'Suppose poisoning in the case of Mrs Thomas had been due to taking these worm tablets, would there have been any difference as to what was discovered in the analysis?'

'I am certain Dr Tickle would have found copper in the organs above the amount spoken of as normal'.

'Supposing, in order that we may follow every possibility, if one or two of those worm tablets had been given on Sunday afternoon, when the genaspirins were given before Mrs Thomas went to sleep, what would you expect to follow on that?'

'I think after taking them she would vomit'.

'Two tablets would cause vomiting, but would not be a fatal dose?'

'No'.

'First of all, as to the suggestion that Mrs Thomas died of food poisoning?'

'Except for the form known as botulism, very few people die of food poisoning – about 1% of those affected'.

'Taking the whole of the details as you know them, what do you say of the possibility of toxins of the kind producing food poisoning?'

'No living microbe entered the body of Mrs Thomas'.

'Did phosphorus poisoning have anything to do with Mrs Thomas' illness?'

'In my view, no'.

'In the case of Mrs Thomas, leaving out the hair and nails, taking what was found in the organs, is there more than you would find in the case of a body of a person who had not died of arsenical poisoning?'

'Yes'.

The judge clarified: 'Is there much more?' 'Yes my lord, much more,' was the reply. Du Parcq then moved on to the case of Miss Everard.

'Do you mean that each dose itself was not large enough to be a fatal dose?'

'Yes. It would produce vomiting, but was not sufficient to cause looseness of the bowels'.

'If there were intervals between the doses of arsenic, with a person suffering from constant and stubborn constipation, would it be likely or not that there would be constipation?'

'Quite likely. The medium dose of arsenic would not produce diarrhoea – at any rate excessive diarrhoea – and the effect would be that the person was constipated'.

'As to the cause of death, having heard Dr Wordley's evidence as to the post-mortem, have you any doubt in your mind as to the question of whether or not Minnie Everard's death was due to colitis?'

'I am quite convinced it was not due to colitis'.

'That is that arsenic poisoning was the cause of death?'

'Yes'.

Having dismissed the possibility that the arsenic-heavy Cornish soil could have contaminated the corpse, Lynch was then asked about the quantity of arsenic found in her nails and hair. The judge asked:

'Do you mean that there is a hundred times more than in a normal body?'

'Comparing these nails, I would say that there was something like 25 times greater than would be expected in a normal human body'.

There was then discussion about arsenic in the water or in the shroud, thus contaminating the body.

'Would that show itself in any appreciable extent in the normal body?'

'No, or should I say extremely minute traces'.

At 11.40 Dr Lynch left the witness box and Du Parcq announced: 'That is the case for the Crown'.[58]

Mrs Hearn later recalled:

'There was an immediate hum in court and everything seemed to grow electric. The judge looked up from the book in which he had been writing, the clerks at the desk below sprang into activity.

All the barristers looked at Mr Birkett and even the wardresses beside me looked down at him from the dock'.[59]

Smith was critical of the Crown's case on a number of points. Firstly, he thought that the emphasis that they laid on Miss Everard having been poisoned by arsenic was wrong. Birkett agreed with this. During the trial Smith passed Birkett notes from time to time (as had Mrs Hearn), drawing his attention to particular points made by the witnesses, and Birkett was not slow to take advantage of these.[60]

Devlin, though, was confident in his and Du Parcq's efforts, later writing 'The case for the prosecution seemed unassailable'.[61] It would have been more so had the evidence from the diary have been allowed as testimony in court, as it had been in the lower court, but this was not permitted.

Chapter 9

Case for the defence, summing up and verdict

It was now the turn of the defence to present their case. Their task was simply to convince the jury that the Crown's case was flawed and to bring out every doubt that could be shown in favour of the defendant and that undermined the prosecution's case. Birkett, in his cross-examination of Crown witnesses, had, he hoped, weakened the Crown's case by pointing out flaws in their evidence.

In the case of a murder trial, the defending barrister has to decide whether to call the defendant as a witness. This has the danger that when the witness is subject to a hostile cross-examination by the prosecution, it may well prove disastrous if the witness is unintelligent and likely to come across badly in the witness box. On the other hand, they may prove very helpful to their own case, as they are literally fighting for their lives.

Furthermore, the defence had the assistance of Smith, who had no doubt that Mrs Thomas was killed by arsenic. However, 'How and when the poison was administered was quite another matter. It seemed to me highly improbable there was in any [arsenic] in the sandwiches she had eaten in the café on October 18'. He thought the evidence of murder in Miss Everard's case was 'even less conclusive' and that the symptoms of arsenic poisoning, such as diarrhoea, were absent (though this was not true).[1]

When Smith had been told of the prosecution's case, he thought:

'This seemed to me unlikely, because all weed-killers containing arsenic are coloured with a purple dye. Surely if this amount of weed-killer was put inside a moist sandwich the bread would seem to be badly stained.

This, at least, is something that could be taken out of the region of doubt. After the first day of the trial when the prosecution made its lines on the sandwiches clear, I put it to the test. I mixed 14.3 grains of the same weed-killer with tinned salmon of the same brand which Mrs Hearn had used and prepared the same sandwiches.

Within half an hour they were stained bluish purple.

It was ridiculous to imagine that anyone would have touched them with a barge pole, let alone have eaten them'.[2]

Meanwhile, in the court room, Mrs Hearn later recalled the scene:

'I wondered what was going to happen because I was still in a dream.

Then everybody seemed to be craning their necks to look at me. Some of them actually stood up to examine my features.

Yet I still did not know why.

I was still in a daze.

It had been kept from me until that very moment that I was to go into the witness box and tell my own story. I suppose Mr Birkett knew I would worry about it if I was told earlier. This was a great act of kindness on his part.

I did not hear my name called. All I knew was that there was still a hum of voices in the court, and that the wardress was touching me on the arm. I seemed to sense that she was trying to convey to me that I was to rise and follow her.

Someone held open the door to the dock. My legs seemed numb after sitting so long. I just stumbled across the floor.

As I walked the few steps to the box, although I could not or did not see them, I sensed that people were straining their necks to get a better view of me.

I suppose they made me repeat the oath but do not remember'.[3]

Birkett decided that it was worth persuading Mrs Hearn to stand as a witness. She recalled:

'Then Mr Birkett asked me a question.

But I could not speak a word. My vocal cords refused to function.

I could hear Mr Birkett's questions quite distinctly, and I knew the answers.

My chief fear was that if I did not reply, people would feel that I was fencing for time and trying to frame in my mind what it would be best to say.

That made me bring all my willpower to bear and at last I managed to speak.

Mr Birkett made it as easy for me as he could'.[4]

Annie went through a number of questions about her family history and in particular about her sick sister. Curiously she said that she had been deserted by her husband after marriage in 1919 and could not tell how old she was. Birkett asked:

'I want to ask you at the outset of this case two very important questions before I go to any details whatever. Have you at any time or in any form given arsenic to Mrs Thomas?'

'No sir'.

'Have you at any time or in any form ever given arsenic to your dead sister Minnie?'

'No sir'.

The family history has already been recounted, though it was invariably selective (no mention of the previous court case for theft in 1920, or of anyone other than her sister dying after her nursing them). Birkett then brought the questioning around to January 1930, when Miss Everard began to be more ill than she had been previously.

'You called in the doctors in January 1930, and they have told us what they saw?'

'Yes'.

'And the visits of the doctors followed through March, April and May and right up to her death?'

Yes'.

'As far as constipation was concerned, was there ever a time when Minnie did not suffer from it?'

At this point Mrs Hearn was given a drink of water and replied 'I don't think so'.

'With regard to the pains in the hands and feet, did they vary at times?'

'Oh yes, the pains seemed to depend on the strength of resistance she had'.

'Do you remember in May Mrs Spear coming to see you and a talk about medicines?'

'Yes'.

'You have also heard Dr Galbraith say that on May 8 or 9 there was a talk also about medicine?'

'Yes. Minnie said "I feel as if I have been poisoned and that the medicine is too strong for me". I said "Oh Minnie" or something in reply and the doctor told her to take half doses'.

'Did you ever give to Minnie any medicine in any form or tea or anything else with arsenic in it?'

'I never did'.

'Did you ever give any medicine or anything other than what the doctor ordered and sent?'

'No'.

'Do you remember if that was the same day that Minnie complained of her medicine?'

'Yes. I gave her a full dose of what the doctor had sent. She said it burnt her and it appeared to me to be too strong for her. I was very anxious and asked Mrs Spear if she would come in. She did, and I asked her to send for the doctor. She told her daughter to telephone Dr Galbraith'.

Birkett then turned to the case of Mrs Thomas.

'Had you become friendly with Mr and Mrs Thomas?'

'Yes'.

'Were they very good friends?'

'Very good friends'.

'And from start to finish did they show you considerable kindness?'

'Yes'.

'On this day, the 18th, what time was it that Mr Thomas came to you and first mentioned to you their intention of going to Bude?'

'It was about noon'.

'Did you know anything about it before October 18?'

'No'.

'And we have the evidence of Mr Thomas that Mrs Thomas wanted you to go and you made the answer you would?'

'Yes'.

'Was anything said about the time you would go?'

'I think Mr Thomas said be all ready about two o'clock'.

'Did he say he would do anything to let you know he was ready?'

'He said he would blow the horn when he passed'.

'Did he then go away?'

'Yes'.

'And was the hour of starting off about three?'

'About that'.

'Now, did you take any food with you?'

'Yes'.

'What food did you take?'

'I took a few sandwiches and some cake'.

'What kind of sandwiches?'

'They were made with some salmon. I had opened the tin of salmon for my dinner and I used some of the same tin to make the sandwiches'.
The judge then asked:

'You mean you had partaken of some?'

'Yes I had eaten some'.

'It was stated in evidence that this was a tin of salmon you had had from Shuker and Reed's. Is that so?'

'Yes'.

'Were you in the habit of buying tins of salmon?'

'Yes. Not very much'.

'Where did you buy them?'

'One from Shuker and Reed's, but I had two or three before from the local shop in Congdon Shop.'

'What is the shopkeeper's name?'

'Mrs Disberry'.

'This was the only one from Shuker and Reed's?'

'Yes'.

'And you made sandwiches from the salmon?'

'Yes'.

'And did you see Mr Thomas in the box giving an indication of the size of the sandwiches?'

'Yes, that was about right'.

'And how many were there? He told us, I think, there were six?'

'Yes, there would be about that'.

'And how were the sandwiches packed or wrapped?'

'I put them into a napkin, but I am not certain whether I put a grease proof paper or not'.

'And the chocolate cake?'

'That was placed in a serviette'.

'Have you ever taken food on trips before?'

'Yes'.

'Why did you take food with you at all on that day?'

'I thought it was very possible, most probable that the Thomases would take food, too'.

'Did you know when you were invited to go to Bude, whether you would be getting tea?'

'I thought we might have stopped on the road on the way back'.

'When you got to Bude, at about what time was that?'

'I suppose it would be about four'.

'Mrs Thomas senior had been dropped at Hele Farm?'

'Yes'.[5]

'What happened at Bude?'

'Mr Thomas went somewhere, I don't know where'.

'What did you do with Mrs Thomas when Mr Thomas was away?'

'We walked along down some sand dunes'.

'Did you say anything about the food you brought?'

'Yes'.

'What did you say about the food?'

'I said "I have brought a few sandwiches. Would you like one?" or "Would you care for one?" I am not sure.'

'Can you say whether one of you took the sandwiches?'

'Mrs Thomas took one, I took one and Mr Thomas took one'.

'Did anyone else have one of the sandwiches?'

'I had one. I cannot be sure whether anyone else. Mrs Thomas had a piece of cake'.

'And when tea was over, do you remember now whether any of the food which you had brought was left over?'

'There was cake left over, and I feel, one sandwich'.

Mrs Hearn did not remember that Mrs Thomas complained of a 'sweety taste' at Bude, but answered questions about her being ill on the way back. She dealt with enquiries about cooking and nursing at Trenhorne Farm and about Mrs Thomas's illness. She answered questions about various visitors to the house. The judge suggested that Birkett ask about the weed-killer.

'Mrs Hearn, as regard to the weed-killer ordered in 1926 from Shuker and Reed, was that the only weed-killer that has been in your house at Trenhorne?'

'No'.

'What was there in addition?'

'There was a little in a tin'.

'Was that before or after you got the pound tin?'

'It was in the house, on the premises, when we got there'.

'Was that used in any way?'

'It was used on the garden... The chief part of the garden was at the back'.

'And then there was the tin ordered in 1926?'

Yes'.

'Was any of it used?'

'Yes'.

'How came it in July 1926 that you ordered a new tin?'

'It was really at my aunt's suggestion'.

'And was some of that used?'

'Yes'.

'And where was that used on the garden?'

'The chief part was on the garden at the back'.

'Did you use it all?'

'Yes'.

They then moved on to what happened after the funeral and Mrs Hearn's subsequent intention to commit suicide, her journey to Looe and then to Torquay and the interview at the police station. Birkett asked:

'And when you saw Superintendent Pill on January 13, did you make the statement that was read out in court and is that statement true?'

'Yes'.

'And I conclude by asking this general question: Sergeant Trebilcock in this case said you said to him these words, "That Mr Thomas used to come to our house every morning with the newspaper, but this was only a blind". Did you ever use such words?'

'I never used such language at all with Sergeant Trebilcock'.

'Is there any shadow of truth in it?'

'Not the least'.

'You were very fond of your sister?'

'Very fond of her'.

'Have you given many years of your life to nursing your sister?'

'I was very happy doing so. She would have done the same for me'.

'With regard to Mrs Thomas, was she always a friend to you?'

'Ever since I have known her'.

'And in her illness did you do everything you could for her?'

'Yes'.

After an hour and three quarters, that was the end of the examination. Then came the less friendly cross-examination by Du Parcq, which began with a discussion of Mrs Hearn's so-called marriage.

'Can you tell of anybody who ever saw your husband?'

'Yes, my sister and my aunt'. [Both being dead, neither could confirm or deny this statement.]

'Anybody else?'

'I don't quite know what you mean. Other people did see him, but I cannot point to anyone who is about just now'.

'Did you have a marriage certificate?'

'I had a paper with names on'.

'I mean the marriage lines? The official record?'

'I have not got it now'.

'Did you ever have one?'

'Yes, at the time'.

Mrs Hearn added that she only briefly lived with her husband, who died six days after the marriage. He was a medical student (this ran contrary to her previous story of his being a doctor) called Leonard Wilmot Hearn.

'Did he leave you or did you leave him?'

'We parted'.

'Did you ever really have a husband?'

'Yes, I did'.

She also said that she was married in a registry office in London, not a church as per her original story. This questioning may have shown that Mrs Hearn was a woman capable of telling lies, but it was not perhaps wholly germane to the main point at hand. However, it is arguable that Du Parcq could have rammed home the fact that Mrs Hearn was a proven liar more forcefully and thus cast a doubt on whatever else she had to say. Mrs Hearn realised the effect the exchange might have had too, and later recalled, 'I felt that in these few questions he had done me a great deal of harm in the eyes of the jury'.[6]

They then moved on to Mrs Thomas and Du Parcq asked:

'Now tell me this. When did you first hear that arsenic was the cause of Mrs Thomas' death?'

'I don't think I heard of arsenic until I read about it in the paper'.

'And when you did realise that she had died from poison not taken accidentally you were very much surprised?'

'Yes'.

'How many times do you think you used weed-killer in the garden?'

'Not many times'.

'Did you use the whole at once?'

'No'.

'If your sister did get arsenic into her body from food that she ate in the ordinary course, it must have been the food which was prepared by you, must it?'

'It must have, unless it was food that did not need any preparation, such as apples'.

'It has never entered your mind as a possibility in this case that your sister would have wilfully taken arsenic?'

'No'.

'And you would not think, would you, that in any of the food that you prepared at any time that weed-killer or arsenic could have accidentally got in?'

'No'.

'At any time before you went to Harrogate did you take in lodgers?'

'Not before'.

'And after you came back, you had lodgers sometimes?'

'Yes'.

'Did you find it was suggested that your sister's illness made it very difficult to take lodgers?'

'Yes, it did make it difficult'.

Du Parcq then asked about the state of the sisters' finances and about Miss Everard's illnesses and the symptoms. He then turned to the question of Mrs Thomas.

'If you had put a little of that weed-killer into the sandwich, you would have a great deal to be afraid of'.

'Oh yes; a very great deal'.

'Let me put it to you quite plainly Mrs Hearn, that it is a fact you put some weed-killer into that sandwich?'

'It is not a fact, it is not a fact'.

'And that you made up your mind not to commit suicide at all, but to run away?'

'No, I did not. Suicide was more preferable to me at the time'.

Du Parcq then went on to suggest that the motive might have concerned Thomas, but Birkett objected to this line of questioning. The judge intervened: 'I do not understand Mr Du Parcq to be suggesting that there was anything between Mr Thomas and Mrs Hearn implicating Mr Thomas'.

'I felt the difficulty that somebody might think that I was making such a suggestion, and I have tried to frame my questions so that there would not be such a suggestion'.

'I do not know that Mr Du Parcq would object, or that any harm would be done, if I inferred the motive. It is that this woman had conceived to marry Mr Thomas if he were free, and was under the impression that Mr Thomas was not unwilling'.

Birkett said:

'I am obliged to know that. But why should my friend not have stated it at the opening of this case?'

'In my judgement he has conducted this case rightly in that respect. I wish you to understand, of course, that I am expressing no view'.

'I make no complaint about my learned friend, but I should have been glad to know that this was the suggestion so that I could deal with it'.
Du Parcq then asked the defendant:

'Did it occur to you at any time that if at any time Mrs Thomas died Mr Thomas might have made a match with you?'

'No, never'.

Birkett then re-examined the witness:

'Mrs Hearn until twenty minutes past four on the sixth day of the trial has anyone in the world suggested that you wanted to marry Mr Thomas?'

'No'.

'Was there at any time in your mind the thought that you might marry Mr Thomas?'

'Never'.

'I want you to understand that it is now suggested you killed Mrs Thomas in order to do that. Is there a word of truth in that?'

'Not an atom'.

The court was then adjourned for that day. [7]

Devlin did not think that the case for the prosecution had proceeded as well as it might have. The prosecution had not got the answers it wanted as to how the arsenic got into the victims. 'This was not the sort of brutal cross-examination that Mr du Parcq knew how to do effectively', he concluded.[8]

Instead of returning Mrs Hearn to the police station in Bodmin, she was taken back to Exeter Prison that evening. This was so she could take more exercise than was possible in a necessarily cramped police station, but also so she could attend church in Exeter.[9]

In his memoirs, Dr Smith commented about this stage of the trial, 'Annie Hearn gave evidence in a clear, firm voice and never faltered under cross-examination'. Likewise, Devlin wrote 'Her manner was perfect. She would have been a marvellous witness if she had had anything to say'. He added that she was 'always entirely composed'.[10] Bowker added 'She was a very fine witness… She carried conviction in every word… Never once did she falter in an answer, and never once was her evidence upset'.[11]

Smith then stated:

'Now Birkett had to decide whether to call me or not. If he did he could reveal the test we made with the weed-killer and sandwiches. He could ask me to give the court my opinion on when Mrs Thomas received the last lethal dose of arsenic. He could show that, because arsenic poisoning is rare in England but commonplace in Egypt, my experience in this matter was vastly greater than that of Lynch and all the other Crown medical witnesses put together. But he would lose the right to address the jury after the Crown Counsel's final speech.

He decided not to call me. I think his decision was correct. He had obtained all the information the defence needed from cross-examination of the Crown witnesses, and having the last word before the summing up was a considerable advantage. Especially in the hands of Birkett'.[12]

Bowker added, 'Mr Birkett was satisfied with the admissions he had been able to obtain from the experts of the Crown, and equally satisfied with the evidence of Mrs Hearn'.[13]

Birkett and Smith conferred on the Sunday prior to the closing speeches and discussed the scientific details. Birkett, a former devout Methodist, then stated that the Cornish people were very religious and therefore he would emphasise the loving care that Mrs Hearn took over his ailing sister and compare this with her allegedly being a fiendish poisoner. He would cite the Bible in this. Then West arrived and told them that when the jury had been given a choice of a trip to the seaside or a church service they chose the former, so he decided against this.[14]

Mrs Hearn recalled her day in court:

'The questions came with machine-like rapidity. I could not see what some of them were leading to. Others were so obvious. My body was becoming numb, but still my brain was alert. I thought it was terrible. How hopeless I was, even with the truth…

For four hours I had been in that witness box, answering questions and I felt more dead than alive. How I crossed that floor and got back to the dock I cannot tell you. The Judge was talking to the jury. I could dimly gather that he was telling them that counsel would speak on Monday and that the case would finish on Tuesday.

That will be a long time I thought.

The wardress touched me on the arm. I rose up. No, I must still fight, must bring my willpower to bear. But, oh, how awful it seemed. Even the walls seemed closing in on me – to crush me.

It had been decided to take me back to Exeter Prison for the weekend. This cheered me just a little. They had been very sympathetic to me there during my long wait for the trial. Perhaps they would cheer me up. That weekend in Exeter gaol was the worst part of my whole experience.[15]

That weekend seemed as if it would never come to an end. Talk about been in the rack. If I had been a guilty woman they could not have punished me more. Not even by hanging me. I felt that weekend dragging more than the five months I spent waiting for trial'.[16]

There was no hearing on Sunday 21 June, of course, so it was on Monday 22 June that the case for the Crown was summed up. Mrs Hearn later recalled:

'Now I was back in the dock. The Judge is on the bench and the jury in their places. I glance at their faces.

They look tired, bowed down by the weight of their duty.

The usher stills the court and Mr Du Parcq is now on his feet, "Members of the jury" he began.

I have very little hope!

I don't think any other woman has had to stand what I stood in the last stages of my trial.

All the time there were scenes which no one who was guilty could have sat through without breaking down.

The first came very early in the day.

Mr Du Parcq was speaking, and slowly and surely, I thought, winding the rope around my neck'.[17]

The question to begin with, Du Parcq argued, was whether Mrs Thomas had died from arsenic or not. He agreed that the symptoms of arsenic and food poisoning were similar, but the doctors in looking back on the case were far more certain. In this case the symptoms: sickness, tingling in the feet and legs, and then the deprivation of all power in the limbs, were consistent with arsenic poisoning. Some of the stages were of peripheral neuritis, which was associated with the latter stages of arsenic poisoning. Gastric poisoning was cleared up and replaced by peripheral neuritis and sickness.[18]

Doctors Saunders and Lister had suspected that Mrs Thomas had arsenic poisoning on 3 November. Then the post-mortem revealed that there was arsenic in the body, not minute amounts but considerable amounts compared to the quantities found in the Cornish water or in fish. Du Parcq then began to deal with how arsenic was introduced into Mrs Thomas when it was noticed that he began to seem pale, and he fought against it, then collapsed into his chair.[19]

Birkett and Devlin helped him to leave the court and took him into the ante-chamber, where he fainted. Before the adjournment, Du Parcq had told the jury:

'Can there be any doubt as to what caused Mrs Thomas' death? The doctors may be wrong – you must judge – but Dr Roche Lynch, who gave his evidence fairly, carefully and with proper appreciation of the gravity of his task, tells you that it is a matter about which he feels no doubt with all those materials before him. No doctor, no scientist, nobody qualified to speak has been called to give evidence that he is prepared to tell you that he can be any doubt. The defence has not put anybody into the witness box qualified to judge and say he is willing to swear that among these findings and figures there can be any doubt about the cause of death.[20]

The suggestion has been made that the cause of her death might have been food poisoning. If there had been food poisoning at that tea on 18 October the onset of the symptoms would have been less rapid than they were. The symptoms of peripheral neuritis would never have appeared at all. Do you think that nobody else would have suffered from food poisoning at the same time? There was something said about poison about toxins without bacteria being discovered. Dr Roche Lynch's answer was that you would not expect toxins, although they might have produced an illness to produce a fatal result. If you take this illness as a whole, it is perfectly plain that the symptoms were the symptoms of arsenical poisoning and not food poisoning'.[21]

There was then a dramatic break in the proceedings as Du Parcq collapsed, so Dr Roche Lynch and Dr Norman Guy Hawtry Salmon (1885–1956) of Bodmin attended to the sick man. Smith recalled taking Du Parcq to the judge's chambers and putting him to bed. Smith did his best to calm Du Parcq and had a doctor see him. On recovering consciousness and despite advice to rest, Du Parcq insisted he return to the court and did so at about 3pm. Later journalists tried to ask Smith about Du Parcq, but he refused to discuss his illness and he was eventually able to resume his speech, after having apologised to the court and thanked those who had helped him. The judge said that he had once had a similar experience, 'And yet, I am still here and am older than Mr Du Parcq'. This unfortunate interruption cannot have made his job any easier. He proceeded:

> 'If you consider that these sandwiches were prepared by Mrs Hearn, you have to consider how the arsenic got into them. You have an answer from Mrs Hearn herself, because she does not suggest in any way that there is an accident or mistake. There was no arsenic in the rest of the salmon, so I think it is proved beyond doubt that if it were in the sandwiches, it was put into the sandwiches. You are forced to follow the line of reasoning that it was arsenic that killed Mrs Thomas, and that the arsenic was deliberately introduced'.

The jury had before them every person who had been in the house during the time that Mrs Thomas had been unwell. Could they doubt that it was more than suspicion but certainty that Mrs Hearn was to blame? As to Thomas, he could be entirely cleared. The only one to speak against him was his brother-in-law, Percy Parsons, who said that the Thomases had argued ten years before.

Du Parcq then brought forward the evidence of Mrs Hearn's letter. Roche intervened to show the letter to both the jury and to Birkett, for he believed it could be interpreted in two ways. The line 'When I am gone' had been revised to substitute 'dead' with 'gone'. There were other deliberate alterations. Du Parcq suggested that the letter meant 'One of us is guilty, and when I am out of the way they will think I am, and you will be cleared'. Put yourself in the position of a man against whom there is no suggestion that he has compromised himself with Mrs Hearn. If he should show that letter to anyone, there would be plenty of suspicious minds and slanderous tongues. People would say "Yes, she had to kill herself, poor thing, so that he could clear himself"'.[22]

> 'Might it not be that at the stage, when she knew that Mr Thomas had no affection for her, she decided to disappear and then pass as dead? Then when she wrote the letter, people would think Mr Thomas was involved in it, and say, "Then so much the worse for him". Yet Thomas sent the letter to the police. Would a guilty man have done that?'[23]

The question of the motive then arose. Du Parcq cited the conversation that Mrs Hearn had had with Pill and Trebilock's evidence:

> '"Mr Thomas used to come every day with the papers, but that of course was only a blind". It was also suggested that she said, "Mr Thomas has been very kind". Mrs Hearn denied she had said these things. Yet if she had done, then the idea that she had was that Thomas was paying attention to her and if so, and he became a widower, she could become the second Mrs Thomas. This might seem to be an inadequate motive for murder, but motive did exist. In the case of Miss Everard, Mrs Hearn had ample opportunity to kill her. Dr Gibson declared that he could not have sent her any medicine without recording it. He suggested that Mrs Hearn was an incorrigible liar and that she had killed Mrs Thomas and Miss Everard.'[24]

According to a journalist:

> 'Carefully, with chosen words and sentences, the Crown counsel reviewed the whole of the evidence, occasionally bringing his hand down sharply on the table to stress a point. In perfect silence throughout the court, his voice rose and fell as he spoke of the dramatic happenings "in this peaceful village community". Occasionally he rested his chin upon his palm. Sometimes as he referred to Mrs Hearn, he looked towards the pale, small figure in the dock'.[25]

Mrs Hearn recalled:

> 'when all the evidence had been given, and the counsel in both sides were making their speeches – I tried to listen as though it did not concern me. I endeavoured to put myself in the place of the jurors as Mr Du. Parcq pieced together all the evidence which I had given'.[26]

It was now the turn of the defence to answer these charges. Mrs Hearn recalled her anxiety at this stage:

> 'His [Du Parcq's] speech had been terrible for me. I did not see how Mr Birkett could ever destroy the effect of his elocution.

When he stopped I felt limp.

Mr Norman Birkett rose at once, and, as he went on, I gradually began to feel a little hope.

Like Mr Du Parcq, he dealt with every point in the case, but with a difference.

I could see that his speech was having a big effect on the jury. Cornishmen like a gifted speaker. They just drank in the eloquence. Even yet I can see them resting their hands on the ledge of the jury box. They listened to every word. Even the Judge seemed to be impressed at the tall figure with the deep chiselled face and the alert eyes towered above the court his rich voice ringing'.[27]

Birkett spoke for four hours from 12.20pm in order to sow seeds of doubt in the jury's minds as to the prosecution's case. He began by submitting to the jury that the Crown had failed to present an adequate case against the defendant and so they should deliver a verdict of not guilty. Mrs Hearn was only being charged on one indictment and therefore anything pertaining to anything else should be discounted.[28]

Birkett began:

'Members of the jury, I am unfeignedly thankful that the moment has at last come when for the first time I can address you on behalf of the defence... I shall have some very severe comments to make to you about the case presented'.[29]

He continued:

'At twenty past one, for the first time in the case, the Crown on Saturday suggested that there might be a motive – a motive, I suggest, fanciful and fantastic – that Mrs Hearn had conceived some kind of idea that if Mrs Thomas were not there, Mr Thomas would marry her. She was poor, and therefore, she killed her. With the exception, which was made by Sergeant

Trebilcock, there is not a breath or hint of any such motive. That ascription of motive was made after every witness of the Crown had left the box. Mr Thomas was never once asked whether by word or gesture or in any other way whether Mrs Hearn had shown that she was fond of him'.[30]

Birkett stressed the lack of motive and that on the day of the expedition to Bude it was not Mrs Hearn who suggested it. That being so, it was surely a huge coincidence that a tin of salmon that had been poisoned was ready to hand, after the arsenic had been bought four years ago. Coincidences, chances and rare possibilities were the foundation of the Crown's case, argued Birkett. There was no evidence of any arsenic bought in the past four years, but he pointed out that Thomas had a tin of arsenic. This contained copper and that was not an ingredient of the weed-killer. 'And in the organs of Mrs Thomas there was found copper', Birkett added, though he did not mention that this occurs naturally.[31]

Birkett challenged Dr Lynch's conclusion that it was arsenic which killed Mrs Thomas. He had never dealt with an arsenic poisoning case before [not true; he had done so in the Croydon arsenic poisoning case in the previous year] and yet he was so emphatic on this instance. Surely the expert should stick to his metier? Birkett suggested that there were five possibilities as to the cause of Mrs Thomas' death. These were, food poisoning on 18 October and arsenic poisoning on 2 November, secondly, arsenical poisoning on both days, thirdly, arsenical poisoning followed by phosphorus poisoning, fourthly, food poisoning then phosphorus poisoning and lastly, arsenic poisoning on 18 October only.[32] Yet arsenic had been found there in quantities vastly greater than would have been expected ordinarily. There is no evidence of phosphorous poisoning and so this seems like a red herring.[33]

He thought that the first possibility was the most likely. Vomiting, diarrhoea, cramps and dizziness were all symptoms of food poisoning.

Suspicion alone formed the basis of the Crown's case. Birkett said that Mrs Hearn had had weed-killer for four years, so why did she wait to use it in 1930? The idea of blue weed-killer in the sandwiches was nonsense because the blue stains would be obvious to the potential eater. They would see it and not eat them. Then there was no evidence that Mrs Hearn poisoned Mrs Thomas afterwards as there were several other people in the house who could equally have done so; Thomas and Mrs Parsons. The arsenic-laden worm tablets could be cut up and given to Mrs Thomas as pills. Apparently, after her death, Thomas said, 'They are going to send some organs to be analysed. They will find out what it is... They will blame one of us. The blame will lie heavier on you than me. People are saying so. A detective might be here at any time'. Birkett claimed that this was strange language for an allegedly distraught husband to use. He also dismissed the evidential value of Mrs Hearn's letter to Thomas after her disappearance.[34]

Birkett went on to say that Mrs Hearn had said that Mr Parsons was an 'awful man'. Birkett said:

'I say that he was an awful man. He was so awful to say, because he saw Mr and Mrs Thomas having words once, that he knew they did not get on together from the first. That shows the kind of man he can be. If all these things do not put the greatest doubt into your minds, it is beyond the power of men and angels to do it.[35]

It is not for me to say that I have to prove that someone else did it. God forbid that that burden should fall to me, but the Crown must prove beyond all reasonable doubt that Mrs Hearn did it. Have they done so?'

That Mrs Hearn fled was not evidence of guilt, but only of her being in a distracted mind. She was being pathetic and foolish in thinking she could escape being found. As to the sergeant's claim about Mrs Hearn alleging that Thomas saw her under cover of delivering papers, well, he might have been wrong in his recollection.[36]

Returning to the case of Miss Everard, there was no evidence that Mrs Hearn had complained about her task of nursing her sister in her illness. There was arsenic in the body, but that might have come from the earth or water in the churchyard and so contaminated her body, or even from her shroud. Had the Crown not considered this? Mrs Hearn had gone into the witness box and her testimony had not been shaken. The jury must find her Not Guilty because the Crown had not proved its case. After four hours Birkett sat down. The court was then adjourned until 10.15 on the following morning.[37]

Birkett made a final and emotional appeal to the jury:

'For over five months Mrs Hearn has laid in Exeter Goal. When the darkness of the winter has now come to this lovely light of this June day, for her upon the trial for her life, it may be said with truth that she has been walking in the valley of the great shadows. It is your hand and you hand alone which can lead her forth into the light. It is your voice and your voice alone which can speak her the word of deliverance.

My appeal is that you will speak that word, that you will stretch forth the hand for every fact and circumstance in this case so fully discussed by every principle of law goes to the time honoured administration of justice of this land.

I spoke to you about the paramount duty of the Crown being undischarged and unproven beyond all reasonable doubt that she is guilty. Your verdict ought to be, and should be, that she is not guilty. For that verdict I now appeal'.[38]

Mrs Hearn was impressed by this performance:

'His last words were grand. They nearly made me cry. I wanted to stand up and say "Oh, Mr Birkett. Even if they hang me now, you have done more than any man could have done to try and prove my innocence".'[39]

She added:

'But, perhaps, I may be forgiven if I say that I simply hung on the words of Mr Birkett when he came to address the jury. I sat spellbound as I noted every inflection of his voice, and every movement of that long tapering finger which he empathised his points one after the other'.[40]

O'Donnell was also enthusiastic about it, calling it 'one of the most eloquent and analytical closing speeches' and as to his overall performance, 'I have never heard him more deadly in cross examination or more eloquent in his final speech'.[41] Devlin was also impressed and gave a backhanded compliment: 'Mr Birkett's speech was a masterpiece of attractive irrelevance'. He claimed Birkett had only said two things of note; that it was four years since Mrs Hearn bought the arsenic and the death of Mrs Thomas, and that there was no motive.[42]

Another commentator observed:

'Mr Birkett's speech for the defence was a remarkable forensic achievement. Turned sideways to face the jury, his arguments followed one after another with scarcely a pause of hesitation. There were passages full of pathos when his voice fell almost to a whisper; there were moments of drama when that voice was raised to strength and power. Throughout he used his hands in eloquence to aid his speech which must rank high in the pages of legal oratory'.

Birkett finished speaking at 6.45pm. As ever, Mrs Hearn seemed self-possessed, but she was also pale, and sat low with her coat collar turned up. Mostly she gazed straight ahead. When her late sister was mentioned, she bowed her head down to the rail of the dock and the women on either side started forward to grasp her arms. She was given a cup of water after Du Parcq's speech.[43]

To summarise, the defence argued that it was open to doubt whether Miss Everard had been poisoned at all, as arsenic could have found its way into her body by cross-contamination from the soil and water in the churchyard. As to Mrs Thomas, they argued that arsenic could not have been conveyed in the sandwiches as the prosecution claimed, and that there was no motive at all for these killings.

On Tuesday 23 June the judge commenced his summing up of the case. Mrs Hearn remarked later: 'He had not spoken for a few moments when I became dismayed. I thought the sand were running out for me – that everything was gone'.[44]

The judge's role was to summarise the arguments used by both prosecution and defence and to highlight aspects of the evidence that the jury must focus on and ponder in order to reach their verdict. Roche began his four-hour speech by making general observations on the nature of circumstantial evidence; after all, no one had seen the accused add poison to the food eaten by the deceased. They must make their conclusion by focussing on a number of specific points.[45]

The first question to answer was whether Mrs Thomas had died due to arsenic poisoning and if so, was Mrs Hearn responsible? The first question was simpler to answer; if negative then it negated the second. However, it was conclusive that arsenic had been found in the body of the deceased. The defence had raised the objection that the doctors called by the prosecution had no prior knowledge of arsenic poisoning, but then few doctors had. No arsenic had been given after 29 October. Neuritis was diagnosed and this could have been the result of botulism, or food poisoning. The defence had suggested ptomaine poisoning. The jury must decide what they would make of these possibilities.[46]

These were possibilities, stated the judge, but the expert opinion was that that these were not the case. Yet the jury did not have to accept the verdict of the doctors. Expert and medical evidence could be rejected, but only if it could be shown to be demonstrably wrong. Some of the medical evidence produced by prosecution witnesses had not been opposed by the defence and the judge seemed to suggest that the jury should pay heed to it.[47]

'You are not trying Mrs Hearn for the murder of her sister', said the judge. 'The prosecution are not being allowed to bring evidence to show that Mrs Hearn is a bad woman given to poisoning, and that therefore she must have poisoned Mrs Thomas. What they are being allowed to do by the well settled law is to bring evidence to show that Minnie Everard died because poison was administered to, and administered to her, they say, by Mrs Hearn, in order to show that there was no accident or suicide about this case with Mrs Thomas'.[48] He continued:

'People do say "Accidents do not happen twice in a short time in the different spheres in the same small circle of people". They say it is improbable to find two or more cases of a particular kind happening in the same place, and they naturally conclude there is something different from accident. It may be probable that one woman would commit suicide in such a horrible way, but they say it must be vastly improbable that two women would be seized with the same desire to achieve the same end about the same time'.[49]

Then there was the question as to whether the jury believed Mrs Hearn and Dr Gibson about the symptoms of Mrs Thomas. The judge then returned to the question of expert evidence. He told the jury that there was more arsenic in Miss Everard than could be accounted for by natural causes. There was no evidence to support the speculation that the arsenic might have entered her by being in the water at Trenhorne Farm or in the soil in the churchyard. He thought that Dr Lynch was wrong in assuming that it would need as much as a pound of dirt to produce the level of arsenic that was found in the woman.[50]

The defence argued that Mrs Hearn's complete denial that she had administered arsenic was true. The jury, then, had to judge her. This did not mean in a moral sense as to her character, but as to the credibility of the evidence she had given. He reminded them that Mrs Hearn claimed that she had married in 1919 but had only lived with her husband for a week and that she was unaware of whether he was alive or dead. The prosecution had stated that this was a fantasy and that by implication, everything she said was untrue. That she had no marriage certificate and was unsure where she was married was also pointed out as being distinctly odd.[51]

This, in conjunction with her disappearance and presumed suicide, discredited her evidence, argued the prosecution. However, the judge said that it was for the jury to make what they would of this. There were letters written by Mrs Hearn. These seemed to negate the possibility that she had given her sister arsenic. The questions were whether she had poisoned her sister and/or Mrs Thomas.[52]

Roche then put the matter bluntly:

'I do not suppose you have any doubt in your minds, whatever doubts you may have, that the issue is down to two people – Mrs Hearn and Mr Thomas. It lies between them. I do not suppose any other person can occur to you. It is no use beating about the bush or declining to face facts. To my mind it does lie between these two people. Here, as elsewhere, it is for the prosecution to satisfy to you that it was not Mr Thomas. It is not for the defence to satisfy you that it was. Mr Norman Birkett has never undertaken the burden of satisfying you that it was Mr Thomas. If at the end of this case you cannot say which it is, you ought to acquit Mrs Hearn, just as if you were trying Mr Thomas you would have to acquit him.[53]

The Crown says that everything points to Mrs Hearn and points away from Mr Thomas. It is for you to judge after considering the evidence. If you think it was arsenical poisoning on 18 October, then the conclusion must surely be that the only source was the sandwiches [clearly it was not considered that poison could have been in the chocolate cake]. If it were the sandwiches, is it not – I will not say inevitable, because that is a very strong word – but is it not very difficult indeed to come to any other conclusion, than the source and origin of the arsenic was the maker of the sandwiches'.[54]

There was an adjournment for lunch and then the judge resumed his speech. He turned to the defence suggestion that ptomaine poisoning was what had happened. Mrs Hearn had undoubtedly prepared the sandwiches. The question of taste was a crucial one. He could not advise them on this point. He then emphasised another point, 'The sandwiches are the very kernel of the case. If you are not satisfied that the arsenic was put in the sandwiches by Mrs Hearn, then you should acquit her.'[55]

The question of the £38 that Mrs Hearn had been lent by Thomas that was readily admitted was not suggestive of guilty knowledge as this would have been suppressed if there was guilt. The next question was one of motive. This was a matter to which Roche had given much thought and considered that both Thomas or/and Mrs Hearn were guilty.

Mrs Hearn might have killed her sister because they were living in difficult financial circumstances and her death would make it easier for Mrs Hearn to cope, being tired of nursing her sister. Her death would also mean that Mrs Hearn could create an income by taking in lodgers. This seemed a weak motive, but then murders were often committed for inadequate reasons by any rational understanding. It was fantastic, but not impossible. For the motive of killing Mrs Thomas, there was no clear motive and no evidence of any romantic motive.[56]

Roche called the jury's attention to the conversation between Mrs Hearn and Thomas. 'Whatever it is, they will find it out', Thomas had said to Mrs Hearn. This did not seem like talk between two conspirators. The letter written to Thomas by Mrs Hearn after his wife's death could be construed as proof of either innocence or guilt. It certainly suggested that Mrs Hearn thought that Mrs Thomas meant a lot to her husband, so unless it was a mockery it was not evidence of a conspiracy between the two. He dismissed the idea of Thomas's guilt: 'With regard to Mr Thomas, there is no aspersion, and it was not for Mr Birkett to discuss him, but he pointed a finger at Mr Thomas. With regard to him, there was nothing so far as I could see, why Mr Thomas should do this, either for money, greed, passion, love or hatred'. Additionally, 'If they supposed Mr Thomas were the guilty person, what could his motive have been... There may have been some other woman who moved him to passion. You do not know, there is no evidence of it. There is no evidence that Mrs Hearn moved him to passion'. He also dismissed the idea that Thomas and Mrs Hearn were working together. Roche then concluded. If the jury agreed, however reluctantly, with the Crown's case, they must find Mrs Hearn guilty. If they did not, they must acquit her.[57] He finished:

'That is all I have to say about it. The case rests with you.

It is wise in matters like these, which excite a good deal of public interest, to hold your tongues as much as possible, and not discuss the reasons for what you have done. Although you do not actually take the oaths administered to the Grand Jury, you would be well advised to keep silent. Will you please conduct your verdict, and say whether you find Mrs Hearn guilty or not guilty'.[58]

Devlin had mixed feelings about the judge's speech when he later read it (at this stage all the barristers had left the court room and were on their way to London, their work being over). He wrote that it was 'a massive presentation of the case for the prosecution, it could hardly be anything else' and 'a masterly summary of the facts and issues'. However, he thought the discussion concerning Mrs Hearn's marriage was irrelevant, 'the pathetic case of a woman who did not want to be known as a lifelong spinster and who wanted the title of Mrs'.[59] Bowker commented 'The summing up was careful, lucid and fair'.[60]

The jury then left the court room at 3.12 to discuss their verdict. Mrs Hearn later recalled:

'As the jury rose I thought I was a lost woman. Every vestige of hope had gone. My endurance had been stretched to the utmost limit. For the second time I broke down and cried. They had almost to carry me from the dock.

Mr Norman Birkett came in to see me. He spoke in a very kindly voice.

"Don't be downhearted" he said, "No matter how this game goes, we shall not leave it here. We don't know what the verdict will be, but even if it is against you, we shall go on fighting".

I tried to smile, but I felt I could not fight anymore. I was completely exhausted, a physical and mental wreck.

During the rest of the time my mind became more or less a blank. It remained so even when I was brought into the Court.

Altogether I must have waited for over an hour with my life in the balance'.[61] In another statement she recalled:

'Then came the cool dispassionate summing up of the judge. Never shall I forget it. No longer could I listen as an onlooker. It came to me as I sat there that it was I – I who was the central figure in this drama which was being played out.

There was a tense silence in the court as slowly, almost ponderously, this solemn looking man in the bright scarlet robe sifted this piece of evidence and that piece of evidence and explained to the jury just what to do.

I realised all that depended in how the jury were taking what was said, and looked towards them trying to read their thoughts. I wondered what the two women were thinking. Harsh – terribly harsh things had been said about me. Evidence – terrible evidence – had been given. What were they thinking? There was no sign upon their faces as I gazed at them, and I turned back to the judge who was still addressing them.

'Only then did I begin to feel the real strain. I had suffered months of imprisonment. I had gone through long days of the trial. Now – very soon I would know my fate. Still in my heart I felt certain that I should be acquitted – but – who could help that gnawing fear of doubt?'[62]

The jury were absent for only 54 minutes. Since the discussions of these twelve people are inviolable, we cannot know what was said, but to discuss such a complex case and come to so decisive a resolution in just under an hour is fast work indeed. On their return, Mrs Hearn was brought back, fully composed.

The Clerk of the Assizes, John William St Lawrence Leslie (1857–1934), asked the foreman:

'Members of the jury, are you agreed upon your verdict?'

'Yes'.

'Do you find Sarah Ann Hearn guilty or not guilty?'

'We find her not guilty'.

The tension then broke.

O'Donnell later wrote, 'For a moment the black clad figure hesitated, not knowing what to do'.[63] Du Parcq rose to his feet and asked about the second charge, on the murder of Miss Everard. The judge replied that this would not be proceeded with, the prosecution putting up no evidence and so Roche told the jury, 'I direct you to return a verdict of Not Guilty', which they did. Roche then addressed Mrs Hearn, saying 'Sarah Ann Hearn, you are discharged' and so Mrs Hearn was acquitted. The jury were thanked for their time and efforts and assured that they would not need to perform the same duty for ten years at least. Mrs Hearn was helped out of the court room. Roche then addressed the court, 'Good order has been singularly marked in the course of the proceedings. I hope it will continue now both inside and outside the Court'.[64]

When the verdict was read out by the foreman, Mrs Hearn was deathly white. She bowed her head and tears rolled down her face. She was hardly able to walk from the dock and had to be supported by wardresses. Many women stood in a semi–circle outside the court waiting to see her, but police kept them from the doors.[65]

Mrs Hearn recalled the events thus:

'I heard him [the clerk] say Not Guilty and yet the meaning of his words did not penetrate my dulled brain. I still remained inanimate and uncomprehending.

I think the explanation is that I had so steeled myself for the worst that I could not appreciate the freedom these words meant to me.

I have no recollection of how I got out of the dock.

All I can recall is sitting outside in a sort of semi-swoon with the wardresses trying to revive me with smelling salts.

Then I heard the voice of my solicitor.

He said to one of the officers, "Does she realise she is free?"

Although I heard him say this, I was still unconvinced.'[66]

In order to leave quietly, a plan had been arranged by O'Donnell and two colleagues. The sisters changed clothes, red coat and blue hat for her brown coat. Mrs Hearn was then driven away in a fast car. Mrs Hearn was initially unable to speak for emotion and had a reunion with her sister, the latter saying 'Thank God it is over and time to forget'. Mrs Poskitt said, 'I have prayed for Annie every day, night and morning. I have believed in her all through. I have always been quite convinced that she could not have done such a dreadful thing'. Mrs Hearn told her solicitor, 'I knew they would find me innocent. I want to go away and forget everything'. West and Mrs Poskitt then left in a car and were cheered by the crowds, pursued by journalists.[67]

George Munro, special correspondent for *The Western Mail*, described the scene in detail:

'Thousands of people lined the roadway and streets of Bodmin today, cheering with obvious sympathy and satisfaction, when I drove Mrs Hearn, radiant with happiness to a quiet spot somewhere in Cornwall, where she and her sister are now quietly resting. For eight days, Mrs Hearn has maintained a brave and apparently stoic calm in circumstances trying even to the most resolute powers of endurance'.

Arthur Smith recalled:

'The crowd which had hissed her so cruelly on the first day of the trial now cheered her like a heroine.

'Then the huge gates opened and we flashed out, the police making desperate and successful efforts to restrain the crowd, who in their obvious enthusiasm, wanted to congratulate Mrs Hearn.

Almost at once a fleet of cars raced after us in pursuit, but in a few minutes later, we were speeding swiftly and far beyond our pursuers through the glorious Cornish countryside'.

The effect on Mrs Hearn was breathtaking:

'Never have I known such joy ecstatic as Mrs Hearn showed as we passed familiar landmarks – familiar to her but not familiar to me – which she identified to me: the raptures possible only to one; who for an eternity of months, has been caged in the darkest shadows of despair.

Again and again she turned, spoke excitedly of the joy which the journey gave her. Then, after the first few moments of quiet thrill, she spoke calmly and soberly of the trial.

"If I had known at first that it would be five months before I should be tried, I don't know what would have happened. The first two months, as it was, were terrible. Apart from the task of steeling myself to endure without complaint the rigours of prison life, there was the bewildering and horrid knowledge of the accusation.

"Oh the terror of those nights, when the brain, stifled and weary, tried to cope with the incredible knowledge that I was being accused of the murder of my sister. It was a godsend during this time to come from Exeter to Launceston for the police court proceedings. It meant movement. Of course, it was all imagination, but on those trips, I used to imagine the next time I would come back, free. No one can ever appreciate the torture I endured whole sitting in the dock. They say I was composed. How little they knew. Inside was an inferno of doubts and fears; and yet always the conviction seemed to grip me that my innocence could not be disproved, no matter how scientific and certain the evidence was against me. Honestly, at times, when I listened to the evidence being piled up against me, I could not believe my ears.

"Then came this morning. I thought of Bessie. I knew she was behind me somewhere in the court. I listened to the judge summing up. When he finished I thought this was the end. There is no escape. Fate is against me. They say I swooned. I do not know. I listened to the last words but did not hear them, and even now I cannot tell you how I walked out of the dock. My mind was in a whirl. You cannot appreciate the terrible feeling, even when one is terribly conscious of innocence, when you sit day after day, hour after hour, and hear amazingly brilliant brains building up facts you know are meant to hang you. God knows I needed courage and only God in his goodness could have given the courage to sustain me.

"Five months in gaol. The very words mean nothing. The reality too awful to describe in words. Yet I was shown every kindness and on the morning I left Exeter Gaol for Bodmin, everyone, from the highest in rank to the lowest, wished me Godspeed".'

When the judge discussed the importance of the sandwiches, Mrs Hearn said:

'When he said that, a mysterious and sweet confidence came on me. I knew of my innocence. There was no need for me to reassure myself on that fact. But somehow as I looked at the jury and remembered the courage given me by the speech of the counsel for my defence I felt no harm would come to me.

I swooned at the end of the judge's summing up, not from fear, but simply because the strain became overpoweringly acute. I do not care now what people say or have said. All I know is that my sister and I are together and happy again. I have no bitterness in my heart towards anyone, but it is only human to feel that somehow or somewhere I have been the victim of a terribly cruel mistake. All I want now is to go quietly with my sister and forget all the trouble I have had.'[68]

We might also want to consider why the verdict of not guilty was given. First, Birkett was a very able counsel and was assisted by an equally able pathologist. Second, Du Parcq's interrupted summing-up did the Crown's case no favours. Most important, though, was Mrs Hearn herself. In her appearance, demeanour, coolness and intelligence under cross-examination, she made a good impression on the jury. Even witnesses for the Crown, such as Thomas, had nothing but good to say about her character. She had come across well on trial in 1920; she did likewise in 1931.

Bowker and Birkett had already left. It was not until reaching Exeter that they learnt the verdict. Bowker congratulated his master.[69] Devlin did likewise and later wrote that it was one of Birkett's 'greatest triumphs'.[70]

Thomas also made a brief statement, saying 'I am glad it is over. I have, of course, held my own opinion on the case throughout, and I prefer to say no more about it. It's a good job it's over: it has been a long time about'. That was his last known word in public on the subject.[71] One wonders if many people, knowing of the not guilty verdict given to Mrs Hearn, thought that if she was innocent then he must be guilty, or whether Thomas thought that they might think so.

There was some disquiet about the trial in official circles and a letter was addressed to Dr Lynch in 24 June from Sir Ernley Robertson Blackwell (1868–1941), an under-secretary at the Home Office, who had read the judge's summing up at the trial's end. He was surprised that a doctor agreed with Birkett when the latter asked if a 'pinch' of soil would produce the arsenic found in Minnie's body. He added that Dr Lynch declared that a pound of soil would be needed in reality. Then the judge in his summing up disagreed with Lynch's estimate and said that only a quarter of a pound would be needed. The letter ended thus, 'I should be very glad to have your observations about this for purposes of record. I think it would be well if you would put your observations in the form of a memorandum which I could send privately to the Judge. I should be pleased to do so if it established the fact that your estimate was right and his was wrong'.[72]

Dr Lynch replied on the next day in the form of a letter rather than the requested memorandum. He stated that he said that the amount of arsenic in Minnie's corpse was one pound and this would equate to a pound of soil, but the defence had not commented on this and the judge thought that he meant that this was the amount of soil which contaminated the samples, but thought this must be too high and so a quarter of a pound of soils was more likely.[73]

It seems that a memorandum was made out as well, though by another. He estimated that the amount of arsenic in the body was 0.776. He also estimated it was 0.075 grains that was in the organs he received. However, this was only that which was taken for a very small proportion of a body that weighed about 80 pounds so that the actual amount of the arsenic would be considerably greater. Dr Lynch's calculations were questioned.[74]

It left, though, three questions. Who killed Mrs Thomas, how and why? The defence had poured scorn on the prosecution's case of the fish sandwiches being poisoned and they thought it was impossible that the weed-killer bought by Mrs Hearn in 1926 could have been used. Rather, they had argued that food poisoning could have been the cause of Mrs Thomas's illness. Yet she had died of arsenic, and the prosecution could not say how this had been administered. They also stated that they were uncertain whether Miss Everard had been poisoned, but the evidence of the diary and Dr Lynch was certainly strong enough.

Chapter 10

Aftermath

The case was over. There would be no more investigations. At the beginning of July there was an announcement that the inquest into Miss Mary Everard and Miss Minnie Everard's deaths would not be resumed. The case was closed, presumably because the coroner either believed that the original natural causes of death recorded held good, or that nothing would be gained by pursuing any other verdict, as Mrs Hearn could not be charged again for the latter death having been acquitted, and there was not enough evidence concerning the first death.[1]

In the following year, Thomas moved from the district where he had lived for over a decade. He disposed of the tenancy in July 1932 and sold the animals in October.[2] In 1939 he was at Vivian Farm, Treswithiam, in Camborne, as a dairy farmer. He was married again, in 1938, to one Ada Ellen Lumbard, ten years his junior, but they separated in October 1945 'without just reason', according to Thomas. He died on 14 December 1949 at Babington Farm, Bradoe, Lostwithiel. He left £2,328 8s 1d in his will to Frederick Stanley Thomas, his brother. He was aged sixty and the funeral was at St Germain's church on 19 December.[3]

Meanwhile, Mrs Hearn and her sister stayed at the Commercial Hotel, Wadebridge, and Mrs Hearn signed her name in the register as Sarah Annie Hearn (though in 1933 she claimed she had 'signed a new name. This name I would have to keep now'). The proprietor drove them to the railway station early the next day, but no one observed their passing. The two sisters and O'Donnell took a train to London.[4]

Mrs Hearn 'looked pale and a little shaken'. O'Donnell had recalled her shuddering when they passed the prison where she had spent so many months.[5] Meanwhile, in Yorkshire, Mr Poskitt told journalists, 'It is a happy ending to a long and anxious period of waiting. Of course, we were convinced that Annie was not guilty of this horrible crime, and our belief in her innocence is borne out by the jury's decision'.[6]

O'Donnell then asked Mrs Hearn if she wanted to see her family. She replied, 'We would like to spend a few days in London before going home'. O'Donnell thought they would want to see Buckingham Palace and the Tower of London, but instead they went to the National Gallery where O'Donnell gushingly wrote, 'I found her a most delightful companion. Quite intelligent and with an intense fondness for all things beautiful'. There, 'I was amazed at the knowledge she revealed of painters and their works and the technical phrases she used concerning the period of brushwork'. At the zoo 'She astounded me with her knowledge of the animals, their place of origin and habits'. They also went to the theatre and to West End restaurants. O'Donnell summed up 'gradually I saw the greyness of sorrow which had shadowed the eyes of Mrs Hearn give way to an expression of content, that the cloud which for so long enshrouded her, had passed over… It was a different woman whom I saw off the train when at length she went back to Doncaster with sister Bessie'.[7]

Mrs Hearn initially went to Grimsby to see friends after the trial. According to one account, Mrs Hearn stayed briefly at her brother's house. She visited St James' church and then met West at the Yarborough Hotel. Mrs Hearn then went to the railway station opposite the hotel and took a train to Doncaster to be with Mrs Poskitt.[8] She was suffering from a bad cold and would stay with her sister indefinitely. She had no plans for the future.[9]

According to her later account she was already thinking about her options:

'Although a jury of my countrymen had said I was innocent, I could never use my own name.

This meant I could not take a post as a teacher of domestic science. My certificate is made out to the name of Mrs Hearn. It would give me away at once.

Nor could I go out and ask for a job as Mrs Hearn in a home.

It seemed to me, that no one, even in face of the verdict, would ever dream of employing me as a cook. And who could blame them?

I soon began to realise what I was up against – what a hard struggle my future was to be. All the peace had gone out of my life. I had to be on guard all the time, to be careful not to say anything that might link me to Cornwall, and in the case in which I was the central figure'.[10]

Mrs Hearn wrote Smith a letter, on 15 July:

'Dear Sir,

I have only just got your address, and I want to thank you so much for all you have done for me, but for you I dare not think what the end might have been. I had no idea all these lonely months, how much, how very much was being done for me. Mr West has told me how you set aside important engagements to come to Bodmin and help to save a life, my life.

I am convinced no one else could have done what you did there, it was wonderful. I feel that I owe my life to you, and I do want to thank you, but it feels too big a thing to put into words, but please accept my heartfelt gratitude and sincere thanks. I should never forget.

Yours very sincerely

Annie Hearn'.[11]

Immediately after her release, Mrs Hearn told her story and it was serialised in *The Empire News*, which had paid in part for her defence. It was published in June and July 1931. The story focussed on her innocence, stressed that her relationship with Thomas had been entirely platonic, and claimed that she had been a great friend of his wife and had lovingly nursed Minnie for years.

In the second issue Annie related how her sister had kept a diary each year and at the end of each year they burnt it. Mrs Hearn wrote 'I am glad that there is the testimony from the dead to show that I was not a callous sister... had I been so minded and had I ever feared what was in the last diary I could have destroyed it'. She demanded sympathy from the reader, telling them that hers was 'one of the saddest human stories ever written'.[12]

In one article Mrs Hearn reproduced initial diary entries to further vindicate her. The entries reproduced in the newspaper show that Mrs Hearn cared for her sister and that they enjoyed visits from Thomas and excursions with him and his wife. Naturally she took care to be selective in this account; there was nothing about Minnie thinking she had been poisoned or about Thomas only visiting when Annie was there or about her denying her sister hospital treatment.[13]

In another article Mrs Hearn tells of her feelings and actions following the death of Mrs Thomas. As for the letter to Thomas, 'When I wrote it I never dreamed that any other eyes but those of Mr Thomas would ever see it'. After her taking the taxi to Looe, she claimed that:

'There was an inner something driving me on to those cliffs at Looe. I went straight there on my arrival with the full intention of hurling myself into the depths below.

I flung my coat away and went to the edge of the cliff and then as I looked down some power outside myself seemed to hold me back.

It was almost tangible this power, and I remember thinking at the time that it was like putting one's finger against the end of a bicycle pump and then trying to blow that finger away. There was some definite resistance holding me back and suddenly I realised I could not do the thing I intended.

My heart failed me as I looked down into the sea. And I turned away walking mechanically. There was no idea, no plan in what I did. I simply walked'.[14]

In one article she wrote about how the playing card of the three of spades had played such an important part in her life. She recalled how she, Minnie and their aunt had played cards in Grindleford and on one occasion that particular card was missing. On another time she and Minnie were waiting for a bus and they saw a face-down playing card in the road. Minnie said 'Wouldn't it be funny if that was the three of spades?' On closer examination it was found that that was just what it was.[15]

Mrs Hearn also told the story of her marriage. She was living in Harrogate with her aunt in 1917, presumably shortly after Mabel's death in Grindleford. She was in Valley Gardens and heard her name being called. She saw a man in khaki, but she could not remember him as an acquaintance. He explained that he had been on the same seat as her and her friend and so knew her name. They walked along together and she mentioned that her sister was ill and that Dr Hearn of Sheffield had been attending her. He told her 'That's funny, my name is Hearn'.[16]

He told her that he was from Australia and had been a medical student before quitting his studies to enlist in the army. They met each other again and became friends. He met Minnie and their aunt. The latter was impressed but Minnie did not like him. Mrs Hearn recalled that he had been the first man in her life (she was then 32) and wrote 'I confess that I became very fond of Leonard Hearn'. Although he returned to the Western Front shortly after, they wrote to one another and he said when he came back he would ask her to marry him. She later wrote 'I told him I would marry him' and thought that they could live together with Minnie.[17]

Hearn told his fiancée that he was returning to London and could meet her. Annie did not hesitate and went there to marry him. Mrs Hearn later wrote, 'I was a very happy woman, but it was the sunshine before the storm'. The pair went to a registry office and saw two men in an office there. Mrs Hearn recalled 'I knew nothing about registry office proceedings'. She recalled a brief ceremony and signing a book. They then went to a hotel near Bedford Square and it was the first time she had been to London.[18]

While at dinner that night she saw a painting called *The Gamblers*, in which the playing card the three of spades was visible. She recalled 'I felt a little cold clutching of fear at my heart'. A fortune teller was at the hotel and people took it in turn to have their fortune told. When it was her turn, she was told 'I don't like the way the three of spades hovers over you' and when the cards were drawn, that one was picked up three times for her. 'What does it mean?' She was told 'It means tears. It means great trouble, in which you will suffer terrible sorrows'.[19]

Her husband talked of returning to Australia. Mrs Hearn recalled talking about how the climate there would be very beneficial to Minnie. Then an argument ensued. Hearn wanted to take his wife to Australia, not his wife and her invalid sister. She explained, 'All my life I have been the nurse of the family. I nursed my sister Mabel through the last two years of her terrible illness until she died of tuberculosis'. Her husband claimed there was another man in her life. Eventually the two decided that they must part. He suggested that she say that he had been killed in the war and that she was now a widow in order to avoid public scandal. She never heard from him again.[20]

These articles are very much a case for the defence. Mrs Hearn wrote in the first 'how the smallest and most innocent actions and remarks were magnified a thousand times against me in my trial'. She concluded, 'I have never considered myself free to marry, and I have never had any desire to marry anyone since that first uncomfortable experience'. She concluded her fourth and final article in the series thus:

'And now I must take life up again where I left it. Homeless – with the exception of the houses of my brother and sister [she actually had two brothers then living] – penniless but with the determination to make some little place in the world where I can live down the unhappy past, although the memories must ever remain'.[21]

Mrs Hearn was economical with the truth in her 1931 autobiography. According to her she and her sister went straight to North Hill when travelling south after 1918, but as we have noted they were not there until 1921.[22]

There is also direct contradiction with previous evidence. The year of the bogus marriage was given here as 1917 rather than 1919 as she previously had claimed it to be (both in 1919 and at the trial). And, in the previous account her 'husband' died rather than left her. In both he was conveniently inaccessible. Certainly nothing in it can be verified; and there is certainly no reference in the indexes to marriages in England to a marriage between anyone called Hearn and anyone of her 'maiden' name, which is now stated as having occurred in a registry office, not a church as previously alleged. As both her sister and her aunt were dead they could not contradict the story. If we are to believe the story we must also believe that the marriage ceremony was faked and that the soldier had no intention of marrying her, but there is no clue in Mrs Hearn's account that he was deliberately acting in concert with the two men in the office to deceive her, and no purpose to do so either. It also suggests that Mrs Hearn could be easily deceived by a fake ceremony. If she was inventing the story, as seems probable, then this is further proof of her being a romantic fantasist and thus that she could have imagined that Thomas could have been attracted to her.

Apart from writing for the *Empire News*, Mrs Hearn also wrote several very similar articles for *Peg's Companion*, a weekly magazine aimed at young women. Her story would take up several issues in August and September 1931, and much of the content was very similar to the story in the Sunday newspaper earlier that year.

As with the earlier pieces, it is very much a self-justifying piece of work. At the onset Mrs Hearn rests her case and calls on the sympathy of the reader:

'In my heart I knew that I was innocent. Innocent of the cruel and wicked crimes with which I was charged. In my heart I felt that the jury must know I was innocent.

'For six months I have lain under the shadow of death. For six months I have suffered the torture of knowing that I was suspected of murdering Mrs Thomas, a very dear and kindly friend.

For three months I have suffered the torture of knowing that I was suspected of knowing that I was suspected of the cruel and prolonged poisoning of my sister, Minnie.

It does not need any great stretch of the imagination to realise what my feelings must have been during the anxious period of waiting for these charges to be dismissed and my innocence proved.'[23]

Mrs Hearn also made much of her late sister's diary, which she clearly had in her possession and which she cites, selectively, in her defence.

'And now I shall turn to the diary of my sister Minnie for a moment. In justice to myself, the dead shall speak, and extracts from the diary must be made public, so that all the mystery that surrounded it may be lifted and so that this testimony from the dead may show that I was not the callous sister I was made out to be.

As you know, the diary was not produced during the trial and doubtless there were many who wondered why. I wondered myself. I am determined that this record of my sister's sufferings, which in ordinary circumstances would have been sacred, and open to none but members of the family, shall be published.

Her last diary was one of the saddest human stories ever written'.[24]

Annie refers to the diary selectively. Of the visits by Thomas, 'his visits were of purely a neighbourly character'. Of herself an extract read 'How I sought help for my sister… Again it was I who sent for the doctor, and I could go on and on giving you extracts… Yet the most outrageous suggestions were made at the trial'.[25]

She excuses her flight to Looe, 'I realise now that it was a very foolish thing to do, but it is easy to be wise after the event, and I daresay that there are many among my readers who can recall how they have done things which they have regretted afterwards'. She referred to her relations with Thomas:

'I never had a single thought of ever marrying anyone and I had gone there at the express invitation of Mrs Thomas to help nurse and look after her. I never expected and never received any payment for my small services which I gave and gave gladly as any woman would have done in the circumstances but everything that could be said to blacken me in the eyes of the jury was said in order to make it appear that my thoughts were in the direction indicated'.

In reference to Thomas's visits, Mrs Hearn wrote he would 'stand chatting to us for a minute or two', or would spend a few minutes playing cards or he and Mrs Thomas would come over to play cards of an evening. She rhetorically wrote 'Does that look like a guilty association?'[26]

As has been noted earlier, Thomas's visits were always rather longer than a minute or two or a few minutes, and in 1930 Mrs Thomas never visited. Possibly Mrs Hearn's memory is at fault; it is certainly selective or perhaps she is deliberately misrepresenting the facts in order to show herself as above all reproach.

Her account fails to shed any light on the mysteries of the case; principally the death of her sister and that of Mrs Thomas, though she spends much time stating how much she loved both sister and friend. The death of her aunt is excluded from her account, as is the theft in 1919. She must have known that the death of Mrs Thomas was not due to natural causes, but she did not speculate about it in public. According to this account the two sisters travelled straight from the Midlands to North Hill in about 1919, yet we know from the reporting of the theft case and the census of 1921 that this was not so. Whether this was a case of simplifying the story or deliberately falsifying it is another question.

Apart from writing to Birkett, O'Donnell stated that he received Christmas cards from Mrs Hearn for a couple of years after the trial. Devlin reported meeting West in 1932 and hearing that Mrs Hearn was now working, under a new name, as a cook-housekeeper.[27]

In 1933 Mrs Hearn appeared in print again in an eleven-part series for *The Weekly News*, part of which has already been cited, though these writings have never previously been brought to light. The new account included a little about the deaths of her mother, two sisters, aunt and Mrs Thomas, as well as her time on the run, her arrest and her trial and acquittal. As in the 1931 newspaper serial, it was designed to show that Annie was wholly innocent regarding both Thomas and the deaths of her family and friends, and that she was a hard-working and devout woman. It also told the story of what happened to her after the trial, and this has never been told since then.

Mrs Hearn also retold the story of her alleged marriage and this was rather different to the story she had retold two years earlier, as well as that known about in 1930. This time she alleged she met her future husband when on holiday with her aunt in about 1917. They were staying in Edinburgh and she was at Portobello, where she met a young man. He was 'a wonderful type of Scots boy', a medical student at Edinburgh University called Leonard Hearn. He had recently enlisted in the RAMC. They married in London and after a seven-day honeymoon she saw him off to France at Victoria and then never saw him again, later learning that he had died in early 1931.[28] There was a Leonard Hearne Smith who was a corporal, later a second lieutenant, in the RAMC, but he lived in London and was killed in action in 1917, leaving his goods to his sister, so he does not seem to be the man she described.

Mrs Hearn then gave an account of her life after the summer of 1931. For the first month after her acquittal, she stayed with her sister and 'lived to help out with the children and take them out. It gave me the distraction I needed'. She noted 'Now that I was free, I thought that everything would be forgotten, that everybody would be good to me'. She added 'My honest endeavour to live a new life, to toil my fingers to the bone for a few shillings a week, to live in the poorest houses rather than take the dole. Yes, and even to spend whole days and whole nights nursing the aged, the infirm – and the dying'.[29]

Then a married woman, knowing her identity, wrote to Mrs Hearn out of the blue offering her a job as a companion-help at her home. It was just what Annie wanted and it filled her with hope and happiness. Mrs Hearn's sister helped her with her journey and she took a train to Oxford and then caught a bus to her new place of work. She called herself Mrs Jones, but her employer did not mention her past and set her to cooking meals for her and her husband. However, the woman alternated between finding fault with her and then praising her work. The woman's husband later explained to Mrs Hearn that his wife was addicted to drugs and this explained her erratic behaviour. Mrs Hearn feared that if the woman overdosed herself and died she would be identified and suspected: 'It would never do for Mrs Hearn to be found in the house of a woman who might accidentally die of taking drugs. They would say I poisoned her when I cooked the food. And who would believe me?' Next day she explained she would have to leave and so gave her notice. 'I walked down the drive with a heavy heart'.[30]

After this Mrs Hearn went to stay at the house of a relative and their children helped distract her. A month or so later she saw an advert for a job in the house of a working man. Her next post was at Derby, where she was employed by a man referred to as Jack, to look after his elderly mother for 7s 6d per week. She had to reveal to Jack her true identity as he needed to complete some paperwork about her employment, but he was not perturbed by who she was. However, she thought that she was identified by a woman in a queue for buying groceries. The woman told an insurance agent and soon her identity was common knowledge locally. She then explained to Jack that she had to leave and he regretfully accepted her resignation and took her to the railway station where she boarded a train to Manchester, where she stayed in a boarding house for a few days.[31]

Annie's next job was working on a farm near Stockport, for an elderly farmer and his son who was a young man. She did a lot of work in the dairy and with the hens. On one occasion the young man made unwelcome advances towards her, but he desisted when she was firm with him. Later his father realised her true identity by looking at pictures of her in (presumably old) newspapers. He and his son confronted her and were very angry that she had deceived them, though she defended herself by stating that she had been found not guilty. This ended her employment there and she left the next day to return to the Manchester boarding house.[32]

Mrs Hearn then returned to Cornwall to work at a small farm belonging to a doctor's widow. On arrival she found that her main job was to look after a frail and elderly lady. This struck her with fear that the lady might die and she would be accused of murder. The two had a discussion of the Hearn case and the old lady said, 'She was found not guilty alright, but I still think she was the luckiest woman alive. She ought to have been hanged'. Mrs Hearn agreed, saying 'Yes, she ought to have been hanged'. Eventually the old lady died after being nursed by Mrs Hearn. She left the job.[33]

The whole tone of these articles is twofold. Firstly, Mrs Hearn stresses how hard-working and loving she was towards her family and friends and how devoted she was to them in times of sickness. Secondly there is a strong strain of 'woe is me'. She wrote, full of self-pity:

'Why if they dug up my aunt why didn't they dig up my mother and my sister Mabel, both of whom I saw breathe their last... why should I have not murdered Mabel, who I nursed for months before the end?... I wish I had been hanged... It would have saved me from a fate far worse. To lose happiness, freedom and all the other privileges that any other woman enjoys... wherever I went the world was dead against me'.[34]

When describing her time on the cliff at Looe she wrote:

'Many times since then I wished I had gone over the cliffs. Even now, with my trial two years behind me, I often feel it would have been better for everyone – and most of all myself – if the waters of the Atlantic had closed over me that day.

What anguish of mind it would have saved. What bitter memories. What persecution. What tortures of soul in my struggle to face the world and begin a new life'.[35]

Mrs Hearn ended her life story with the following:

> 'At present I am out of employment and still feeling the strain of nursing
> and the mental blows... Wherever I go it will always be the same. I shall
> always be in the shadow of Trenhorne House... The shadow of the past.
> I can never escape it'.[36]

Again, as with the newspaper and magazine articles of 1931, we must question how accurate this information is. Some details are certainly not right: Mrs Hearn was born in 1885 not 1890, and she did not immediately leave her aunt in Harrogate to tend to her ailing mother. The theft in 1919 is never mentioned; nor is Mrs Aunger and her death. Most of the material, however, cannot be verified. For example, none of the employers nor their addresses are revealed, so they cannot be traced. Their anonymity is preserved. This reticence might be quite natural and understandable, of course. The discrepancies in the accounts of her marriage are also remarkable. Which version, if any, is correct? It is noteworthy that on her sister Grace Mabel's death certificate on 26 November 1917 the name of the informant is Annie *Everard* (my italics), which does not accord with her alleged marriage earlier that year when her surname would have changed to Hearn. The court case of 1919–1920 goes naturally unrecorded, and the account of Minnie's death does not match previous versions. Could the remainder be true, or was Mrs Hearn a brazen liar and fantasist?

Mrs Hearn, in these accounts, does not discuss why her sister died and who poisoned Mrs Thomas at all. No explanation is offered for these two deaths. Naturally, if she was guilty she would not do so (though she no longer ran the risk of another trial under double jeopardy laws), and she could hardly accuse anyone else in print and risk libel. She was vague in suggesting that her sister died of her long-term illnesses, and ignored how and why Mrs Thomas died. Perhaps, if guilty, she really believed her public persona as a kind and sympathetic nurse and friend and wished to preserve this. Other murderers have reiterated that they were not really guilty and gloss over their crimes, despite all evidence to the contrary, and it seems that perhaps Mrs Hearn was just such a fantasist.

After this, Mrs Hearn returned to the obscurity from which she had emerged in the autumn of 1930. Under a new name, she flitted from job to job, assuming her writings in 1933 about that part of her life were accurate. She changed her name to Margaret Day (the latter being her mother's maiden name) and she was living with her sister Betsy at 16 King Street, Shrewsbury from at least 1939 until her death on 4 May 1948, a year before Thomas. Annie referred to herself in 1939, as ever, as being a widow and engaged in unpaid domestic duties, which presumably included nursing her elder sister who was referred to as being 'incapacitated', though she outlived her by a decade. It will be noted that Mrs Hearn retained the fantasy of having been married, but gave her correct birthday. It is also worth noting that she did not leave a will or administration, indicating that she had no money on death. On 7 May 'Margaret Day' was buried in Emstrey Cemetery, extension 006-313.

Let us turn now from the fate of Mrs Hearn to the mystery of what happened in Lewannick. A Cornish newspaper summarised the case and then asked, 'Will the mystery ever be solved? How can it be?' They argued that 'We must, like the judge, accept their verdict, but whilst many were ready to cheer the deceased woman, others will sympathise with the bereaved and defenceless husband, who was pointed at by the counsel and who returns to his lonely life, knowing that in all probability, the mystery of the administration of that fatal dose of arsenic, will remain as insoluble as the poison itself'. On the other hand, 'Mrs Hearn, as an acquitted woman, is entitled to seek the sunshine and forget, if possible, the most terrible ordeal any human being can pass through, the trial for her life in the charge of a most diabolical inhumanity to a fellow creature. The ordeal was almost as unbearable as the sufferings of the unfortunate women who died from the poison found in their bodies'.[37]

The question remained, however, as to who killed Mrs Thomas. The court had decided that it was not Mrs Hearn, or at least that the prosecution had not come up with sufficient evidence that that was the case. The judge had stated that either she or Thomas must have administered the arsenic.

Most writers on the case have confessed that the whole matter is an unsolvable mystery, though anyone writing when Mrs Hearn could have still been alive, could hardly accuse her in print and risk committing libel. Likewise, anyone writing before Thomas's death in 1949 could not accuse him outright. Winifred Duke covered the case in a book about six trials, published in 1934, and she wrote, 'the conclusion of the trial offered no answer to the riddle' as to who killed Mrs Thomas and Minnie Everard. She had no doubt that 'both these women were given arsenic, and that arsenic caused their deaths is indisputable'. She added that the judge offered no comment on the verdict – and judges often pronounce that the jury have made the right decision if they think this is the case. This is as close as Duke could get to accusing Mrs Hearn of the double murder. She clearly agreed implicitly with the prosecution but could not be more explicit. Thompson, writing in 1937, reached no conclusion about Mrs Hearn and nor did Felstead, two decades later. Even in the 1980s writers including a chapter on the case confessed themselves baffled, as Williams wrote of 'this unfinished jigsaw puzzle of a crime'.[38]

Some thought Mrs Hearn was entirely innocent. Participants in the trial retained the stance they had taken in 1931. Smith later described the case, concluding:

'She was a foolish woman but not a murderess. I am ready to stake my reputation on that. If she had not bolted I doubt if she would have been charged… Who then killed Mrs Thomas? Apart from the doctors and her mother at the end, only one person besides Annie had access to her. That was her husband. We are unlikely to know the truth now because on December 14 1949, William Thomas died… So far as I know, Annie Hearn is still alive. I do not think she has any more secrets to tell'.[39]

Smith clearly thought that Thomas was the murderer, although he did not put it explicitly, though by then it was legally safe to do so. However, he did not formulate a case against him to explain why he should have killed his wife.[40]

Smith also seems to err in some of the analysis offered in his memoirs. To write that Minnie did not have diarrhoea when she did and that 'most of the other signs of chronic arsenic poisoning were missing' is to have overlooked or forgotten much of the relevant medical evidence. She did suffer from it, and the fact that this happened less than might be expected is surely accounted for by the number of times that she is recorded as having vomited, which would have reduced the amount of diarrhoea.[41] He added that many of the symptoms described by the prosecution witness could be interpreted differently, which is true, but taken together they present a rather different picture which he did not acknowledge.[42] Likewise, Smith's attack on Lynch about his estimate of the amount of arsenic in Minnie's body is hard to substantiate, for, as Lynch noted, the weight of her body was vastly reduced due to undernourishment, and so he adjusted the proportions accordingly. The amount of arsenic in the hair should also have been seen as a decisive indicator of murder.

A biographer of Birkett follows Smith's assessment, writing three years later, 'There is little doubt that Mrs Thomas was murdered, perhaps by her husband, who had the poison and the opportunity... Birkett himself never had the slightest doubt of Mrs Hearn's innocence'.[43] O'Donnell wrote that 'Some person has committed a foolish or thoughtless act that has aroused suspicion' and he was convinced that Mrs Hearn fell into this category; again he could not or would not proffer a solution except to imply that the arsenic in Minnie's body had come from the soil in the graveyard.[44]

Conversely, Devlin thought she was guilty. He wrote in his memoirs, 'For myself, I think it was a Jekyll and Hyde case, a case of split personality'. He believed that the jury had seen Mrs Hearn as Dr Jekyll and he saw her as Mr Hyde. He wrote 'There was Mrs Hearn who devoted her life to nursing the sick and there was the Mrs Hearn who poisoned, in the most painful way, three women whom she was nursing'.[45]

There was a rather different view in an account of the case by a non-participant. Daniel Farson wrote up the case for a magazine in 1984 and followed Smith's interpretation of the case, but added fresh material. As well as stating Mrs Hearn's innocence, he thought that Thomas killed his wife while Mrs Hearn bore the brunt of the consequences. His conclusion was reached as follows. Firstly, that the judge had said that 'There may have been some other woman who moved him to passion'. Secondly, in 1984 a woman living in Lewannick told Farson that she remembered the postmistress gossiping after the murder, saying 'He'll be able to have Mrs Tucker now'. Thirdly, there was copper in Thomas's wife's body as well as arsenic. The worm tablets in his possession contained copper. Farson said that if this was so, then Miss Everard was not murdered after all, but died a natural death as noted at the time.[46]

The difficulty with this thesis is that as regards Mrs Tucker and Thomas, there is no evidence that the two had any affection for one another and they certainly never married. Farson also discounted the arsenic found in the body as well as all the symptoms that Minnie endured in her final months of life, and clearly did not know that copper can be found naturally in humans, even though this was stated at the trial.

A recent anthology of stories of real-life Cornish murders included a chapter retelling the story, concluding that there was not enough evidence to charge Thomas. It added that Mrs Hearn probably changed her name and went northwards and was 'never seen again'.[47]

More recently, however, the pendulum has swung against Mrs Hearn. There is a YouTube video, 'Who killed Alice Thomas: The Trial of Annie Hearn, 1931' which first appeared online in 2019, in a series of videos called 'They got away with murder' by Mark John Maguire. This has presented a radically different solution. Maguire discusses the various possibilities. Could it have been food poisoning? To that he says no. Perhaps Mrs Thomas committed suicide, but he disregards this. Could a visitor have been responsible? No. Then he ponders which, of the two main suspects, as identified by the judge, committed the crime. Was it Thomas or Mrs Hearn? Both had the opportunity. Or was it a joint enterprise? He could find no motive for Thomas to kill his wife and no evidence that he felt romantically inclined towards Mrs Hearn, despite gossip thereafter (such as that noted by Farson above). However, he did not have the evidence of the diary, which points to Thomas's very frequent visits to the house, but only when Mrs Hearn was there.

Maguire is strongly of the opinion that the person with both means and motive was Mrs Hearn. She had the only opportunity to poison the sandwiches and then made all Mrs Thomas's meals for the next week, giving her opportunity. The evidence about Miss Everard's death also seems important. The death of the aunt was similar in symptoms, and shortly followed the purchase of the arsenic. He also noted that she was a strange character: cold, peripatetic, a fantasist and obsessed with death and doctors. He thinks Mrs Hearn had developed an attraction to Thomas, but her invalid sister and his wife were obstacles, yet he probably found her unattractive. He also stresses the lack of the diary, which, though there was probably nothing directly against Mrs Hearn (or else she would have destroyed it), may have provided indications about Mrs Hearn's character and actions which could be suggestive at the least, and that was why the defence wished it to be suppressed. The tea party at Bude gave Mrs Hearn the unique opportunity to give food to Mrs Thomas. Had Thomas wished to do so he would have had plenty of other opportunities. It is a plausible theory, and better argued than Farson's.

There has also been a novelisation of the case, *Arsenic and Mercy Quint*, with names mostly changed. A retired journalist recounts the tale in 1965, after having covered the case for his newspaper. The first half of the book is a fairly factual overview of the case, with occasional comments about how it was mishandled. Then the journalist reinvestigates the case. There is no doubt throughout that Mercy Quint, as Mrs Hearn is called, is guilty. The second half of the book is more speculative; by interviewing people (some clearly based on real individuals) we learn that Mercy and the elder Dr Quint had an affair in Derbyshire in the 1910s, and she subsequently blackmailed him, receiving cash to pay for legal defence in 1920 and in 1931. She also poisoned her younger sister in 1918, having taken white arsenic from a neighbouring taxidermist. Her killing in Cornwall was to silence her sister who knew too much and, as regards Mrs Lucy Trahair (Mrs Thomas), in order to procure the farm to live with the survivor, whether this was Lucy or Henry Trahair. Mercy's surviving brother is illiterate and we learn that he had incestuous relations with the sister that Mercy killed in 1918. We also discover that Mercy returned to Cornwall to work as a housekeeper in the 1930s, but went back to Yorkshire. Her brother visits her and, having retained a packet of white arsenic he stole nearly fifty years ago, poisons the woman who killed the love of his life. The conclusion is that this is natural justice. The book is unsourced, there is no bibliography and it is not possible to tell where fact ends and fiction begins.[48]

The most recent book – in fact the first book solely about the case – is extremely lengthy and thorough, using material from both The National Archives (including, for the first time, Miss Everard's diary of 1930) and from the press, as well as the memoirs of some of the senior figures in the medical and legal aspects of the case. The majority of these sources have never been utilised by any of those writing admittedly very short accounts of the case.

This is the most important book so far about the case and concludes that Mrs Hearn was guilty, having killed both her sister and Mrs Thomas; the latter by inserting arsenic into the sandwiches shortly before they were eaten, in the brief moment of opportunity when the two women were apart, thus ensuring the dye did not show up. It would then be easy enough to position the poisoned sandwich uppermost and nearest to Mrs Thomas so that she would naturally select it. The author also believes that Minnie was murdered, given the level of arsenic in her body that could not have got there in any other way. In fact, the author stresses that this is an even clearer case of poisoning than that of Mrs Thomas. He concludes, 'Her drives were internal, emotional, personal, secretive and untouched by the usually softening effects of the human conscience'.[49]

The author also postulates that evidence for the poisoning of Minnie by her sister was strong, as arsenic was found in her body, and that only Mrs Hearn had the opportunity to poison her. He dismissed the defence's suggestion that arsenic from the soil could have infiltrated the coffin or entered the sample jars during the exhumation. He suggests that although these two murders can be safely attributed to Mrs Hearn, there is less evidence for the earlier deaths, such as those of Miss Aunger and Miss Mary Everard, not to mention Grace Mabel Everard. She could have been responsible but the evidence is not strong enough to do more than suggest the possibility.

The book also notes the eventual fate of Mrs Hearn, using information from a recently published novel. The author is critical of the errors that previous authors have made about the Hearn case as part of wider studies, for example misnaming key characters and stating that Mrs Thomas had to be exhumed. The only drawbacks are occasional factual inaccuracy (for example Mrs Hearn was born in 1885 not 1884), assumptions, such as Mrs Hearn being a true crime enthusiast, frequent deviation into other cases known to the author, frequent shifts in chronological narrative, and the fact that some primary sources were not utilised. The author does not highlight the frequency of Thomas's visits to Mrs Hearn. Admittedly these are minor points in an otherwise impressive book.[50]

One additional difficulty in this case is that the file of papers created by the Cornish Constabulary in 1930–1931 is closed to public inspection until 2030 because of data protection laws. Its contents are currently unknown. It is possible that there might be comments made by policemen about their suspicions, and there might be reports, letters and statements which were not used in the public proceedings but which might reveal background about the people involved in the case. There may be information that was passed to the police following the trial. The contents may or may not reveal additional important information. We must thus fall back on what is currently publicly available.

Much of what we know can be interpreted in differing ways and the evidence is, as always, incomplete. Both Thomas and Mrs Hearn are noted as having got on well with Mrs Thomas. Mrs Hearn's constant nursing of relations and others may have been wholly natural and admirable, as Mrs Poskitt stated. Or it may have been the cover for something more sinister.

Thomas seems to have been exonerated by recent authors, though earlier writers often pointed the finger at him, though without developing a properly thought-out thesis. To be a murderer, the killer must have the means, the opportunity, the motive and the will to kill. To take the means first, it is worth noting that Thomas, like all farmers, had ready access to arsenic in the form of worm tablets, which are not soluble in water, as Gilbert Freak noted. These contained arsenic in sufficient quantity to kill. Therefore, Thomas had the means for the murders. Means alone are insufficient.

Secondly, he admitted that he went to Trenhorne House on an almost daily basis from January to July 1930 and Minnie's diary backs this up, and he never went with his wife. Furthermore, he only came when Mrs Hearn was present. He was also present on the night of Minnie's death. This is important on two counts. Firstly, it provided opportunity to kill Minnie should he desire to do so. Secondly, it gives substance to Parsons's allegation that he had a motive for both murders if he was carrying on an affair with Mrs Hearn, but this is not certain.

Parsons thought that there was animosity between the Thomases and certainly there was a frostiness between Thomas and his in-laws, and he did not let them know that his wife was so unwell. Differences between the Thomases in religious matters may also have created difficulties in the marriage. Furthermore, his visits to the two sisters without ever bringing his wife can also be seen as suspicious, as can his wish for Mrs Hearn's company. The degree of intimacy between himself and Mrs Hearn can never be known. It can be suggested that he killed Minnie and then his wife in order to marry Mrs Hearn, but that he shied away from the final step once it was obvious that the death of his wife would not be passed off as being from natural causes, whereas that of Minnie had been.

The question is, how realistic is this scenario? It has been postulated here as an alternative solution that needs consideration. Thomas had both means and opportunity to kill Minnie. Whether he had the motive and the desire to do so is unanswerable, as this is in part dependent on the true nature of his relations with Mrs Hearn as well as Mrs Hearn's role in all this. As to the murder of his wife, it seems, again, that he had the means at his disposal and possibly the motive; again the latter is dependent on the conclusions one draws about his relations with Mrs Hearn (and even if he did have romantic feelings for her it is not axiomatic that he would necessarily kill for them; he may have been content with the status quo). The difficulty with this scenario is that it seems impossible for him to have had the opportunity to poison his wife in a way that meets the known facts, as he could not have interfered with the foods that Mrs Hearn fed the three of them and it seems hard to believe that this was not where the arsenic was. This would seem to rule him out as the killer.

Or could this have been a joint enterprise between Thomas and Mrs Hearn, assuming they were, or wished to be, lovers? Thomas could have supplied the poison and Mrs Hearn was the poisoner and then when the truth about the method of Mrs Thomas's death came out, the plot collapsed. It is not unknown for two people to poison as a joint venture, but it is rare, as it puts each in the other's power.

However, these hypotheses have many holes, as has been noted. They are possible, but no more than this. Instead it is Mrs Hearn who seems the far more likely murderer in terms of means, opportunity and motive, and perhaps character. One issue worth pondering is whether Mrs Hearn could have been a serial poisoner. She had been involved with at least nine people who died, possibly prematurely; her mother in 1915, her sister Mabel in 1917, two unnamed friends at the same time as the previous two, Priscilla Aunger in February 1926, her aunt Everard in August 1926, her father in 1928, Minnie in 1930 and Mrs Thomas later that year. However, her father, her aunt and Mrs Aunger were all elderly, aged well over seventy, and her mother was sixty-eight and may well have died of natural causes. Yet her sisters were only aged twenty-eight and fifty-four respectively on death and her friends were presumably in their twenties or thirties.

Miss Mabel Everard apparently died of tuberculosis, Mrs Aunger died of senile decay, Miss Everard of cerebral obtulism and Miss Minnie Everard of chronic gastritis and catarrh and colitis. Could the symptoms of any of these have been mistaken for anything more sinister? Alas, we do not know the names of the two friends, assuming her sister is correct in this.

Grace Mabel died of tuberculosis, but the symptoms are not dissimilar to those of arsenic. Margery Radford died in a sanatorium in Surrey in 1949 after having been ailing for two years and she was certified as dying from pulmonary tuberculosis. After someone else nearly succumbed to arsenic poisoning, she was exhumed and enough arsenic was found in her to have been fatal.[51] Whether Grace Mabel was poisoned by arsenic is another question, as we do not know for certain. But it is a possibility that cannot be ruled out.

As to Minnie, it seems certain she died of arsenic poisoning; this was noted in 1930 by Dr Lynch and Birkett's remark at the trial was, in reality, more of an observation about the faulty nature of the post mortem and does not invalidate the findings. There is additional evidence too. Minnie commented that she was being poisoned and being given 'special medicine' by her sister, not that given by the doctors. Her emaciated and well-preserved body also suggests death by arsenic. Mrs Hearn had a motive and opportunity for her murder. Only she had access to all these people as she was feeding and nursing them.

Did Mrs Hearn have a motive for any of these crimes? It is unlikely to have been monetary, for although she gained just over £100 from her aunt, there was nothing from any of the others, though the sum in question represented nearly a year's wages for a working man in 1926 and would have helped her pay the rent and for food. It is not known whether she materially benefitted from the death of either parent, though it is probable that she might have gained some trinkets of sentimental value. The other deaths probably brought no monetary gain, though her older sister's death in 1930 resulted in an end to paying medical bills and spending on medicines, and allowed the possibility of taking in lodgers and so receiving a steady income.

There are other motives for poisoners, of course, apart from money. Drs Bodkin Adams and Harold Shipman made some cash from their killings, but this was not their prime motivation. Rather it was power, wanting to play God with people's lives, which is a frequent motive for those feeling insignificant and unhappy with their worldly lot. In some ways Mrs Hearn seems to have been reasonably intelligent and capable, but she lacked an outlet for this aspect of her character, being held back as an unmarried woman whose lot was to tend to family members who were unwell due to physical ailments or old age. She may well have resented this. In the case of her elder sister, Mrs Hearn had been her main carer since at least 1919 and her sister was in constant poor health. It may be that she became tired of this constant burden.

If Mrs Hearn was a serial poisoner, she was certainly a clever one, choosing victims who were elderly or ill or would not be missed. Their deaths would not be examined closely by any doctor. Serial killers tend to begin their murders cautiously, leaving time between each crime to minimise detection. Then, feeling bolder and more experienced, they leave shorter gaps as the drive to kill blunts their instinct for self-preservation. In 1915–17 the deaths were two years apart; in 1926 the deaths were six months apart; and in 1930 they were three months apart. In the final case, the whole process of death took a matter of days; earlier that year it had been almost seven months. Mrs Thomas's death guaranteed an enquiry as she was relatively young and healthy, so if Mrs Hearn was a serial killer she had reached the final stage of recklessness which often leads to arrest and conviction. By this stage the killer is so confident in their powers and in the ineptitude of doctors and the police that they think they are invincible and thus are over-confident. Yet this is a theory. There is little contemporary realisation save for a question at the inquest that she was killing en masse and when Mrs Spear reeled off the list of those who had died at Trenhorne House in 1926–1930, there seems no suggestion that she was listing poison victims.

It is worth exploring what we know of Mrs Hearn's character. She seems to have been a woman who made few friends and kept herself very much to herself. This may have been due to shyness or from a sense of superiority or because she was naturally cold and unloving. She was reasonably well educated, but liked reading light fiction, thrillers and romances. She was a trained cook. She claimed to be a practising Christian. She was capable of appearing respectable and trustworthy. Yet she may have been a figure of pity; unmarried, with little money and burdened by caring responsibilities since at least 1915. She clearly wanted to have been married and this led her into deceit; as well as the fake marriage of 1917/1919, all her three aliases in 1930 were prefixed by Mrs, either as a widow (when with Powell) or as having a live husband as with Mrs Marker. This may have led her to entertain fantasies about Thomas (possibly encouraged by the romantic fantasy novels she enjoyed) who was the man she most had dealings with. It is not hard to think that a man who shows friendship might harbour deeper feelings than he does, and if he is married, that the one infatuated might think his wife is the only barrier to the two being together. Furthermore, his frequent visits to the sisters could be taken as additional proof of this. When this bubble was burst in the aftermath of Mrs Thomas's death, Mrs Hearn took flight, being not only suspected of murder but also, more importantly perhaps, having the object of her desires put beyond her reach. What Thomas had seen as being neighbourly she saw as a symptom of something more. Thus if Trebilcock was right, then this would fit with her alleged reference. She was also deceitful, not only about the marriage stories but also about the theft in 1919. But there was worse.

The account of the painful and prolonged sufferings leading to the death of Minnie, as outlined in Chapter 5, is horrific. Doubly so because her sister was present throughout. To kill a family member is bad enough, but to watch them suffer horribly at close quarters and then die is far worse and is not only suggestive of an utterly callous and unmerciful nature, but also of a sadist who enjoys witnessing long drawn-out torture lasting not days or even weeks, but months. This does not make her unique, regrettably. From 1897–1902 George Chapman slowly poisoned the three women who passed as his wives.

There seems even less reason why anyone else who came into contact with Mrs Thomas, such as Mrs Tucker, Mrs Parnell, Mrs Parsons or the Pearces, would kill her, and their opportunities were severely limited at best. They did come into contact with Mrs Thomas and that is all. Only Mrs Parsons was on close enough terms, but then only from 29 October.

If suicide can be ruled out – arsenic is a slow and agonising death – even if Mrs Thomas had access to the arsenic in the farmhouse, and given her immobility this seems unlikely, then can the same be said about an accident? Could any of the medicines given by the doctors to either Miss Everard or Mrs Thomas possibly have contained arsenic? The only evidence for what they gave her comes from themselves and naturally none were going to admit to this and neither were they seriously questioned about it. Thus it is hard to continue this line of reasoning, but perhaps it should not be ignored without consideration.

Perhaps it is worth discussing how Mrs Thomas died. That she was killed by arsenic is clear. The question is how and when it was administered. Was it put in the food consumed at Bude? Or was it given to her in the next eleven days, when Mrs Hearn fed and nursed her by herself? Birkett and Smith argued that the former was not possible because the arsenic would turn blue in contact with moisture and so would be seen by the eater. In this case, could Mrs Thomas have succumbed to food poisoning initially (and as Thomas and Mrs Hearn also claimed to having been slightly unwell soon afterwards this is not impossible) and then was fed arsenic in her food and drink?

However, although Mrs Thomas did die of arsenic, it is probable that it was white arsenic and so not visible, or that it had been inserted very shortly before the eating of the food in question before staining would occur. Yet there is no record of any such purchase. However, Mrs Hearn was in Harrogate and Grimsby and perhaps elsewhere from 1926–28. She could have bought arsenic there, as it is not known whether there was a national search of poison books.

Gilbert Arthur Freak, chief chemist of Cooper, McDougall & Robertsons Ltd, a laboratory, made the following observation about the weed-killer in question:

'As long as it is in a powder the colours are retained and would be discernible as it is now. In my opinion the colour would show up a trifle more if damp.

The pigment in the weed-killer is insoluble in water, the dye is soluble, the idea being to give the powder itself a blue colour and a blue colour to the solution when the powder is dissolved. For a reasonable time after making the mixture into solution it retains its blue colour. By reasonable time I mean 2 to 7 days or possibly longer. The colouring would gradually become less until the solution became colourless except for any grains of the pigment which remain in suspension and probably form a sediment. After a period of days or possibly weeks it would be possible to decant a colourless liquid'.[52]

The other possibility is that only a relatively small amount of arsenic was introduced to the food eaten at the café. This could have been enough to have made Mrs Thomas very ill but not enough to have caused major staining, and if introduced shortly before the meal might not have had time to show up. More arsenic could then have been introduced when Mrs Hearn was at Trenhorne Farm, which was the case from the time of Mrs Thomas's illness until she was sent to hospital. She had sole charge of the cooking until 29 October and then was helping in the house so opportunity remained throughout.

The question is whether Mrs Hearn killed Mrs Thomas. The answer to this is dependent on the answer as to whether Miss Everard was killed or not; she certainly had sufficient arsenic in her body and her diary recounts all the symptoms of the poison, so it would seem inescapable that she was. Birkett argued that arsenic in the soil and water contaminated her body, though those present said not. Yet the former is to ignore the evidence of the diary, Dr Lynch's examination and other witnesses. If she was killed, and it seems difficult to think that she was not, then Mrs Hearn killed her and thus almost certainly killed Mrs Thomas. She had a motive and opportunity in both cases. The evidence, incomplete though it is, suggests it is more likely than not that Mrs Hearn was a multiple poisoner, responsible for earlier deaths too, but this is not wholly conclusive. Because of this it was reasonable that she was given the benefit of the doubt during her trial.

However, we can lay this to one side and look at what is most likely. The conclusion which seems most probable is that Mrs Hearn poisoned her aunt for her money, her sister because she was a burden and her neighbour because she entertained fantasies about her neighbour's husband. The arsenic purchased in 1926 was probably used to kill Miss Mary Everard, Minnie and Mrs Thomas and was then disposed of thereafter.

An additional reason for Mrs Hearn to kill her sister may have been this. Although Thomas preferred her to Minnie, to a woman with an obsessive and possessive nature, even the fact that Minnie took up some of his attention was too much. She wanted him all to herself. So she had to die. Once this was achieved, Mrs Hearn was one step nearer to her ultimate goal. She still had to share Thomas with Mrs Thomas and thus her days were numbered too.

Appendix: Agatha Christie and Annie Hearn

(Warning: includes spoilers. Read *Sad Cypress* before reading this)

T he 1940 novel by Agatha Christie, *Sad Cypress*, has already been referred to and the single explicit reference in that novel to the Hearn case has previously been stated. Ironically, a writer discussing the Hearn case reported, 'the whole thing has an air of Agatha Christie fiction'.[1] It is actually the other way around. There was also a five-part BBC Radio 4 adaptation of the story in 1992, in which John Moffatt played Hercule Poirot. The TV dramatisation of the book starring David Suchet as Hercule Poirot in the long-running series *Agatha Christie's Poirot* appeared in 2003 and does not refer to the Hearn case; there are many true crime references in the Agatha Christie books, but these are usually chopped from the TV adaptations.

Most of the book's readers will not have heard of the Hearn case it alludes to and it certainly made no impression on this author, who read the book for the first time in 1987 and a couple of times afterwards.

In the novel, set in 1939, Roderick Welman and Elinor Carlisle are engaged but receive an anonymous letter alleging that their aunt, the wealthy and elderly Laura Welman of Hunterbury near Maidensford, is being preyed upon by a potential gold-digger. They visit her and the 'threat' is revealed as the young and beautiful Mary Gerrard, apparently the daughter of the lodge keeper, who has been favoured by Mrs Welman.

Roderick falls in love with Mary. The engagement with Elinor is over and Mrs Welman, who has already had two strokes, dies apparently from natural causes on 28 June, just before she was to have made a will. Elinor inherits her fortune of about £200,000 as next of kin. However, Jessie Hopkins, the local district nurse, who helped tend Mrs Welman in her final illness, finds that a tube of her medicine is missing, and this contains morphine. This goes officially unreported.

Elinor sells Hunterbury and on Thursday 27 July meets Mary (to whom she has already given £2,000 from her aunt's estate) and Nurse Hopkins, who has taken an interest in Mary and has persuaded her to make a will in favour of her aunt, Mary Riley, a nurse in New Zealand. Elinor takes fish paste sandwiches for them to eat, having bought the bread and butter and then a pot of salmon and shrimp paste and a pot of salmon and anchovy paste from a grocer en route to Hunterbury and after mentioning to the grocer about the dangers of food poisoning. She has murder in her heart. Leaving the sandwiches in the kitchen, she goes to the Lodge to invite Mary and Hopkins to lunch with her. The three women have lunch together. Elinor first offers the plate of fish paste sandwiches to Mary and then to the nurse. The two also drink tea which Hopkins makes. Mary apparently dies of morphine poisoning, of the 'foudroyante' variety, which means that the victim falls asleep and dies within ten minutes. Elinor's antipathy towards Mary is well known and she is arrested for her murder, having had both opportunity and motive. Mrs Welman's corpse is exhumed; morphine is found in her body too.

Dr Peter Lord, a local physician, is in love with Elinor and consults Poirot, wanting him to investigate the case and find evidence that will acquit his beloved. At first Poirot appears reluctant and examines the case against Elinor.

The two men discuss the case. A suggestion is made that the death might be passed off as food poisoning. Yet Poirot dismisses this as morphine poisoning and food poisoning have different symptoms so it would be hard to expect to have one taken for the other. Lord also has to explain that while he suspected that the death of Mrs Welman was suicide not natural, he did not voice his suspicions and signed the death certificate as the latter in order to avoid scandal. The defence is planning to argue that the engagement was one made for family reasons and was not one of passion, and so Elinor lacked the necessary passionate animosity to kill Mary. They also wonder if the sandwiches could have been poisoned after Elinor left them in order to ask the other two women to join her for lunch. They wonder if Mary could have seen someone take the morphine to kill Mrs Welman and so she in turn had to be silenced.

Poirot agrees to investigate. He then questions the *dramatis personae*: the two nurses; former housekeeper, Mrs Bishop; Ted Bigland, a mechanic in love with Mary; Welman; Elinor, and various officials. Some believe Elinor guilty with others disagreeing and Mrs Bishop posits food poisoning as the cause of Mary's death. Poirot also learns much that is useful in building up an alternate case. It is learnt that Mary was the illegitimate daughter of Mrs Welman, that Mary made a will in favour of her aunt in New Zealand, due to the legacy she received from Mrs Welman, that Welman met her in London when he said he was abroad and that Elinor's will leaves her fortune to him, and that Dr Lord was near the crime scene.

Elinor is put on trial for murder at the Old Bailey. According to the prosecution only Elinor had the opportunity and the motive to murder Mary. The defence argues that Mary could have committed suicide, but that Elinor lacked a real motive and had opportunity alone, before launching into an alternate theory as supplied by Poirot and so she is acquitted. That is, that the real murderer is revealed as Nurse Hopkins who killed Mrs Welman and then Mary so the former's fortune would pass to the latter (as her daughter) and then to her, as Mary's aunt (Mary Riley) who is from New Zealand (she thus killed her own niece). It turns out that the poison was in the tea not the sandwiches and that Hopkins injected herself with apomorphine hydrochloride, an antidote (it is not stated why Elinor did not drink the poisoned tea; in the TV version she states that she is not a tea drinker), thus enabling her to drink the poisoned tea with few ill effects. Poirot deduces this because Hopkins said that she had been pricked by a rose thorn when she could not have been because the roses in question were thornless and because she appeared to have been sick, a side-effect of the antidote. It is noted that the killer previously poisoned a woman whom she inherited a legacy from and was suspected of other poisonings. Elinor and Dr Lord are united at the book's end. Ironically the solicitor in the story, Seddon, shares the same name as an infamous Edwardian arsenic poisoner. Nurse Hopkins's fate is unknown; she leaves the court room before the end of the case for the defence and so whether she is later arrested is left unknown. No one makes any further comment about her.

Throughout the novel there is an ambiguity over whether Elinor is innocent or guilty and in her attitudes. On page one there is concern expressed by her defending counsel at the trial about whether she will plead guilty or not guilty. We see her harbour hatred (not unnaturally) against Mary Gerrard as her fiancée falls for her and when Elinor sees Mary making a will she laughs and states how funny that is. Elinor is a passionate woman and later tells Poirot about her feelings toward Mary and that she had murder in her heart and thus is guilty of that. He tells her that that is not the same as committing murder and that she is judging herself by standards which are too high.

Compared to some Agatha Christie stories, the book is emotionally engaging, especially when it concerns Elinor, and to a lesser extent Dr Lord and Roderick Welman. The murderer's personality is perhaps less well drawn and psychologically she is a closed book.

In the TV adaptation, Elizabeth Dermot Walsh plays Elinor, Rupert Penry Jones is Roderick Welman, Phyllis Logan plays Nurse Hopkins, Diana Quick is Mrs Welman and Paul McGann is Dr Lord. Given the limited running time of just under 100 minutes, Mrs Bishop's role is vastly cut and Horlicks the gardener and Ted Bigland's roles are merged. Mary is described as being the gardener's not the lodge keeper's daughter and her apparent father does not appear in the drama.

Deviating from the book, the story is set in 1937 and Poirot appears throughout, rather than being introduced at mid-point. It transpires here that Elinor had made an appointment to meet Mary and Nurse Hopkins in Hunterbury prior to their lunch (therefore giving the killer time to prepare the poison) and that Elinor does not drink the tea that is poisoned. Elinor has not made up one plate of sandwiches, but has a separate plate for each person, and the sandwiches are salmon paste (for Mary) and crab and shrimp paste (for her and Hopkins). Furthermore, in order to add to the tension, Elinor is found guilty of murder in court and is sentenced to death. At the last moment Poirot discovers the truth and meets Dr Lord, Mr Welman and the murderess at Hunterbury. The latter tries to poison him with a cup of tea but fails, as Poirot never drinks tea, and is apprehended after Poirot has revealed her plot.

There are many differences between the novel *Sad Cypress* and the real case. In the book, the majority of the characters are upper middle class or servants/ nurses and the action takes place in the Home Counties, not far from London, rather than among more lowly folk in a relatively remote Cornish village. Murder occurs in a country house rather than a more modest dwelling and a tea shop and the poison used is rather more immediate in taking deadly effect. The motive in the book is entirely monetary; to gain a vast inheritance. The murderess in the book does not kill her sister. The novel ends with the exposure of the guilty whereas in reality the case was left unsolved. It also ends with a happy romantic ending, as do most of Agatha's books; no such ending ensued for any of the characters in real life.

Likewise, in reality there was never a suggestion by the defence that Mrs Thomas or Minnie committed suicide. Nor did they strongly posit another suspect as the killer, though there was a faint suggestion that Thomas was guilty.

However, apart from the central scene of the alleged poisoned sandwiches, there are some similarities. In the story the killer has killed by poison before and her victim was an elderly woman. Both killer and victims are all female and poison is used throughout. This first murder is not suspected until after the murder of Mary Gerrard. This matches the reality. This first murder is the killing of what will be the accused's aunt; and Mary Everard was Mrs Hearn's aunt. It is suggested that the killer had poisoned before – Poirot notes that 'anyone who has once committed a murder finds it only too easy to commit another'. In the fatal meeting there were three characters; murderer, victim and one other, as in reality. The murderess in the book is a middle-aged woman who is not well off and has much experience of nursing the sick. She appears respectable and competent. She is introduced as 'a homely looking middle aged woman with a capable air and a brisk manner' and a character later refers to her as a 'sensible, shrewd, middle aged woman, quite kindly and competent'. She clearly resembles Mrs Hearn. The true identity of the murderess's character is unknown until near the novel's end and Mrs Hearn often deceived people about her real name and other personal details, especially her marital status. There is the suspicion that the accused woman's motivation is jealousy, as her fiancé Roddy Welman has fallen in love with Mary Gerrard and broken off his engagement with her. In both story and reality a male character acts as the accused's supporter, whether Herbert Powell in reality or Dr Lord as in the book, though from different motivations. Powell was Mrs Hearn's ex-employer and Dr Lord is the accused's would-be lover. In both the novel and real life the story ends with the acquittal of the accused.

It is also possible that the first verse of the song from *Twelfth Night*, Act II, scene IV, cited at the novel's opening, might provide a clue:

'Come away, come away, death
And in sad cypress let me be laid;
Fly away, fly away, breath;
I am slain by a fair cruel maid'

Of course, in the novel the 'fair cruel maid' would appear to be Elinor but is actually the spinster Nurse Hopkins, but with reference to the real-life case of Annie Hearn arguably points to her, another spinster.

It is quite possible that Agatha Christie, with her often unerring insight into murder mysteries, was, implicitly at least, pointing the finger at Mrs Hearn by identifying the murderer as a middle-aged woman with experience of the sick bed. Or perhaps it could be argued that she was 'acquitting' Mrs Hearn as she has the accused but innocent woman (Elinor Carlisle) acquitted in the book. Or perhaps neither hypothesis is true and we are reading far too much into a novel that only has one explicit reference to the real case and where the main intention is to entertain the reader.

A critique of the book's central plot was made by John Curran. How could Nurse Hopkins ensure that Elinor did not drink the poisoned tea? And how, as Elinor called on Hopkins and Mary without prior notice, could Hopkins have had poison and antidote to hand immediately? No answers are given in the book and the author's notebooks do not suggest even a consideration of a possible solution.[2]

Authors writing about Agatha Christie have referred to this case. In 2010 Michael Holgate related it to the Agatha Christie novel *After the Funeral* (1953) in which an accusation of murder is made after the funeral, as Percy Parsons did in real life (albeit beforehand). Holgate then gives a brief account of the case. However, he refers to Annie Hearn as Sarah Anne Hearn and Sarah Hearn, and Alice Thomas is referred to as Annie Thomas. Mrs Hearn is referred to as being a widow, as she pretended to be, but not as she actually was. It also states that Mrs Thomas was in Plymouth Hospital for two weeks before she died. Curran, in his analysis of the Agatha Christie notebooks, discusses the novel but makes no reference to the Hearn case.

There have been two recent books about true crime and Agatha Christie's works and both refer to this case. Unfortunately both suffer from insufficient research, as is common with books that cover numerous stories. The first adds nothing to what is already known and is full of errors; Alice Thomas is called Annie Thomas and the author focusses on the arsenic in the Cornish soil as having contaminated the bodies.[3] Then there was another which defended Mrs Hearn, asking that as arsenic is tasteless then why was Mrs Thomas ill shortly after imbibing it; how could Mrs Hearn have ensured her victim took the poisoned sandwich; and finally asserting that the sandwiches would have been stained blue and that in the trial blue-stained sandwiches were passed to the jury. Mrs Hearn is apparently exonerated and so implicitly Thomas is noted as the killer.[4]

Unfortunately, as with the other book, this is only slightly researched and all three points can be easily answered. First, on imbibing the arsenic there is no taste but the first symptom is when the victim's body tries to eliminate the poison by being sick, which Mrs Thomas was. Second, ensuring a victim takes the poisoned food is easy; place it on the plate nearest to them (an experiment that can be tried by any doubtful reader). Third, no sandwiches, blue-stained or otherwise, were shown to the jury. It is not necessarily the case that the blue dye would even have been there, as it can be distilled. In this the author is taking the ploy of the defence as being accurate.

There are two other connections between Agatha Christie and Mrs Hearn. The first concerns Torquay, a place that Agatha knew very well, though Mrs Hearn was only there two months. This was where Agatha was born on 15 September 1890 at a detached house called Ashfield, on Barton Road, now long demolished. She lived there with her parents Frederick (1846–1901) and Clarissa (1854–1926) and her older siblings, Margaret (1880–1950) and Louis Morant (1878–1929). It was to Ashfield that Mrs Margaret Miller (1828–1919), Agatha's 'Auntie-Grannie', moved to from Ealing in 1914, and it was there that the inspiring novelist first learnt about poisons while employed by the Voluntary Aid Detachment during the First World War. It was at the Grand Hotel opposite Torquay railway station that Agatha and her first husband, Archibald Christie, enjoyed their honeymoon in December 1914, and it was at Ashfield that the couple's only child, Rosalind, was born on 5 August 1919. The Christies only briefly resided at Ashfield. The action in one of her Poirot novels, *Peril at End House* (1932), takes place in and near Torquay, though the seaside town is called St Loo and the Majestic Hotel, which overlooks the sea, is the name given to the Grand Hotel. Torquay trades on Christie's connection with the town; the International Agatha Christie conference is held there, there is bust of her in a prominent public place near the seafront and there is even a Christie's Fish and Chip shop!

Then there is Harrogate, the place where Mary Everard had her cookery school and where her niece learnt the skills that stood her in good stead in the decades after. It was Harrogate, at the Hydropathic Hotel, where Agatha Christie was discovered on 14 December 1926 (ironically Mrs Hearn and her sister were in Harrogate at this time) after a highly publicised disappearance lasting eleven days. She used an assumed name and discussed the disappearance of the famous novelist with fellow guests, just as Mrs Hearn discussed her own disappearance with others.

Bibliography

Primary sources

Manuscripts

National Archives
ASSI 26/47
HO 144/16306
MAF34/407/44

Wellcome Institute for the History of Medicine
PP/SP1/C7

Newspapers

Ballymeena Weekly Telegraph, 1931
Belfast Telegraph, 1931
Blyth News, 1930
Birmingham Gazette, 1930
Cornishman, 1930-1931
Coventry Ealing Telegraph, 1931
Daily Herald, 1930-1931
Daily Mail, 1930
Dundee Courier, 1930
Empire News, 1931
Evening Herald, 1930
Exeter and Plymouth Gazette, 1931
Gloucester Citizen, 1930
Harrogate Advertiser, 1919, 1930.
Hartlepool Daily Mail, 1930-1931
Illustrated Police News, 1931
Lancashire Daily Mail, 1930
Lancashire Evening Post, 1930
Launceston Weekly News, 1926, 1930-1931
Leeds Mercury, 1930
Lincolnshire Echo, 1930
Liverpool Echo, 1930, 1959

Londonderry Sentinel, 1930-1931
Northampton Chronicle and Echo, 1930
Nottingham Journal, 1930
Nottingham Evening Post, 1931
Peg's Companion, 1931
The People, 1959
Portsmouth Evening News, 1930-1931
Scotsman, 1930-1931
Sheffield Daily Telegraph, 1930-1931
Sheffield Independent, 1930
Taunton Courier, 1931
The Times, 1930-1931
Torquay Herald and Express, 1930.
Torquay Times, 1931
Weekly News, 1933
Wells Journal, 1920
Western Evening Press, 1930
Western Morning News, 1930-1933, 1949
Western Mail, 1930-1931
Western Times, 1931
Yorkshire Post and Leeds Intelligencer, 1930
Yorkshire Evening Post, 1930-1931

Directories

Cornwall, 1914, 1919, 1930
Crockford's Clerical Directory
Lincolnshire, 1887, 1891, 1896, 1905
Medical Directory, 1931
Who's Who, 1931

Published primary sources

W. Auternriech, *Detection of Poisons* (1928).
A.Bowker, *Behind the Bar* (1947).
Patrick Devlin, *Taken at the Flood* (1996).
Launceston Medical Officer of Health Annual Report (1937).
Bernard O'Donnell, *Crimes that made the news* (1954).
Keith Simpson, *Forty Years of Murder* (1978).
Arthur Smith, *Lord Goddard* (1959).
Sydney Smith, *Mostly Murder* (1959).

Books and articles

Dean Bardens, *Lord Justice Birkett* (1962).

Valentine Carla, *Murder isn't easy: the forensics of Agatha Christie* (2022).
Agatha Christie, *Sad Cypress* (1940).
John Curran, *Agatha Christie's Secret Notebooks* (2009).
Winifred Duke, *Six Trials* (1934).
Daniel Farson, 'Annie Hearn: The Case of the salmon sandwiches' *Unsolved* 28, (1984).
S.T. Felstead, *Shades of Scotland Yard* (1959).
P. Gray, *Cornish Murder Files* (2010).
Mark Holgate, *Stranger than Fiction: Agatha Christie's True Crime Inspirations* (2010).
H. Montgomery Hyde, *Norman Birkett: The Life of Lord Birkett of Ulveston* (1964).
Brian Lane, ed., *Murder Club Guide to South West England and Wales* (1989).
Mark John Maguire, *They got away with murder*, Vol 2, (2023).
Kathryn Markup, *A is for Arsenic: the poisons of Agatha Christie* (2015).
Janet Morgan, *Agatha Christie: An Autobiography* (2017).
M.W. Oldridge, *The Case of the Salmon sandwiches* (2021).
John Rigeby, *Arsenic and Mercy Quint* (2016).
C.J.S. Thompson, *Poison Mysteries Unsolved* (1937).
Michael Williams, *Cornish Mysteries* (1980).

Electronic sources

Ancestry.co.uk; censuses, civil registration indexes, electoral registers, medical directories.
Findmypast.co.uk, 1921 census
Will of Miss Mary Everard
Will of William Thomas
YouTube: Who killed Alice Thomas? The trial of Annie Hearn, 1931

Notes

Introduction

1. Agatha Christie, *Sad Cypress* (1940).

Chapter 1

1. *Western Morning News,* 17 June 1931.
2. Ibid, 14 January 1931.
3. *Weekly News*, 30 September 1933.
4. *The Times*, 27 November 1930; *Western Morning News*, 25 November 1931.
5. *Western Morning News*, 26 February 1931.
6. The National Archives, ASSI26/47.
7. *Western Morning News*, 25 November 1930, 17 June 1931.
8. *The Times*, 27 November 1930; *Western Morning News*, 26 February 1931, 17 June 1931.
9. *The Times*, 27 November 1930; *Western Morning News*, 25 November 1931 and 17 June 1931.
10. *The Times*, 27 November 1930; *Western Morning News*, 25 November 1931 and 17 June 1931.
11. *Western Morning News*, 25 November 1930.
12. *Daily Herald*, 26 November 1930.
13. *The Times*, 27 November 1930; *Western Morning News*, 25-26 November 1930, 16 June 1931.
14. *Western Morning News*, 25 February 1931 and 16 June 1931.
15. Ibid, 26 February 1931.
16. Ibid, 17 June 1931.
17. *The Times*, 27 November 1930; *Western Morning News*, 18 June 1931.
18. *Western Morning News*, 24 November 1930.
19. Ibid, 13 March 1931.
20. Ibid, 12 March, 12 and 17 June 1931.
21. Ibid, 27 October 1930.
22. Ibid, 27 November 1930.
23. *The Times*, 27 November 1930.
24. *Western Morning News*, 25 November 1931.
25. *Dundee Courier*, 18 November 1930.
26. *Cornishman*, 20 November 1930.

27. *The Times*, 27 November 1930; *Western Morning News*, 27 November 1930.
28. *The Times*, 27 November 1930; *Western Morning News*, 25 November 1930 and 20 June 1931.
29. *Western Morning News*, 25 November 1930.
30. Ibid, 25 and 27 November 1930.
31. Ibid, 27 November 1930.
32. Ibid.
33. Ibid, 25 November 1930.
34. *Western Morning News*, 27 November 1930; *The Times*, 27 November 1930.
35. *The Times*, 27 November 1930.
36. Ibid.
37. Ibid.
38. *Western Morning News*, 25 February 1931.
39. TNA, ASSI26/47.
40. *The Times*, 25 February 1931; TNA, ASSI26/47.
41. *The Times*, 31 January 1931.
42. *Western Morning News*, 27 November 1930.
43. Ibid, 22 June 1931.
44. *Peg's Companion*, 1 September 1931.
45. *Western Morning News*, 17 June 1931.
46. Ibid, 25 November, 17 and 22 June 1931.
47. Ibid, 16 and 17 June 1931.
48. Ibid, 22 June 1931.
49. *Peg's Companion*, 1 September 1931.
50. *Launceston Weekly News*, 15 November 1930.
51. *Western Morning News*, 22 June 1931.
52. Ibid, 27 November 1930.
53. Ibid, 22 June 1931.
54. Ibid, 27 November 1930.
55. *The Times*, 12 March 1931.
56. Ibid, 25 February 1931.
57. *Western Morning News*, 27 November 1930.
58. Ibid, 18 November 1930.
59. *Launceston Weekly News*, 8 November 1930.
60. *Western Morning News*, 24 November 1930.
61. Ibid, 16 June 1931.
62. *The Times*, 12 March 1931.

Chapter 2

1. Ancestry.co.uk; census returns.
2. *Lincolnshire directory*, 1887.
3. *Lincolnshire directory*, ancestry.co.uk, census returns.
4. *Hull Daily Mail*, 26 August 1897.

5. *Weekly News*, 16 September 1933.
6. Findmypast.
7. Ibid.
8. *Peg's Companion*, 25 August 1931.
9. Ancestry.co.uk, census returns.
10. Ancestry.co.uk, census returns; *Western Morning News*, 21 June 1931.
11. *Weekly News*, 16 September 1933.
12. *Western Mail*, 24 June 1931.
13. Ancestry.co.uk census returns.
14. Ibid; *Launceston Weekly News*, 28 August 1926.
15. Ibid; Ancestry.co.uk, census returns.
16. Ancestry.co.uk, census returns, soldiers' pension records.
17. Ancestry.co.uk census returns.
18. *Peg's Companion*, 25 August 1931.
19. Ibid.
20. *Western Morning News*, 19 June 1931.
21. *Peg's Companion*, 15 September 1931.
22. Ibid, 25 August 1931.
23. *Weekly News*, 16 September 1933; *Yorkshire Post and Leeds Intelligencer*, 20 November 1930.
24. *Peg's Companion*, 25 August 1931.
25. Ibid.
26. *Sheffield Independent*, 21 November 1930; death certificates of Betsy and Grace Everard.
27. *Sheffield Daily Telegraph*, 20 November 1930; *Western Morning News*, 20 June 1931.
28. *Western Morning News*, 20 June 1931.
29. *Western Mail*, 24 June 1931.
30. *Peg's Companion*, 25 August 1931.
31. Ibid.
32. *Yorkshire Post and Leeds Intelligencer*, 19 and 20 November 1930.
33. *The Harrogate Herald*, 25 June 1919.
34. *Crockford's Clerical Directory*.
35. *Leeds Mercury*, 16 December 1930.
36. *Daily Herald*, 19 November 1930.
37. *Sheffield Independent*, 18 November 1930.
38. *Harrogate Advertiser*, 22 November 1930.
39. *Yorkshire Post and Leeds Intelligencer*, 19 and 20 November 1930.
40. *Lincolnshire Echo*, 17 December 1930.
41. *Nottingham Journal*, 21 November 1930.
42. *Daily Herald*, 19 November 1930.
43. *Peg's Companion*, 25 August 1931.
44. *Weekly News*, 16 September 1933.
45. *Yorkshire Post and Leeds Intelligencer*, 19 and 20 November 1930.

46. *Wells Journal*, 2 January 1920; *Western Daily Press*, 1 January 1920.
47. *Western Daily Press*, 2 and 9 January 1920.
48. Ibid, 1 January 1920.
49. *Wells Journal*, 2 January 1920.
50. *Western Daily Press*, 1 January 1920.
51. Ibid, 1 January 1920.
52. Ibid.
53. Ibid, 9 January 1920.
54. Will of Miss Mary Everard.
55. Census returns, 1921.
56. *Western Morning News*, 16 December 1930.
57. 1921 census.
58. *The Times*, 25 February 1931.
59. *Western Morning News*, 20 June 1931.
60. Ibid, 19 July 1931.
61. *Western Morning News*, 20 November 1930.
62. *Yorkshire Post and Leeds Intelligencer*, 21 November 1930.
63. Ibid, 19 and 20 November 1930.
64. *Western Morning News*, 11 December 1930.
65. *Western Morning News*, 12 December 1930 and 16 June and 19 June 1931; *Torbay Herald and Express*, 22 December 1930.
66. Ibid, 16 September 1937.
67. TNA, ASSI 26/47.
68. *Western Morning News*, 18 November 1930.
69. Ibid, 20 June 1931
70. *Peg's Companion*, 15 August 1931.
71. Ibid, 25 August 1931.
72. *Launceston Weekly News*, 22 November 1930.
73. TNA, ASSI41/16.
74. Ancestry.co.uk, census returns.
75. *Cornwall Directory*, (1930), pp.194-195.
76. *Western Morning News*, 12 March 1931.
77. *Cornwall Directory (1930); Western Morning News*, 17 June 1931 and 7 July 1932 and 30 September 1932.
78. *Western Morning News*, 25 November 1930.
79. Ibid, 24, 27 November 1930.
80. *Launceston Weekly News*, 15 November 1930.
81. *Peg's Companion*, 25 August 1931.
82. *Western Morning News*, 27 November 1931.
83. *Western Morning News*, 16 and 17 June 1931; TNA, ASSI 26/47.
84. *Peg's Companion*, 22 September 1931.
85. TNA, ASSI26/47.
86. *Weekly News*, 23 September 1933.

87. *Empire News*, 5 July 1931.
88. *Weekly News*, 23 September 1933.
89. TNA, ASSI 26/47.

Chapter 3

1. *Western Morning News*, 27 November 1930.
2. Ibid, 18 June 1931.
3. Ibid.
4. Wellcome Institute for the History of Medicine, PP/SPI/C7.
5. W. Autenrieth, *Detection of Poisons* (1928), pp.264–266.
6. *The Times*, 13 March 1931.
7. *Western Morning News*, 25 November 1930.
8. Ibid.
9. *Western Morning News*, 16 March 1928; *Launceston Weekly News*, 2 August 1930.
10. *The Times*, 25 February 1931.
11. *Western Morning News*, 13 March 1931.
12. *Weekly News*, 30 September 1933.
13. *Peg's Companion*, 1 September 1931.
14. *Western Morning News*, 13 March 1931.
15. Ibid, 12 March 1931.
16. Ibid, 17 June 1931.
17. *Western Morning News*, 17 June 1931.
18. *The Times*, 12 March 1931; *Western Morning News*, 12 March 1931.
19. *Western Morning News*, 18 June 1931.
20. *Torbay Herald and Express*, 17 November 1930.
21. *The Times*, 18 November 1930, 25 February 1931.
22. *Sheffield Independent*, 18 November 1930.
23. *Western Morning News*, 13 March 1931.
24. TNA, ASSI26/47.
25. *Yorkshire Evening Post*, 20 November 1930.
26. *Sheffield Daily Telegraph*, 21 November 1930.
27. *Yorkshire Evening Post*, 20 November 1930.
28. *Western Times*, 5 December 1930.
29. *Belfast Telegraph*, 5 January 1931; *Taunton Courier*, 7 January 1931; *Leeds Mercury* 18 November 1930.
30. *Western Morning News*, 15 November 1931.
31. *Northampton Chronicle and Echo*, 25 November 1930.
32. *Western Morning News and Mercury*, 27 November 1930.
33. *Western Morning News and Mercury*, 27 November 1930.
34. *Western Morning News*, 29 November 1930.
35. *Hartlepool Northern Mail*, 21 November 1930.
36. *Gloucester Citizen*, 27 November 1930.
37. *Lancashire Evening Post*, 22 November 1930.

38. *Western Morning News*, 22 November 1930.
39. *Sheffield Daily Telegraph*, 26 November 1930.
40. *Daily Herald*, 29 November 1930.
41. *Western Morning News*, 22 November 1930.
42. *Sheffield Independent*, 22 November 1930.
43. *Daily Herald*, 19 November 1930.
44. *Yorkshire Evening Post*, 22 November 1930.
45. *Leeds Mercury*, 18 November 1930.
46. Ibid, 17 November 1930.
47. *Yorkshire Evening Post*, 20 November 1930.
48. *Yorkshire Post and Leeds Intelligencer*, 21 November 1930.
49. *Lincolnshire Echo*, 17 December 1930.
50. *Birmingham Gazette*, 18 November 1930.
51. *Yorkshire Post and Leeds Intelligencer*, 20 November 1930.
52. *Daily Herald*, 19 November 1930.
53. *Dundee Evening Telegraph*, 21 November 1930.

Chapter 4

1. *The Times*, 27 November 1930.
2. *Western Morning News*, 25 November 1931.
3. Ibid.
4. *Daily Herald*, 25 November 1930; *Western Morning News*, 25 November 1930.
5. *Evening Herald*, 26 November 1930.
6. *The Times*, 27 November 1930.
7. *Londonderry Sentinel*, 27 November 1930.
8. *Western Morning News*, 27 November 1930.
9. Ibid.
10. *The Times*, 27 November 1930.
11. *Western News and Mercury*, 27 November 1930.
12. *The Times*, 27 November 1930.
13. Ibid.
14. Ibid.
15. *Londonderry Sentinel*, 27 November 1930.
16. *The Times*, 12 February 1931.
17. *Lancashire Evening Post*, 28 November 1930.
18. Bernard O'Donnell, *Crimes that made the news* (1954), pp.143-144.

Chapter 5

1. *Western Morning News*, 1 December 1930.
2. *Launceston Weekly News*, 6 March 1926.
3. Oldridge, *Salmon Sandwiches*, pp.313-314.
4. *Yorkshire Post and Leeds Intelligencer*, 19 and 20 November 1930.

5. *Weekly News*, 23 September 1933; *Launceston Weekly News*, 28 August 1926.
6. *Western Morning News*, 18 November 1931.
7. *Weekly News*, 23 September 1933.
8. *Western Morning News*, 16 June 1931.
9. TNA, ASSI 26/47.
10. *The Times*, 25 February 1931.
11. *Yorkshire Post and Leeds Intelligencer*, 19 and 20 November 1930.
12. *Launceston Weekly News*, 28 August 1926.
13. Ancestry.co.uk, wills.
14. *Weekly News*, 23 September 1933.
15. *Yorkshire Post and Leeds Intelligencer*, 19 and 20 November 1930.
16. *Western Morning News*, 20 June 1931.
17. Ibid, 17 June 1931.
18. *Yorkshire Post and Leeds Intelligencer*, 20 November 1930.
19. *Western Morning News*, 12 December 1930.
20. Ibid, 22 June 1931.
21. *Western Mail*, 24 June 1931; death certificate.
22. *Western Morning News*, 22 June 1931.
23. Ibid, 27 February 1931.
24. Ibid.
25. TNA, ASSI 26/47.
26. *The Times*, 25 February 1931; *Western Morning News*, 19 and 22 June 1931.
27. *Western Morning News*, 25 February 1930.
28. *The Times*, 25 January 1931.
29. TNA, ASSI 26/47.
30. Ibid.
31. Ibid.
32. Ibid.
33. *Western Morning News*, 17 June 1931.
34. TNA, ASSI 26/47.
35. Ibid.
36. Ibid.
37. Ibid.
38. Ibid.
39. *The Times*, 25 February 1931; *Western Morning News*, 27 February 1931.
40. *Western Morning News*, 22 June 1931.
41. TNA, ASSI 26/47.
42. *Western Morning News*, 19 June 1931.
43. Ibid, 18 March 1931.
44. TNA, ASSI 26/47.
45. Ibid.
46. *Western Morning News*, 19 June 1931.
47. Ibid.

48. Ibid, 18 March 1931.
49. TNA, ASSI 26/47.
50. *Western Morning News*, 12 March 1931.
51. Ibid, 22 June 1931.
52. Ibid, 19 June 1931.
53. Ibid, 22 June 1931.
54. Ibid, 19 June 1931.
55. TNA, ASSI 26/47.
56. *The Times*, 25 February 1931.
57. TNA, ASSI 26/47.
58. *The Times*, 25 February 1931.
59. *Western Morning News*, 27 February 1931.
60. TNA, ASSI 26/47.
61. *Western Morning News*, 19 June 1930.
62. *The Times*, 25 February 1931.
63. *Western Morning News*, 19 June 1931.
64. TNA, ASSI 26/47.
65. Ibid.
66. Ibid.
67. *Western Morning News*, 19 June 1931.
68. TNA, ASSI 26/47.
69. Ibid.
70. *The Times*, 25 February 1931.
71. *Western Morning News*, 25 February 1931.
72. Ibid, 19 June 1931.
73. *The Times*, 24 February 1931; TNA, ASSI 26/47.
74. *Western Morning News*, 24 June 1931.
75. Ibid, 19 June 1931.
76. Ibid.
77. *The Times*, 24 February 1931.
78. TNA, ASSI26/47.
79. *Weekly News*, 23 September 1933.
80. *Western Morning News*, 19 June 1931.
81. Ibid.
82. Ibid.
83. *Western Morning News*, 17 June 1931.
84. TNA, ASSI24/47.
85. See online database with toxicological profile of arsenic https://wwwn.cdc.gov/
    TSP/ToxProfiles/ToxProfiles.aspx?id=22&tid=3
    https://www.atsdr.cdc.gov/ToxProfiles/tp2-c3.pdf
    This information was kindly supplied by Dr Anna-Lena Berg.
86. *The Times*, 9 December 1930.
87. *Yorkshire Post and Leeds Intelligencer*, 19 and 20 November 1930.

88. *The Times*, 27 February 1931.
89. TNA, ASSI26/47.
90. Ibid.
91. *Western Morning News*, 29 November 1930.

Chapter 6

1. *Portsmouth Evening News*, 2 December 1930.
2. *Scotsman*, 29 November 1930.
3. *Western Morning News*, 1 December 1930.
4. *Hartlepool Daily Mail*, 4 December 1930.
5. *Lincolnshire Echo*, 1 December 1930.
6. *Western Morning News*, 12 December 1930; TNA, HO 144/16306.
7. *The Times* 19, 25 February 1931.
8. *Western Morning News*; 8 December 1930; *Lancashire Daily Post*; 9 December 1930.
9. *Birmingham Daily Gazette*, 10 December 1930; *Western Morning News*, 19 June 1931.
10. *Liverpool Echo*, 6 July 1957.
11. Ibid, 19 December 1959.
12. *Western Morning News*, 25 and 28 February 1931.
13. Ibid, 11 December 1930.
14. *Daily Mail*, 9 December 1930.
15. *Western Morning News*, 11 December 1930.
16. Ibid, 4 December 1930.
17. *Blyth News*, 1 December 1930.
18. *Lincolnshire Echo*, 2 December 1930.
19. *Western Morning News*, 22 December 1930.
20. Ibid, 3 January 1931.
21. *Belfast Telegraph*, 5 January 1931.
22. *Taunton Courier*, 7 January 1931.
23. *The Times*, 31 January 1931.
24. *Torbay Herald and Express*, 12 November 1930.
25. TNA, ASSI 26/47; *Western Morning News*, 16 June 1931.
26. *The Times*, 14 March 1931, 25 February 1931.
27. *Medical Directory*, 1930, p.1327.
28. *Western Morning News*, 14 January 1931.
29. Ibid.
30. *The Times*, 31 January 1931; *Western Morning News*, 13 February 1931.
31. *Western Times*, 16 January 1931.
32. *The Times*, 31 January 1931; *Western Morning News* 13 February 1931; *The Western Times*, 16 January 1931.
33. *Weekly News*, 7 October 1933.
34. *The Times*, 31 January 1931
35. Ibid, 12 March 1931.

36. *Western Morning News*, 16 June 1931
37. Ibid.
38. *The Times*, 12 March 1931.
39. Ibid.
40. Ibid.
41. Ibid, 31 January 1931.
42. *Western Morning News*, 22 June 1931.
43. Ibid, 13 March 1931
44. Information supplied by Roger Winnen, Cornwall Railway Society.
45. *Peg's Companion*, 8 September 1931.
46. *Western Morning News*, 18 June 1931.
47. *The Times*, 14 March 1931, *Western Morning News* 14 March 1931.
48. *Weekly News*, 7 October 1933.
49. Ibid.
50. Patrick Devlin, *Taken at the Flood* (1996), p.125.
51. *Launceston Weekly News*, 17 January 1931.
52. Ibid.
53. *The Torquay Times and Devon Advertiser*, 16 January 1931.
54. *Torquay and South Devon Advertiser*, 16 January 1931.

Chapter 7

1. *Western Morning News*, 14 January 1931.
2. Ibid.
3. *Weekly News*, 14 October 1933.
4. *Peg's Companion*, 25 August 1931.
5. Ibid, 8 September 1931.
6. *Illustrated Police News*, 29 January 1931.
7. *Londonderry Sentinel*, 29 January 1931.
8. *Western Morning News*, 14 January 1931.
9. O'Donnell, *Crimes*, pp.147-148.
10. Devlin, *Taken*, p.126.
11. A.E. Bowker, *Behind the Bar*, (1948), p.198.
12. O'Donell, *Crimes*, pp.147-149.
13. *Illustrated Police News*, 29 January 1931; *Daily Herald*, 6 February 1931; *Western Times*, 20 February 1931.
14. *Western Morning News*, 23 January 1931.
15. Ibid.
16. Ibid, 25 February 1931.
17. *The Times*, 25 February 1931.
18. Ibid.
19. Ibid.
20. Ibid.
21. Ibid.

22. *Daily Herald*, 27 February 1931.
23. TNA, HO 144/16306.
24. Ibid.
25. Ibid.
26. Ibid.
27. Ibid.
28. *Portsmouth Evening News*, 25 February 1931.
29. *Western Morning News*, 26 February 1931.
30. Ibid.
31. Ibid.
32. Ibid.
33. *Sheffield Daily Telegraph*, 26 February 1931.
34. *The Times*, 27 February 1931.
35. *Daily Herald*, 27 February 1931.
36. *The Times*, 28 February 1931.
37. *Ballymeena Weekly Telegraph*, 7 March 1931.
38. *Western Morning News*, 11 March 1931.
39. *The Times*, 12 March 1931.
40. Ibid.
41. Ibid.
42. Ibid.
43. Ibid.
44. *The Times*, 13 March 1931.
45. Ibid.
46. Ibid.
47. Ibid.
48. Ibid.
49. Ibid.
50. Ibid.
51. *The Times*, 14 March 1931.
52. Ibid.
53. Ibid.
54. Ibid.
55. Ibid.
56. *The Times*, 16 March 1931.
57. Ibid.
58. Ibid.
59. Ibid.
60. Ibid.
61. Ibid.
62. Ibid.
63. Ibid.
64. Ibid.

65. Ibid.
66. Ibid.
67. Ibid.
68. Ibid.
69. Ibid.
70. Ibid.
71. *The Times*, 20 March 1931.
72. Ibid.
73. Ibid.
74. Ibid.
75. *Western Morning News*, 20 March 1931.
76. Devlin, *Taken*, p.133.
77. *Exeter and Plymouth Gazette*, 19 February 1931.
78. *Western Morning News*, 26 February 1931.
79. *Northern Whig*, 28 February 1931.
80. *Peg's Companion*, 25 August 1931.
81. *Who's Who*, 1931, p.939.
82. *Gloucester Citizen*, 17 April 1931.
83. *Western Morning News*, 5 May 1931.
84. H. Montgomery Hyde, *Norman Birkett: The definitive biography of the legendary barrister*, (1964), p.xi.
85. Bowker, *Behind*, p.198.
86. *Sheffield Independent*, 12 May 1931.
87. *Peg's Companion*, 25 August 1931.
88. TNA, ASSI 26/47.
89. Ibid.

Chapter 8

1. K. Simpson, *Forty Years of Murder* (1978), p.32.
2. *Liverpool Echo*, 18 December 1959; Sydney Smith, *Mostly Murder* (1959), p.177.
3. *Hull Daily Mail*, 12 June 1931.
4. *Weekly News*, 24 October 1933.
5. Ibid.
6. *Peg's Companion*, 25 August 1931.
7. *Daily Herald*, 15 June 1931.
8. *Western Morning News*, 16 June 1931.
9. Arthur Smith, *Lord Goddard* (1959), pp.53-54.
10. *Western Morning News*, 16 June 1931.
11. *Weekly News*, 14 October 1933.
12. *Peg's Companion*, 25 August 1931.
13. *Who's Who*, 1931, p.2721.
14. *Western Morning News*, 19 June 1931.
15. *Launceston Weekly News*, 20 June 1931.

16. *Western Morning News*, 16 June 1931.
17. Smith, *Mostly Murder*, pp.179-180.
18. *Western Morning News and Mercury*, 17 June 1931.
19. *The Times*, 17 June 1931.
20. *The Times*, 17 June 1931.
21. *Western Morning News*, 17 June 1931.
22. Ibid.
23. *The Times*, 17 June 1931.
24. Ibid.
25. Ibid.
26. Ibid.
27. *Western Morning News*, 17 June 1931.
28. *Peg's Companion*, 25 August 1931.
29. *The Times*, 18 June 1931.
30. *Western Morning News*, 18 June 1931.
31. Ibid, 19 June 1931.
32. Ibid.
33. *Weekly News*, 21 October 1933.
34. *Peg's Companion*, 25 August 1931.
35. *Western Morning News*, 19 June 1931.
36. Ibid.
37. Daniel Farson, 'The Case of the Salmon Sandwiches' *Unsolved*, 28 (1984), p.553.
38. *Western Morning News*, 20 June 1931.
39. Bowker, *Behind*, p.201.
40. *The Times*, 20 June 1931.
41. Ibid.
42. Ibid, 21 June 1931.
43. Ibid.
44. Ibid.
45. Ibid.
46. Ibid.
47. Ibid.
48. Ibid.
49. *Western Morning News*, 21 June 1931.
50. Smith, *Mostly Murder*, p.175.
51. *The Times*, 21 June 1931.
52. Smith, *Mostly Murder*, p.185.
53. *Western Morning News*, 21 June 1931.
54. *Dundee Courier*, 21 June 1931.
55. Bowker, *Behind*, p.203.
56. *Western Morning News*, 21 June 1931.
57. *Weekly News*, 21 October 1933.
58. *Western Morning News*, 22 June 1931.

59. *Weekly News*, 21 October 1933.
60. *Liverpool Echo*, 18 December 1959.
61. Devlin, *Taken*, p.131.

Chapter 9

1. *Liverpool Echo*, 17 December 1959.
2. Ibid, 19 December 1959.
3. *Weekly News*, 21 October 1933.
4. Ibid.
5. *Western Morning News*, 22 June 1931.
6. *Weekly News*, 21 October 1933.
7. *Western Mail*, 22 June 1931; *Western Morning News*, 22 June 1931.
8. Devlin, *Taken*, p.130
9. *Sheffield Daily Telegraph*, 22 June 1931.
10. *Liverpool Echo*, 19 December 1959; Devlin, *Taken*, pp.130, 133.
11. Bowker, *Behind*, pp.204-205.
12. *Liverpool Echo*, 19 December 1959.
13. Bowker, *Behind*, p.205.
14. Smith, *Mostly Murder*, pp.187-188.
15. *Weekly News*, 21 October 1933.
16. Ibid, 28 October 1933.
17. *Weekly News*, 28 October 1933.
18. *The Times*, 23 June 1931.
19. Ibid.
20. *The Times*, 23 June 1931.
21. Ibid.
22. Ibid.
23. Ibid.
24. Ibid.
25. *Western Morning News*, 23 June 1931.
26. *Peg's Companion*, 18 August 1931.
27. *Weekly News*, 28 October 1933.
28. *The Times*, 23 June 1931.
29. *Western Morning News*, 23 June 1931.
30. *The Times*, 23 June 1931.
31. Ibid.
32. *The Times*, 23 June 1931.
33. *Launceston Weekly News*, 27 June 1931.
34. Ibid.
35. *The Times*, 27 June 1931
36. Ibid, 23 June 1931.
37. Ibid.
38. *Western Morning News*, 23 June 1931.

39. *Weekly News*, 28 October 1933.
40. *Peg's Companion*, 18 August 1931.
41. O'Donnell, *Crimes*, pp. 141, 151.
42. Devlin, *Taken*, p.131.
43. *Western Morning News*, 23 June 1931.
44. *Weekly News*, 28 October 1933.
45. *The Times*, 24 June 1931.
46. Ibid.
47. Ibid.
48. *The Times*, 24 June 1931.
49. Ibid.
50. Ibid.
51. Ibid.
52. Ibid.
53. Ibid.
54. Ibid.
55. Ibid.
56. Ibid.
57. *The Times*, 24 June 1931; *Western Morning News* 24 and 26 June 1931.
58. *Western Morning News*, 24 June 1931.
59. Devlin, *Taken*, pp. 131-132.
60. Bowker, *Behind*, p.205.
61. *Weekly News*, 28 October 1933.
62. *Peg's Companion*, 18 August 1931.
63. O'Donnell, *Crimes*, p.154.
64. *The Times*, 24 June 1931; *Western Morning News* 24 June 1931.
65. *Exeter and Plymouth Gazette*, 26 June 1931.
66. *Weekly News*, 28 October 1933.
67. *Exeter and Plymouth Gazette*, 26 June 1931.
68. *Western Mail*, 24 June 1931.
69. Montgomery Hyde, *Norman Birkett*, p.321.
70. Devlin, *Taken*, p.134.
71. *Western Morning News*, 24 June 1931.
72. TNA, HO 144/16306.
73. Ibid.
74. Ibid.

Chapter 10

1. *Western Morning News*, 1 July 1931.
2. Ibid, 7 July and 30 Sept 1932.
3. Ancestry.co.uk, 1939 registers, wills index; *Western Morning News*, 17 December 1949, TNA, MAF34/407/44.
4. *Western Morning News*, 26 June 1931; *Weekly News*, 28 October 1933.

5. *Hull Daily Mail*, 25 June 1931.
6. *Western Morning News*, 24 June 1931; O'Donnell, *Crimes*, p.156.
7. O'Donnell, *Crimes*, pp.156-157.
8. Farson, 'Annie Hearn', p.567.
9. *Leeds Mercury*, 13 July 1931.
10. *Weekly News*, 28 October 1933.
11. *Liverpool Echo*, 15 July 1959.
12. *Empire News*, 5 July 1931.
13. Ibid.
14. Ibid, 12 July 1931.
15. Ibid, 19 July 1931.
16. Ibid.
17. Ibid.
18. Ibid.
19. Ibid.
20. Ibid.
21. Ibid and 5 July.
22. *Peg's Companion*, 25 August 1931.
23. *Peg's Companion*, 25 August 1931.
24. Ibid, 1 September 1931.
25. Ibid.
26. Ibid.
27. O'Donnell, *Crimes*, p.157; Devlin, *Taken*, p.133.
28. *Weekly News*, 23 September 1933.
29. Ibid, 28 October, 16 September 1933.
30. Ibid, 16 September 1933.
31. Ibid, 4 November 1933.
32. Ibid, 11 November 1933.
33. Ibid, 18 November 1933.
34. Ibid, 16 September 1933.
35. Ibid, 7 October 1933.
36. Ibid, 18 November 1933.
37. *Cornishman*, 2 July 1931.
38. W. Duke, *Six Trials* (1934), pp. 235-236; C.J.S. Thompson, *Poison Mysteries Unsolved*, (1937); W.T. Felstead, *Shades of Scotland Yard*, (1959); Michael Williams, *Cornish Mysteries* (1980), pp.13-17; Brian Lane, ed., *Murder Club Guide to South West England and Wales* (1989).
39. *Liverpool Echo*, 19 December 1959.
40. Ibid.
41. Smith, *Mostly Murder*, p.177.
42. Ibid, p.180.
43. Deans Bardens, *Lord Justice Birkett* (1962), p.177.
44. O'Donnell, *Crimes*, p.141.

45. Devlin, *Taken*, p.134.
46. Farson, 'Annie Hearn', pp.566, 568.
47. Patricia Gray, *Cornwall Murder Files* (2010), pp.30-43.
48. John Rigbey, *Arsenic and Mercy Quint* (2016).
49. Oldridge, *Salmon Sandwiches*, p.332.
50. Ibid.
51. Simpson, *Forty Years of Murder*, pp.269-272.
52. TNA, ASSI26/47.

Appendix

1. Williams, *Cornish Mysteries*, p.13.
2. John Curran, *Agatha Christie's Secret Notebooks* (2009), p.378.
3. Kathryn Markup, *A is for Arsenic: The Poisons of Agatha Christie* (2015), p.199.
4. Carla Valentine, *Murder isn't easy: The forensics of Agatha Christie* (2022), pp.317-318.

Index